FLYING MAN

Number Twenty | Centennial of Flight | Roger D. Launius, General Editor

Professor Hugo Junkers in 1922. Technikmuseum Hugo Junkers, Dessau, 2013.
(From author's collection)

FLYING MAN

Hugo Junkers and the Dream of Aviation

Richard Byers

Texas A&M University Press
College Station

This paper meets the requirements of ANSI/NISO Z39.48–1992 (Permanence of Paper).
Binding materials have been chosen for durability.
Manufactured in the United States of America

Library of Congress Cataloging-in-Publication Data

Names: Byers, Richard, 1971– author.
Title: Flying man : Hugo Junkers and the dream of aviation / Richard Byers.
Other titles: Centennial of flight series ; no. 20.
Description: First edition. | College Station : Texas A&M University Press,
  [2016] | Series: Centennial of flight ; number twenty | Includes
  bibliographical references and index.
Identifiers: LCCN 2016024063| ISBN 9781623494643 (cloth : alk. paper) |
  ISBN 9781623494650 (ebook)
Subjects: LCSH: Junkers, Hugo, 1859–1935. | Junkers Flugzeug- und
  -Motorenwerke AG—History. | Junkers-Flugzeugwerk AG—History. | Junkers
  Motorenbau GmbH—History. | Aeronautical engineers—Germany—Biography. |
  Junkers airplanes—History. | Aircraft industry—Germany—Dessau
  (Dessau)—History—20th century. | Germany—Politics and
  government—1918–1933.
Classification: LCC TL540.J8 B94 2016 | DDC 338.7/62913334092 [B]—dc23 LC
record available at https://lccn.loc.gov/2016024063

CONTENTS

Gallery follows page 102.

PREFACE

Dessau: The City in Green

Dessau, Germany, known to locals as the "city in green," lies two hours south of Berlin by train. Travel to the city from the "old West" means passing through the bones of the Cold War borderlands, still distinctly obvious due to the architectural differences and the train stations—spotlessly clean and modern in the "old West" but decrepit and graffiti-covered in the "former East." The city received a face-lift after reunification, but remains as it has been for centuries—a quiet, beautiful place. Dessau is also architecturally renowned, having been home to many in the modernist Bauhaus movement in the 1920s. Small enough to walk across in half a day, but large enough to act as regional center in an otherwise rural region, it sports a mixture of Cold War-era "Ostalgic" reminders, such as a Russian restaurant, and newer additions including a post-reunification industrial park like the ones found in most modern urban areas today, which encloses the former Junkers corporate headquarters and airfield. On these grounds is the hangar-sized Technikmuseum Hugo Junkers, a museum staffed by welcoming volunteers and former employees that celebrates the career and achievements of Professor Hugo Junkers. The Museum displays several rusting East German Air Force fighters and helicopters, as well as the broken, skeletal traces of the Junkers Corporation's research facilities, including a weathered portion of its concrete wind tunnel. Behind the wind tunnel is an abandoned research building, its open windows and damaged roof attesting to the decades since its last use. Hardly an auspicious backdrop, but it was here, one hundred years ago, that the essential features of modern aviation first took shape.

Working with his design teams in Dessau, and later in Munich, Professor Hugo Junkers (1859–1935) combined extensive knowledge of aerodynamics, structural engineering, and combustion engine design to produce the Junkers J-1, the world's first all-metal airplane, which flew in April 1915. By 1917, his later designs were in service for Germany's air force, flying close support and ground-attack missions over the western front trenches. Two years later in 1919, with the war over and Allied bans on military production in place, Junkers's ambitions produced arguably his most important aircraft: the F-13, a luxury passenger and freight carrier with a fully enclosed cabin that also possessed cutting-edge performance and rugged durability. The F-13 went on to lead the way across much of the global air route network over the next decade. As his F-13 fleet crisscrossed the globe, Junkers created even more amazing designs, such as the Ju-52 transport plane, which carried German soldiers and equipment during World War II and still flies today, and futuristic concepts like the R-1 and J-1000, massive multiengine, multilevel aircraft designed to carry hundreds of passengers across the world's largest oceans—the intellectual and spiritual ancestors of today's long-haul passenger and freight carriers.

Today, Hugo Junkers is a member of the International Aerospace Hall of Fame in San Diego, and not much else; beyond Dessau and his adopted state of Sachsen-Anhalt, where he was recognized as a local hero alongside Johann Sebastian Bach and other famous sons during the 800th anniversary celebrations in 2012, he remains outside wider public consciousness. Virtually none of the tens of millions of air passengers that travel every year know his story. Yet it was his dream, the dream of a global, interconnected network of fast, safe, and reliable air travel that has been realized in the twenty-first century. Although he saw his achievements through the bifocal lenses of business opportunities and technological innovation, like many of his industry contemporaries he also held higher, almost messianic aspirations for his aircraft. Part

Thomas Edison, part Richard Branson, Hugo Junkers envisaged afford-able, open-sky air travel as both a key component of global prosperity and human progress, and also a means of conquering distance and open-ing up opportunities for greater interaction and collaboration between cultures and societies—a benevolent deus ex machina. A century after the first short flight of the Junkers J-1, his vision has been realized, and we are all the better for it. It is time his story was told and his achieve-ments recognized outside Dessau, and this account represents a small part of his far larger legacy.

ACKNOWLEDGMENTS

This work could not have been completed without the guidance and help of many people spread out across Australia, North America, and Europe. Jackson Hughes at the University of Adelaide first showed me the way, and William Leary and John Morrow at the University of Georgia finished me off. The faculty at the University of North Georgia have provided great inspiration and friendship over the years while this book took shape between teaching duties, and the staff and archivists at the Deutsches Museum archives in Munich, Germany, provided invaluable assistance during research trips over a fifteen-year span. Special thanks to Dr. Helmuth Trischler and Dr. Wilhelm Füssl, who welcomed me to the Deutsches Museum's wonderful facilities and archives, and archivists Marlinde Schwarzenau and Wolfgang Schinhan for digging tirelessly and unearthing the documentary sources that made this work possible. Thanks also to Geschäftsführer Leeb and his staff at the Technikmuseum Hugo Junkers in Dessau for their support and assistance. Thank you also to Jay Dew, Patricia Clabaugh, and all the staff at Texas A&M University Press, who supported this project and oversaw its completion. Finally, this work is dedicated to my wife, Ashley, who carried me through years of graduate school, and my children, Riley and Will, who now safely and effortlessly travel over oceans and between worlds in ways Hugo Junkers would have both recognized and loved.

FLYING MAN

INTRODUCTION

Munich's *Englischer Garten* (English Garden) winds tranquilly through the Bavarian capital's northern suburbs. Only seconds from the city's vibrant business district, the "Garten" provides an escape from work's anxieties. Trails run for miles through copses of oak trees, stretch out over mowed soccer fields and wide meadows, and follow diverted streams of the Isar River. After lunch on February 2, 1934, Professor Hugo Junkers walked through the Garten toward his office on Königinstrasse. Junkers, by now a vigorous seventy-four years of age, continued to maintain a daily walking schedule even when at work. As he approached the Garten's edge, two policemen stepped off a small bridge and moved toward him. Minutes later, Junkers sat in a police car bound for his mountain home in Bayrischzell, in the snowy foothills of the Bavarian Alps. Munich police officers instructed him to remain at his house and await further instructions.

The same police officers returned the next day, cut Junkers's telephone line, and established permanent surveillance. They informed the professor that any travel from the residence, including skiing, required police escort. All contact with employees of his former firms, even his son Klaus and his lawyer, was forbidden. It was Junkers's seventy-fifth birthday. Twelve months later he died, leaving behind assets that included his aircraft complex in Dessau and the results of twenty-five years in aviation research, including highly valuable patents and license agreements across several industries. These assets now passed into the hands of the Third Reich's *Reichsluftministerium* (German Air Ministry) as it rearmed Germany and prepared for war. By 1938, the now state-owned

Junkers Flugzeugwerke employed over 45,000 workers and served as one of the foundations of the Third Reich's aerial rearmament programs. During World War II, thousands of Junkers-badged aircraft served on all fronts in a variety of roles, and the firm's factories expanded across the Nazi empire, employing thousands of Eastern European forced laborers. It would be this legacy, completely unconnected to the man whose name still headed the state-controlled firm, that partially accounts for Junkers's obscurity today as one of the key pioneers in modern aviation and air travel history.[1]

During the twentieth century, international aviation development owed a fundamental debt to the nation-state. As awareness and recognition of aviation's military potential increased, nation-states intervened and fostered their indigenous aircraft industries in an attempt to sustain and enhance national military power. Integral to this process was a gradual increase in state involvement in the aircraft industry, from client to supervisor and patron to owner of many formerly private firms. From the state's perspective, two circumstances justified these actions: first, increased threats to national security and the industrial demands of modern war and, second, the recognition that the nascent civilian market lacked the means to sustain private manufacturers during peacetime. Within aviation history, these developments have received considerable attention.[2]

However, the consequences of this involvement, particularly its effects on private industry's freedom of action, have attracted less attention. Aviation technology's rapid technological progress brought with it increased design complexity and costs that required the development of extensive command technology and procurement systems. Command systems appeared to channel and coordinate aviation's technical development in directions suitable for state requirements. In Europe, creation and refinement of these systems occurred during World War I, as states realized private producers lacked the means to produce massive numbers of aircraft quickly. Within these new state agencies, as a result of these wartime experiences and personnel continuity, certain assumptions developed regarding the relative power relationship between private manufacturers and national regimes that would persist through the two world wars, and even in some ways to many modern defense-related industries.

Acting as both principal financial source and patron, nation-states possessed enormous influence over aircraft producers in the first half of the twentieth century. Attempts to assert this influence led to conflicts between the state and private industry. To suit their needs, states increasingly intervened in all areas of aviation, including technological development. After World War I all nations recognized the importance of industrial preparation and central coordination of industrial resources for quick military mobilization, and state supervision of militarily valuable industries increased. In Germany, these developments took place between 1914 and 1934 despite military defeat and the destruction of two separate regimes, the German Empire and the Weimar Republic. The remarkable continuity of these efforts, despite political and economic turmoil, clearly demonstrates increased state power at private industry's expense.

In Germany, the ability of private aircraft manufacturers to resist state advances never really solidified. Before and during World War I, only military markets existed. After the war, the Treaty of Versailles explicitly and directly disadvantaged German aircraft firms, particularly those in possession of superior technology, such as the Dornier and Junkers aircraft companies. By the time the Versailles restrictions ended in 1926, the international aviation marketplace was saturated, both in supplies of aircraft and numbers of competitors, increasingly from the United States. For German firms, these circumstances reduced market opportunities and created an environment scarcely better than that of wartime. State organs such as the Aviation Department of the *Reichsverkehrministerium* (Reich Transport Ministry, or RVM) recognized private industry's dilemma and tailored their plans accordingly.

If these agencies determined that state interests required intervention in the private sector, then more often than not their efforts proved irresistible. State participation in the industry rose during the fifteen years after the end of World War I while the ability of private manufacturers to chart their own courses commensurately fell. As aircraft rose in military importance, the state gradually assumed more industry tasks through the creation of new agencies and increased supervision of the private sector. Aviation's rapid technological pace and the demands of industrial mobilization required centralized control of research, procurement, and manufacture. By 1930, nation-states regarded these demands as beyond the abilities of private industry. Transforming the industry's capacity to produce thousands of aircraft at short notice required universal adoption of assembly-line manufacturing and extensive standardization, as World War II would prove. Within this perspective, aircraft became just another mass-produced military item built to official specifications. By 1933, even before the National Socialist *Machtergreifung* (the bombastically—and inaccurately—named "seizure of power") and the resumption of open military rearmament, Germany's remaining private aviation firms faced two choices: accept the status quo and adhere to state priorities or face bankruptcy.

Junkers's aviation career exemplifies these developments. Between 1915 and 1934, Junkers attempted to create a global, interconnected aviation network that also encompassed aviation research, aircraft and aero-engine production; joint-venture airline networks; and dedicated maintenance facilities. Junkers believed that technological superiority guaranteed market dominance; this belief led to the creation of a vertically and horizontally integrated concern, the Junkers Works at Dessau, southwest of Berlin, which combined research and development, testing, production, and spare parts manufacturing. His firms were organized and integrated according to what contemporaries called the "Junkers System." This system placed an overwhelming emphasis on prioritizing and funding research and development at the expense of long-term financial prudence, eschewed assembly-line manufacturing in favor of small batch serial production, and sought to employ patent litigation and license revenue as a key source of corporate funding in lieu of reliance on public or private credit. This approach not only helped support Junkers's obsessive emphasis on maintaining personal and corporate independence, but also encouraged the creation of a fragile corporate financial framework that exposed his aviation interests to economic volatility and an underdeveloped marketplace, with ultimately disastrous results.

The Junkers Works interdependent corporate structure reflected Junkers's commitment to a business paradigm that stressed technical innovation and pure research as connected means to a common end safeguarding the concern's independence from external influences, whether financial in the form of German and foreign banks, economic in the form of conglomerates such as the Hugo Stinnes steel group, or governmental in the form of military and civilian aviation agencies. Also, as the founder of a German *Mittelstand* (medium-sized business) family concern, Junkers strove for financial and administrative self-reliance and sought to minimize his external obligations to other stakeholders. He was also extremely stubborn and self-confident, often excessively so. Throughout his career, his ambitions often outstripped his resources.

At the same time Junkers tried to establish his aviation business interests, his research achievements led to increased state intervention and coercion as three successive regimes—the German Empire, the Weimar Republic, and the Third Reich—sought to use Junkers's innovative and technically advanced aviation technology for military purposes. Junkers resisted these pressures but consistently found himself unable to continue aviation research without state assistance. From a technical standpoint, Junkers reached his goals, but recurring capital shortages ultimately led to the loss of his concern. Between 1916 and 1933, state agencies took control of the Junkers Works three times; although Junkers managed to escape permanent state oversight twice, negative consequences resulted from these processes, particularly as the relationship between the firm and the state declined. State officials came to view Junkers himself as an obstructionist and a liability. In 1932, state agencies tired of Junkers's machinations and combined their efforts to remove him from the Junkers Works and exile him to Bavaria; within two years, he was dead and the firm he created was nationalized. This work follows and analyzes the course of these developments, and charts a new approach to our historical understanding of Junkers and his era by arguing that his story reveals the steady erosion of individual power and initiative within aviation as the technology matured and became viable as an instrument of the state. It also seeks to balance this perspective by highlighting the personal responsibility that must be attributed to Junkers himself for his downfall.

Junkers's career has attracted little attention from non-German scholars, due largely to erroneous connections between the Junkers name and the Third Reich. Anglo-American aviation history has tended to focus on American, French, and British contributions to aviation technology at the expense of German designers such as Junkers. German historians devoted more attention to Junkers, but contemporary politics permeated their analyses, both after 1933 and then between 1945 and 1990, as the Dessau complex and most archival material stayed in the Eastern zone. East German historians produced most of the material currently available, much of which is well researched and written.[3] Unfortunately, rigid historiographical orthodoxy lessens the value of these accounts as East German researchers, often under direct political pressure, struggled to encompass Junkers's life and actions within a Marxist framework. Within these accounts, Junkers appears as half sinner, half saint, praised for his contributions to aviation and resistance to *Grosskapital* (Big Capital) but condemned for his embrace of capitalism. These accounts underplay Junkers's own role in his demise in favor of conspiracies involving alliances between German business and Fascist opportunists, arguments that available evidence fails to support. Since 1990, two works have appeared that challenge these interpretations. Wolfgang Wagner's comprehensive *Hugo Junkers, Pionier der Luftfahrt: Seine Flugzeuge* appeared in 1996 and provides a definitive analysis of the technical development of Junkers aircraft from 1915 to 1945. Wagner, a veteran pilot and great admirer of Junkers, aims his work at an aviation audience, and although his narrative charts the course of Junkers's career, it is not the work's focus, and Wagner makes no claims on scholarly precision. The second work, Lutz Budrass's massive and comprehensive *Flugzeugindustrie und Luftrüstung in Deutschland 1918–1945* (1998) provides the best available scholarly analysis of Junkers's career during the Weimar era. Budrass's work is a landmark of scholarship that covers the entire aviation industry and, for the first time, definitively charts connections between the state's rearmament course and that course's implications for private manufacturers. Budrass's exhaustive analysis includes Junkers's experiences as part of a larger story, however, and does not examine circumstances before 1918. Currently, no scholarly works examining Junkers's life and career exist in English, and as yet, Budrass's important work has not been translated. This work helps address and rectify these omissions for an English-speaking audience.

Chapter 1, "The War Years," focuses on Junkers's early life and entry into aviation research, which began just as official interest in powered flight's military applications grew. From small beginnings as a research project, Junkers's aviation involvement steadily deepened, and by 1915, he commenced construction of the world's first all-metal aircraft at his factory complex in Dessau. Junkers's efforts aroused the interest of army officials within the *Inspektorat der Fliegertruppen* (Inspectorate of Flying Troops, or Idflieg), who sought to utilize Junkers's innovative designs in the escalating war against the Allies. These demands led to tension between Junkers and Idflieg officials as Junkers resisted army attempts to alter his design and construction characteristics to suit military needs. By 1917, with demands for aircraft reaching new heights, Idflieg officials grew tired of Junkers's intransigence and forced him to merge with the Fokker firm, then one of Germany's largest producers. This "marriage from above" proved a disaster as the clash of personalities between Anthony Fokker and Junkers precluded successful collaboration. The Junkers-Fokker union failed, and Junkers emerged from World War I determined to avoid future collaboration with either state or private interests.[4] On the army side, Junkers's actions during the war convinced military officials that he placed his own interests above state requirements. Many of these officials found employment in the new shadow departments of the newly constituted Weimar German Army, called the Reichswehr, where, in deliberate violation of the Treaty of Versailles, they initiated secret plans for Germany's rearmament.

Chapter 2, "The Russian Affair," examines events between 1918 and 1924, as Junkers attempted to establish himself as the world's leading aircraft producer. The firm's development of the world's first all-metal transport aircraft, the revolutionary F-13, during 1920 appeared to guarantee success, but Versailles restrictions forbade German aircraft production, and Junkers's forays into the emerging US market proved unsuccessful. Facing financial difficulties by 1921, Junkers decided to reenter collaboration with German military agencies, this time the Reichswehr. German rearmament strategy, directed by Reichswehr Commander Hans von Seeckt, favored the establishment of military relations with Communist Russia as a way around the Treaty of Versailles. Part of these plans called for the secret erection of aircraft production facilities at Fili near Moscow without the knowledge of the Weimar government. Initially optimistic concerning Russia's aviation potential, as negotiations continued, Junkers found himself caught between divergent German and Russian agendas. These agendas offered little place for Junkers, whose financial problems increased during the course of the Russian venture while his erstwhile partners vacillated and argued over financing the project. Desperation drove him to break silence and alert other government agencies to the Fili plans, an action that provided temporary financial respite but earned him the permanent enmity of Reichswehr officials. Over time, the latter consequence proved decisive for Junkers's fortunes.

Chapter 3, "Diverging Paths," charts the development of Junkers airline networks between 1921 and 1926, as the concern sought to erect and expand airline partnerships throughout Germany, Eastern Europe, Asia, and the Americas. As these networks grew, Junkers encountered opposition not only from domestic and foreign competitors but also from state agencies such as the RVM, who desired greater efficiency in aviation subsidy use and closer connections with military aviation priorities. Junkers's financial problems due to his Russian activities were magnified by poor accounting practices in the firm's airline department, Abteilung Luftverkehr, and rising production costs. By September 1925, these costs reached insurmountable levels and forced Junkers to appeal to the German government for assistance.

Officials within the Reichswehr and the RVM used Junkers's financial problems to merge Germany's two largest domestic airlines, Junkers Luftverkehr (ILAG) and Deutscher Aero-Lloyd (DAL), into a state-run concern, Deutsche Lufthansa, whose descendants still fly today. Both agencies now used the state airline as a mechanism for Germany's covert rearmament. RVM trustees also entered Dessau and took over the Junkers Works for eleven months. The RVM proved unable to rectify the firm's poor financial position during this period and returned control to Junkers in September 1926. Terms of this exchange included Junkers's removal from German airline networks and the dissolution of the Fili project. Although Junkers regained control of his concern, he now found himself excluded from German airlines and air routes and was forced to search further afield for market opportunities. For its part, the RVM developed a derisive attitude toward Junkers that persisted for the rest of his aviation career. After 1926, both civilian and military aviation officials resolved to remove Junkers from German aviation at the earliest possible opportunity.

Chapter 4, "On the Edge," analyzes the concern's path from 1927 to 1932. After emerging from state control, the Junkers Works aviation divisions embarked on a series of costly but ultimately unsuccessful projects. Market sales remained elusive due to increased competition, while internal costs, particularly in the area of engine research, continued to rise. These circumstances once again exhausted the concern's capital reserves by 1929, just as the international depression began. Germany's economic collapse also forced changes in covert rearmament strategy, as the military and allied state agencies accelerated rationalization programs to protect dwindling aviation subsidies. As the financial woes of the Junkers Works deepened, Junkers came under fire from members of his own management team, who argued the concern's large research expenditures were not sustainable. Junkers stubbornly resisted these criticisms and responded with sweeping leadership changes, but he failed to address the concern's inherent structural problems. In 1932, with bankruptcy looming and state agencies refusing his aid requests, Junkers began insolvency proceedings.

Germany's political shift to the right after 1930 greatly increased the power of the Reichswehr within the government, and under Chancellors Heinrich Brüning, Kurt von Schleicher, and Franz von Papen, steps were taken to abandon Versailles restrictions and commence open rearmament. Aviation policy and agencies became centralized under Reichswehr control, and under this new leadership, state representatives increasingly intervened in the private sector. The firm's financial difficulties provided an opportunity to achieve two core state priorities: first, bring Germany's largest aircraft manufacturer into this widening rearmament initiative and, second, remove Junkers from control of the concern. Junkers resisted these pressures but lacked the resources to solve his financial problems independently. Attempting to retain majority ownership of his aviation interests, he was forced to sell the concern's core firm, Junkers & Company (ICO), in November 1932. This sale removed Junkers's last consistent revenue source and effectively compromised his corporate vision. When the National Socialists assumed power in January 1933, Junkers had already given up daily control of his companies.

But as chapter 5, "Twilight and Eclipse," shows, Junkers's ordeal was not over. Despite achieving its aim of removing Junkers from control of his aviation firms, the Nazi state increased pressure on him throughout 1933. National Socialist aviation rearmament policy continued the course established by its Weimar predecessor and incorporated the creation of a state-controlled "patent pool" that allowed swift distribution of technology throughout the entire industry to accelerate licensed mass production. Although now separated from his concern at Dessau, Junkers retained sole ownership of patents coveted by the state, and despite agreeing to hand these patents over as part of the insolvency proceedings, Junkers refused to transfer ownership without just compensation. National Socialist aviation officials, led by former Junkers employee—and later Luftwaffe Field Marshal—Erhard Milch, replaced negotiation with coercion and increased pressure on Junkers by banning him from Dessau, reducing his freedom of movement, and threatening him with criminal charges. Junkers resisted stubbornly until state authorities widened the circle of intimidation to include his family. Isolated and in poor health, Junkers fought to the end, continuing to doggedly resist the state's actions through the courts, but he passed away on February 3, 1935, before judicial proceedings concluded.

With his death, nothing stood in the way of complete state takeover of the Junkers Works, and the Reich Air Ministry concluded the purchase of all Junkers assets and patents with Junkers's widow, Therese, on April 30, 1935. After twenty years of struggle, state interests decisively prevailed over Junkers and severed all connections between his descendants and the firm he founded. His story demonstrates two things: the loss of individual power inherent within twentieth-century technological progress and the tragic gap between Junkers's visions and his means. The work concludes by briefly examining Junkers's posthumous legacy and considers his life and career within both the context of his era and the significance of his achievements today. Endnotes and a bibliography point interested readers and researchers toward additional resources.

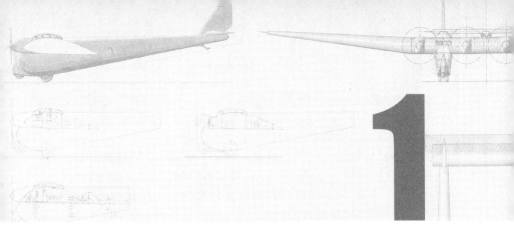

The War Years, 1914–1918

In only four years, World War I created much of the world we still live in today. Modern aviation was no exception, having been born just a decade before the war began and emerging from it, in accelerated fashion, as a mature technology with considerable military applications. Hugo Junkers, a German engineer and manufacturer, found himself engulfed by the conflict, as were all members of his generation, and called upon to lead an unprecedented industrial war effort. For Junkers, a renowned inventor and innovator who represented the intersection between applied research and commercial application, the war meant opportunities for augmentation through military contracts. For the German Empire, Junkers was just a small piece in a massive mosaic of highly educated and talented human capital that could be called upon to sustain and ensure military victory. By 1918, both sides had achieved their goals to some extent, but not without creating lasting mutual feelings of aggrievement. The war established a relationship dynamic between Junkers and the German government that would last for twenty years and would decisively impact his life, career, and historical legacy.

Junkers entered the world before the German nation existed. Born to a weaving family in the Rhineland town of Rheydt on February 3, 1859, Junkers inherited from his father, Heinrich, a love of nature and a strict sense of family obligation combined with shrewd business acumen.[1] Other family traits included stubbornness, self-confidence, and cheerfulness, characteristics common among Rheydters.[2] As a child and adolescent, he showed early aptitude for technical tasks and soon developed an ability to solve complex technical problems through unconventional means. After passing his final exam at the Barmen Vocational School in 1875, he continued his education at technical high schools in Berlin, Karlsruhe, and Aachen.[3]

While studying at the technical high school in Berlin-Charlottenburg, Junkers took a thermodynamics class under Professor Adolf Slaby, who became one of Junkers's most important mentors. Slaby and his students studied the theoretical and technical problems of the combustion engine, a technology then still in its infancy, and with Slaby's encouragement, Junkers and the other students built and studied several engine designs. Here young Junkers's technical gifts bloomed, and Slaby's methodology, which focused on linking theoretical research with practical experimentation, stayed with Junkers throughout his life. Slaby also emphasized the importance of linking scientific research to industry's practical needs; these tenets formed the cornerstone of Junkers's professional career.[4]

After passing his final exam in 1883, Junkers spent the next five years dividing his time between working in several machine factories in Berlin and the Rhineland, traveling, and assisting Slaby. In 1887, Heinrich Junkers died of gas poisoning and left his seven sons a considerable inheritance that included the family weaving concern, a brickworks, real estate, and other property.[5] Junkers's share of this wealth was enough to provide financial security and the freedom to pursue his research aims independently, in cooperation with his former teacher and mentor. Slaby maintained extensive contacts with engineers and researchers in private industry. In 1888, he received word that the technical director of the Deutsche Continental Gesellschaft in Dessau, William von Oechelhauser, whose father owned the firm, needed an engineer to help him develop high-efficiency engines for electricity generation. Slaby recommended his protégé, and Junkers began a working relationship with the town of Dessau that would continue throughout his lifetime.[6]

On October 28, 1888, Junkers began work with Oechelhauser on gas engines, with the aim of increasing their size and efficiency. Conducting their first experiments in a stable on the factory grounds, they founded a research center in 1890 for gas engine development in Dessau, die Versuchsstation für Gasmotoren von Oechelhauser und Junkers. The terms of the partnership allowed Junkers the widest possible degree of independence in pursuing research aims, a condition he sought to maintain throughout his working life. By 1892, the research led to a mock-up of a new 100-horsepower gas engine, suitable for work in blast furnaces.[7] Junkers saw this engine as an intermediate solution, adequate only as a developmental module but not the final product, but Oechelhauser pressed for immediate manufacture of the current design, given that he provided the majority of the research funds and wished to recoup them as quickly as possible. This disagreement, so characteristic of Junkers throughout his life, led to the partnership's dissolution in April 1893.[8]

A free agent, Junkers now began his own career. His first company, a civil engineering firm registered as Hugo Junkers-Zivilengineur, appeared in 1892, and during the following two years, it produced three patents for calorimeter (devices used for measuring the calorific level of gas and liquid).[9] Proceeding systematically from these breakthroughs, in 1894 Junkers developed a gas-fired boiler, for which he received the patent for the following year. After attempting unsuccessfully to sell a manufacturing license, he established his own factory and incorporated it under the name Junkers & Company (ICO). Beginning with one plumber, the firm's workforce numbered thirty by 1898, and by 1914, it had increased to over three hundred.[10] Further developments of the original design led to the development of the gas-fired water heater in 1906; the modern water heater retains the same basic design characteristics today.

Junkers's inventions led to his appointment as a teaching professor of thermodynamics at the Aachen Technical High School in 1897. There, in addition to his teaching duties, he founded a research laboratory, called the Versuchsanstalt Professor Junkers, where he and a staff of assistants and students studied the application of Junkers's research to gas engines for the development of oil engines. Soon an experimental oil engine appeared, which by 1910 developed into a 1,000-horsepower tandem engine suitable for maritime applications. Under a license agreement with the English firm Doxford and Sons, Junkers's engines were manufactured in England between 1913 and 1920. Funding for the laboratory came from ICO, and the laboratory continued its work long after Junkers himself returned to corporate life.[11] While in Aachen, Junkers assembled a circle of engineers and designers who would stay with him throughout his working career. These men, including Otto Mader, a professor at Aachen who would become a crucial part of Junkers's aviation research team, enjoyed the informal atmosphere of Junkers's research laboratory and would take that atmosphere with them to Dessau, where it became part of corporate culture.[12] Already at this early stage, Junkers established four key features of his career arc: a penchant for original thinking and technical innovation, an informal leadership style, a keen awareness of the importance of patents and intellectual property protection, and finally a willingness to engage in international business partnerships to generate research funding.

During his time at Aachen, Junkers met another professor, Hans Reissner, whose experiments in the burgeoning field of aviation attracted Junkers's attention. Junkers always showed interest in the most intractable technical problems, those others believed insoluble. In the early twentieth century in Europe, aviation remained both a dream and a scarcely plausible reality. Although news of the Wright brothers' flights at Kitty Hawk had circulated around the world, many Europeans could not bring themselves to accept the Americans' success, particularly in France, whose aviators considered themselves the world's best.[13] In Germany, Count Ferdinand von Zeppelin's enormous creation, the 128-meter-long Luftschiff Zeppelin, would initially spark little interest during its maiden voyages in 1900, but then created national rapture in 1904, focusing both public and military eyes on the zeppelin as the primary aerial platform.[14] On the whole, German aviation seemed to be well behind its French and American counterparts, particularly after the loss of its "father," Otto Lilienthal, in a gliding accident in July 1896.[15] Nevertheless, a few inventors like Hans Reissner carried on their work despite receiving little notice. In 1909, Junkers joined Reissner in his endeavor to create Germany's first viable powered aircraft.

Prior to Junkers's collaboration Reissner had completed one design and flown it short distances before a crash forced the construction of a new aircraft. With Junkers providing a set of corrugated iron wings—the first such use of metal in a fixed-wing aircraft design—the Reissner Ente

(Duck, so named for its rearward design that resembled a flying duck) flew in Berlin for the first time on August 7, 1912.[16] Yet this was not the first time that Junkers had considered aviation as a research interest. Three years earlier, in December 1909, he applied for a patent for a hollow aircraft wing form constructed of metal. The German Empire's Patent Office awarded the patent, number 253788, in February 1910. The theoretical foundations set by this patent were revolutionary—an all-metal internally constructed wing design that incorporated all nonaerodynamic parts of the aircraft, maximizing lift and efficiency. Today, these design features can be seen in the US Air Force's B-2 "Nightwing" stealth bomber, the most advanced manned bomber aircraft ever built. At the time, contemporary aircraft possessed wooden wings wrapped in fabric supported by struts, demonstrating the trade-offs necessary due to aero-engine weakness and weight. Junkers's patent opened a window into a radically different future for aviation, one where metal construction and advanced applied aerodynamics superseded contemporary limitations. Here was Junkers as an aviation visionary, successfully imagining a world yet to be realized.

At the same time Junkers pondered a radical future for aviation, the German state began to shake itself out of its self-imposed apathy toward heavier-than-air craft. Despite remaining committed to the belief that the empire's new symbol of might and menace, the Zeppelin, would prevail in any current or future conflict, Germany's military leaders eyed events in France with concern. The appearance of designs by the Voisin brothers and Henri Farman, with their superior range, speed, and structural reliability, together with Louis Bleriot's cross-Channel achievement in 1909, both demonstrated the burgeoning military potential of airplanes. A year before, in 1908, the German General Staff created a technical section for aviation under Captain Hermann von der Lieth Thomsen, who in 1907 had warned "of the dangers inherent in merely observing the aeronautical progress of others."[17] In October 1908, this section came under the control of Captain Erich Ludendorff, a man destined for great influence in the twentieth century. Ludendorff displayed immediate enthusiasm for the promotion and support of aviation and advocated the dual support of airplanes and airships to his superiors.

However, the influence of the airship lobby within the Prussian War Ministry—most notably that of the Inspectorate of Transport Troops

Airship Battalion, who sought to protect their imperial funds from their heavier-than-air competitors—meant that official financial support for state construction of aircraft remained half-hearted and sporadic until 1910. After a failed attempt to build their own plane, costing over 42,000 marks, the War Ministry responded to increasing public and internal pressure by embarking on a new strategy, the subsidization of several embryonic domestic firms that sprang up in 1908–9 in response to several well-publicized flying competitions. Official support remained limited, however, as increased expenditure on the Imperial Navy's battle fleet provoked compromises within the defense budgets between 1909 and 1913.[18] The Zeppelin lobby's activities also offered a window into the political elements intertwined with the growth of German aviation—interservice rivalries and vested interests were there at the creation and would play a decisive role in shaping the future of the industry and its major players, including Junkers.

At the same time, the department within the Inspectorate of Transport Troops responsible for aircraft testing, the Research Unit, began to outline the role of the military in aviation design and development. Captain Wolfram de le Roi, the unit's leading aviation authority, published a memorandum on March 15, 1910, recommending the army take an active role in ensuring that aircraft and aero-engine designs correspond to military needs by creating a specific military oversight organization. De le Roi noted the example of the automobile industry, whose designs only became militarily useful after such a move. As John Morrow notes, "This is the first evidence of the realization that military demands on airplanes would differ so significantly from civilian needs that the Army would have to shape the industry's development according to its own ends."[19]

Within this larger context, Junkers, having left his teaching post at Aachen in 1913, began working on the construction of a completely new design, an all-metal monoplane incorporating his patented thick wing. Two immediate problems needed solutions: finding the best aerodynamic profile and developing an efficient and powerful engine. In pursuit of the first objective, Junkers constructed two wind tunnels—one near his residence at the Frankenburg Castle in Aachen in 1913 and another at the Junkers Works in Dessau in 1916. On May 1, 1914, the Aachen wind tunnel became operational. Utilizing the theoretical research of Gustav Eiffel and Ludwig Prandtl, Junkers and his research team tested more than five hundred profiles with wooden models. The results confirmed his belief that the thick-wing design of his 1909 patent provided the best lift and stability characteristics. The design also offered the additional advantage of providing storage areas for fuel within the wings themselves, thus reducing drag, engine size, and overall weight. Junkers himself noted, "It then becomes possible to build a smaller, cheaper aircraft capable of transporting the same payload."[20]

Interestingly, Junkers was not the first to attempt construction of an internally braced monoplane in Europe. In 1911 a French engineer, Leon Levavasseur, employed by the firm Aviation Aeroplan Ateliers, constructed such an aircraft out of wood. Unfortunately, he never persuaded it to fly. This failure led most aircraft designers to dismiss the design as unworkable. Certainly this belief existed in Germany, where Junkers's dual aims of pursuing this design and using metal as the primary material received much derision from both aircraft aficionados and Junkers's friends. Later he commented on this sentiment:

> It was 1914. How to build an all-metal aircraft was a problem that was regarded as being insoluble. My friends asked themselves: How did Junkers get the idea to get engaged in such fantasies? Iron cannot fly, an aircraft must be light! They reproached me, saying my engine and equipment construction business—which until then had been successful and was full of promise for the future—would almost certainly be ruined if I withdrew labor and finance from it.
>
> But everything that these friends said against me—and they really did withdraw their trust—was based on their traditional way of thinking. Their businesses were secure, as they followed a traditional course. For them the unknown seldom occurred. But what I wanted on this occasion—just like at any other time—was to go forward into unknown territory, undertaking the task of the pioneer.[21]

While wind tunnel tests continued, work began on the wings of the aircraft, named the Junkers J-1, on May 1, 1915. ICO, which had built the wings for the Reissner Ente, constructed three sets of large experimental wings based on wind tunnel findings and subjected them to stress and load tests.[22] Profits gained by ICO's boiler and water heater operations supplied funds for the project, and for the next six months, research personnel built and tested various components of the aircraft and also examined various aero-engines.[23]

Junkers's interest in aero-engines preceded his interest in aircraft design—in 1911 he discussed construction of a light gas engine for use in aircraft and U-boats, or submarines, with his associates, and his experience in engine manufacturing, where his efforts focused on maximizing energy conservation and power transmission, seemed to promise excellent prospects for success.[24] Unfortunately for Junkers, circumstances prevented the realization of this goal during the war, which broke out as testing continued. Choosing to pool his resources, Junkers closed his motor engine manufacturing facility, Junkers Motorenbau GmbH, located in Magdeburg, and transferred most of the Aachen research personnel to Dessau, where another research institute, the Forschungsanstalt Professor Junkers, appeared on July 1, 1915.[25] In early 1915, Junkers ceased commuting between Aachen and Dessau and remained in Dessau for the rest of the war.

The war brought orders to Junkers in Dessau: orders from the army for field kitchens, field baths, cooking implements, metal lockers, gas ovens, grenades, and detonators, and heaters and radiators for the navy.[26] During May 1915, a military commission from the Heeresverwaltung (Army Administration) visited the Junkers Works and, after inspecting the work being done on the J-1, ordered a trial model of the aircraft.[27] This order, along with the orders for field kitchens and other items, placed Junkers firmly within the state's sphere of interest. A relationship began between the firm and three successive German regimes that lasted for the rest of Junkers's professional and personal life.

The German Army's initial confidence in the adequacy of its aircraft program shattered in the first three months of the war. Although the creation of the National Aviation Fund in 1912—along the lines of the earlier Zeppelin Fund—raised enough capital together with increased army contracts to shelter the nascent domestic aviation industry through the tough economic times of 1911–13, belief that the war would only last weeks meant that reserves of aircraft did not exist in the event of a longer conflict. As battle lines became entrenched across France by the end of 1914, it became clear that the airplane now represented the vital reconnaissance tool in the hands of the opposing armies. At the end of July 1914, the Prussian Army possessed only forty serviceable airplanes. Frantic orders for 202 more by the Idflieg brought the German total up to about 250 by the outbreak of war, most of which were the monoplane Taube (Dove) type, already obsolete by August 1914.[28]

As the war began, air units began to mobilize, but it soon became apparent that no logistical apparatus existed to monitor performance in the field or to relay technical data back to the aircraft manufacturers. Nor did any effective supply apparatus exist. Morrow notes in his study of the German air forces, "Equipping a unit with different types of aircraft unnecessarily complicated the supply of spare parts. Intermediate air parks often had no liaison with their frontline units. . . . Pilots who had crashed their machines at the front could be found lounging around factories in Germany waiting their turn for new airplanes. Unit leaders zealously sent flying officers in lorries to aircraft factories to commandeer airplanes and drive them to local railway stations for shipment to the front." Adding to these problems, conscription drained aircraft firms of desperately needed skilled workers. Army officials only reluctantly granted exemptions to aircraft employees, and many firms experienced labor shortages. An Idflieg order on August 1 decreed that all firms should begin maximum production immediately, leading to the hoarding of raw materials, creating production bottlenecks and price increases.[29] Against this background, 40 percent of the army's operational air strength was destroyed in August alone. Air units demanding two replacement planes per day often only received one per week.

Despite these problems, the military continued to maintain a tough stance in its dealings with aircraft manufacturers, refusing in a meeting with the largest firms on August 4 to grant long-term contracts or to raise aircraft prices. Justifying this stance, army officials argued they did not possess enough information to determine the length of the war and thus the numbers of additional aircraft needed. Military authorities, cautious given the record of other armaments manufacturers such as Krupp, also wished to preclude "unjustified enrichment" of the manufacturers due to favorable market circumstances. At a meeting three days later, which also included several important Reichstag deputies, army and industry representatives reached an agreement: in exchange for contracts, labor exemptions, and the use of company flying schools, the firms accepted the army's control of aircraft prices and also agreed to relinquish lesser patent rights. In exchange for orders, the industry accepted the military's hegemony over aircraft design and development, thus perpetuating the status quo of the relationship since the industry's founding.[30]

Meanwhile work continued at Dessau on the J-1 design. After wing design experiments ended, work began on the fuselage and tail section of the aircraft in September 1915.[31] Being the first aircraft of its type, the J-1 presented many challenges. The metal selected for the aircraft, sheet iron, was difficult and unwieldy. Junkers wanted duralumin, a lighter and more malleable alloy, but no sources existed as the Zeppelin program received top priority in duralumin allocation. Master Otto Siefert, who worked on the J-1, later recalled that the sheet iron proved extremely difficult to shape and would repeatedly warp if subjected to too much stress.[32] Few workshop drawings of the design existed, and the necessary welding techniques developed during construction. With fifteen workers, Siefert constructed the J-1 in six weeks, after which the craft, now nicknamed the "Blechesel" (Tin Donkey), underwent stress tests that suspended the aircraft upside down and loaded the wings with sandbags. After passing these tests in December 1915, the J-1, now ready for flight experiments, arrived at the army's testing facility, Döberitz Airfield.[33]

The radical nature of the new design astounded the army's test pilots. Later, Lieutenant Mallinkrodt, who first flew the aircraft over a distance of several hundred yards on December 12, recalled that none of his comrades wished to be the first to fly the plane, believing it would crash.[34] Mallinkrodt's successful flight in front of Idflieg personnel, Junkers, and his engineers proved otherwise. After several more flights, the army reached its verdict; the design was a success, but the excessive weight of the aircraft, over 1,010 kilograms (2,020 pounds), meant that the J-1s speed and climbing ability did not match those of its wooden contemporaries. On January 11, 1916, Junkers wrote to Captain Felix Wagenführ, commander of Idflieg's testing department, requesting financial assistance for further development, noting that Junkers continued to bear "constantly greater emerging costs."[35] Wagenführ's reply on February 15 confirmed that the War Ministry had approved an order for six further aircraft at a cost of 25,000 marks apiece.[36] The order vindicated Junkers's belief in his design, and he immediately began work on the new craft, known as the J-2.

It is worth mentioning here that despite the granting of the order to Junkers for six further machines, the two sides already held different perceptions of the aircraft's potential. For Junkers, the J-1 was an intermediate step toward a final system of aircraft manufacture, whereas the military, represented by Idflieg, viewed the J-1 as an end product in itself.[37] This difference in view widened throughout 1916 as production delays caused by material and labor shortages delayed the completion of the six J-2s. Junkers wrote to Idflieg explaining the delays on September 1, noting that "despite great efforts only 28 extra workers had been gained in three months. . . . The problem of personnel is the greatest hindrance to the healthy development of the aircraft. . . . With only 100 workers, about two thirds of whom are completely occupied with modifications, improvements, repairs and so forth, one cannot operate a serious aircraft factory."[38]

Junkers also found himself in financial difficulty; aircraft development costs greatly increased while revenue from other sources, such as license payments from the English engine firm Doxford and Sons, stopped due to the war. A partial advance of 48,000 marks for the six J-2s in March failed to alleviate the problem.[39] Junkers decided to bypass Idflieg and appeal directly to the War Ministry. In a series of long letters between August and October 1916, Junkers pleaded his case, outlining the merits and obvious military potential of his designs along with the difficulties he faced in realizing them. Junkers noted that his aircraft were nearly invulnerable due to their metallic construction, were impervious to fire, and required no hangars in bad weather. He also noted that the character of the metal construction allowed for cheap and relatively unskilled mass production. To achieve this aim, he proposed the War Ministry provide support in four ways. First, compensate him for construction of the Dessau Research Institute and wind tunnel. Second, place more orders for aircraft. Third, publicize his achievements

to encourage an influx of private capital, and fourth, assist him in finding more skilled workers and engineers.[40] Receiving no reply, he wrote
again on October 6, asking for a one-third advance of 250,000 marks
against ministry orders placed for field kitchens in July and August.[41] On
October 24, Colonel Paul Oschmann replied, noting that "the military
authorities have a great interest in the further development of your aircraft types. . . .[However,] currently none of your aircraft are ready for
the front. . . . The firm will continue to receive support to the greatest
possible extent."[42] Junkers tried again on December 19, again asking for
a one-third advance based on army orders for ICO products.[43] These
appeals failed to elicit results. The War Ministry stuck to its stance of
October 24—as soon as Junkers aircraft were ready for the front, the
ministry would provide orders. This response infuriated and embittered
Junkers, who no longer possessed the financial means to reach this goal.
Faced with this circumstance, he began to search for a partner with the
necessary capital to fund his aircraft research.

Junkers's difficulties coincided with those of the German armed
forces generally and those of the German air forces in particular. In an
effort to win the war in August 1916, the German High Command in-
voked the Hindenburg Program with the aim of fully mobilizing Germany's resources, a belated recognition of the conflict as "total." For
the aircraft industry, this meant a huge increase in production to one
thousand planes a month. However, not just improvements in quantity but also quality were needed. Poor engine performance, a circumstance that hindered the aircraft industry throughout the war, began
seriously retarding aircraft capability, with the result that Allied aircraft
now clearly outperformed their German rivals. One type sorely needed
was a ground attack, infantry support model that could fly low over the
trenches and engage enemy ground forces at close range. By this time,
many Idflieg officials had concluded that Junkers was only capable of
producing heavy, slow aircraft. On November 18, 1916, Idflieg called for
designs of this type from three firms: Junkers, Albatros, and Allgemeine
Electricitäts-Gesellschaft (General Electricity Company, or AEG).[44] The
notice also mentioned that armored protection for the crew would be
essential. Immediately, tension appeared between Junkers and Idflieg
officials; Junkers submitted a monoplane design, but Idflieg wanted a

biplane configuration. After much wrangling, a compromise design appeared, a sesquiplane with a large upper wing and small lower wing. This new aircraft, designated J-4, featured a 5-millimeter armored cockpit. After the J-4 underwent tests at Döberitz in January 1917, Junkers received an order for fifty of the new planes on March 20, 1917. After two and a half years of struggle, Junkers finally achieved his wartime goal—a large aircraft order.

However, despite the new order, Idflieg remained pessimistic about both Junkers's financial situation and the firm's ability to produce large numbers of aircraft in a short time. The head of Idflieg's research department, now Major Wagenführ, sought to address this situation by bringing Junkers together with one of the larger aircraft producers, who possessed facilities capable of large-quantity production in a short time. One such producer was Anthony Fokker, whose Fokker Aircraft Works met these requirements. Wagenführ called for a meeting between the two men.

On December 16, 1916, Junkers, Fokker, and their company representatives met in Berlin. Junkers was fifty-seven years old; Fokker was twenty-six. During this first meeting, both men described their methods, resources, and current relations with the army authorities.[45] Fokker's situation was almost as precarious as Junkers's; his most recent designs contained a multitude of structural and engineering problems, resulting in Idflieg refusing to order any of his aircraft. Furthermore, his chief designer, Martin Kreutzer, had died in a crash of one of his own planes in June.[46] Choosing to ignore his own role in recent setbacks, Fokker blamed chance, competitor envy, and poor engine quality as chief causes behind his current problems.[47] He expressed interest in the J-4 design and declared himself ready to undertake production in the near future. Responding to Fokker, Junkers remarked that he was not in a position to guarantee large orders of the J-4—that was up to Idflieg.[48]

Two days later, Fokker visited the Junkers Works at Dessau, where he viewed the plans of the J-4 and inspected the Research Institute. Continuing to express his enthusiasm for the proposed joint venture, Fokker waxed eloquently over the seminal importance of Junkers's work.[49] After taking a test flight of the J-4 prototype on January 22, Fokker announced his readiness to negotiate. He offered Junkers 500,000 marks for the right to manufacture the J-4 under license, together with compensation for the use of Junkers's patents and any other assistance granted by the Junkers Works. Junkers, no doubt aware of Fokker's propensity for "intellectual property takeover," responded with more strict conditions—a nonrefundable 500,000-mark deposit, together with a 10 percent unit charge per plane produced. Additionally, Junkers reserved the right to issue further licenses to whomever he wished and reserved the right to control the use and application of his patents within the design. Furthermore, Fokker committed himself to neither directly nor indirectly take any action against the furtherance of patents or licenses granted to others by Junkers. Finally, all aircraft produced must have a shield installed in plain sight with the inscription "Patent Junkers."[50]

Fokker declined to accept Junkers's terms, particularly the stipulation that the deposit be nonrefundable. The following day, representatives for the two firms met to continue the negotiations at the Hotel Bristol in Berlin. Fokker, having "suddenly fallen ill," could not attend and instead sent his business manager, Wilhelm Horter. The Junkers representative, Director Lottmann, asked what had occurred to change Fokker's mind regarding a partnership. Horter replied that he had no influence over Fokker in these matters, "He does what he wants."[51] Lottmann noted that the latent worth of the Junkers license far exceeded that asked for by Junkers in his letter of February 1, and that Junkers only sought to protect the future financial security of the Research Institute and his firm. Horter promised to discuss Junkers's terms with Fokker again, although by now the damage was done.[52]

Thus the "marriage from above," decreed and arranged by military authorities, fell apart from the start in an atmosphere of mutual suspicion and distrust. Despite these problems, however, Idflieg forced both parties together through a combination of coercion and incentive. In April 1917, Fokker informed Junkers that he no longer desired to produce the J-4 under license; he wanted only to use Junkers's patented wing designs.[53] For Fokker, the agreement with Junkers served a tangential purpose—his return to favor with Idflieg and the War Ministry. The development of the J-4 was little more than a vehicle to achieve this goal. For Junkers, however, the stakes were much higher. Having spent over 1.5 million marks of his own money on aircraft research between 1915 and 1916, he no longer possessed the means to continue his work independently.[54] Faced with Idflieg's stance, that no large orders would be granted to the firm without an amalgamation with an established producer, he sought to influence the state-decreed amalgamation with Fokker as best he could. Refusing to grant Fokker the right to use the patented wing design in his own aircraft, Junkers demanded that only a new joint-stock company, and not the Fokker Aircraft Works in Schwerin, would be granted this privilege. Fokker, eager to retain independence for his Schwerin factory, agreed, and on October 20, 1917, a new company, the Junkers-Fokker-Werke AG Metallflugzeugbau (known thereafter as IFA), appeared.[55]

Terms of the agreement indicated the level of compromise worked out over the previous six months. Initially, Fokker refused to enter into a union with Junkers without the financial backing of a larger industrial concern. Through Wilhelm Horter in a meeting with Junkers representatives in Berlin on June 13, and then again six weeks later in a letter to Junkers on July 27, Fokker pressed for the involvement of a large established firm in the agreement, such as the Stinnes steel concern or AEG, to provide fiscal support.[56] When Junkers refused to consider this or Fokker's additional demand that he control all operational aspects of the new firm, Idflieg stepped in and ordered the creation of a new joint-stock company with a capitalization of 2,630,000 marks, 630,000 marks of which would be funded by a War Ministry subsidy.[57]

Junkers provided all fixed assets for the new enterprise: land, buildings, equipment, and raw materials from the Dessau Works. Shares valued at 2 million marks went equally to Junkers and Fokker, who agreed to buy his stock from Junkers at the rate of 118.5 percent. Fokker received the title of director with responsibility for production, while Junkers as chief designer was responsible for research and development. With army subsidies, new production facilities appeared at Dessau, and the workforce in the aircraft production department grew from two hundred to more than one thousand by the end of 1917. Junkers retained control of the Dessau Research Institute, and the terms of IFA's founding stipulated that advances in design based on Junkers's patents and research work would be utilized only by the new firm, or could be granted either to the Fokker Works in Schwerin or to ICO for 250,000 marks plus a 9 percent subsidy per aircraft built. The new firm immediately began production of the J-4, known in the army as the J-I, and 220 of the armored infantry-support aircraft, known as Möbelwagens (furniture vans) because of their box-like fuselages, were delivered between October 1917 and January 1919.[58] The design fared well at the front, particularly during the spring offensives in 1918, and the firm received many grateful messages from German aviators who had been saved by the plane's "steel bathtub."[59]

The state-directed union appeared to give Fokker a distinct advantage. By separating the new firm from his other facilities, Fokker seemed to be in the best position possible, having redeemed his relationship with Idflieg authorities. He returned to Berlin and, with technical knowledge gained during his time at Dessau, focused on regaining his position as Germany's preeminent aircraft manufacturer.[60] For Junkers, the union saved his aviation research and provided much needed financial assistance, as well as a large aircraft order, but meant that the army no longer considered Junkers's core firm, ICO, as a viable aircraft production concern in its own right.[61] Correctly assessing Fokker's ultimate intentions, Junkers sought to end the partnership as soon as possible. He characterized these intentions in a note on March 6, 1918, sarcastically entitled "Fokker's Patriotism": "Just as he [Fokker] has disowned his congenital Dutch nationality, in view of his character traits there is not the least doubt that he will seek to conceal his German nationality if he sees an advantage in it.

1. Characteristics: Ambitious, inconsiderate, brutally self-interested, and unscrupulous in the use of methods to achieve his goals. . . .
2. Goals: Wealth, prestige, a dominant position in aircraft, weapons, and motor science. Inconsiderate pursuit of all those who stand in his way, especially competitors (Junkers, Siemens.)"[62]

Junkers's attitude toward his erstwhile partner stemmed both from Fokker's recalcitrance during IFA's foundation and his crash landing of another Junkers aircraft, the J-7, during army trials in December 1917. The J-7, a duralumin development of the J-1 design, was a product of ICO and appeared to be superior to all other designs in the army trial, including Fokker's own entrant. Although no direct evidence exists to suggest Fokker deliberately crashed the aircraft, the circumstances of the incident and Fokker's capabilities as a pilot suggest his intentions were to destroy the J-7 and obtain the army's new fighter contract, worth 10 million marks, for himself.[63]

The stakes were high, as the beginning of the High Command's "America Program" demanded two thousand aircraft per month from the industry, and new fighter designs were eagerly awaited at the front, where once again Allied aircraft commanded the skies due to superior performance. Idflieg authorities hoped their enforced Fokker-Junkers union would boost production of Junkers's designs, and that Fokker's involvement would encourage Junkers to compromise on the composition of his aircraft and merge the reliability and security of metal with the easier and more rapid workability of wood. When it became clear that Junkers had rejected Fokker's involvement in any design decisions involving metal aircraft, and Fokker himself showed no interest in developing an active role in the enterprise, Idflieg's Wagenführ suggested the two parties arrange a separation. Reflecting on this proposal at his vacation home in Bayrischzell, Bavaria, on March 24, 1918, Junkers noted that he favored a separation from Fokker only if a new partner could be found who would both "guarantee a harmonious union" and "support the activities of the research institute."[64] He observed that many directors of IFA, especially those who had come from Fokker, sought to destroy the freedom of the Research Institute by controlling its ability to allocate licenses and thus maintain an independent financial support base. In his view, attempts by IFA's board to spin off the Research Institute from his other companies would destroy the entire enterprise. Lacking the financial resources to buy Fokker out, his hands at that moment seemed tied.[65]

Chafing under the imposed union, Junkers sought a viable exit strategy. In April 1918, Junkers drafted a letter to Idflieg's Major Siegert, in which he noted the IFA board's attempts to circumvent his authority by decreeing research priorities and allocating funds for specific tasks. Junkers argued this practice, aimed at him, worked directly against the interests of the state by curtailing research into areas not deemed immediately profitable. Faced with this environment, Junkers informed Siegert that he intended to take back control of the Research Institute by absorbing it into ICO. He noted that IFA would use all means at its disposal to prevent such a move, but that he would press on, regardless. He remarked, "The great influence and intensive efforts of Fokker have succeeded in bringing about a situation where the Aircraft Construction section of Junkers & Co. is prostrate and the existence of the research institute has been undermined, and no quick cure will work. . . . Major Wagenführ doesn't see things correctly, he misjudges the purpose of the research institute (scientific, not economic!). He overestimates the importance and help of Fokker . . . Fokker has demonstrably harmed us more than helped us."[66]

Despite his entreaties, Junkers appeared to face an uphill battle. The same day Junkers drafted his letter to Siegert, ICO Director Paul Spaleck telephoned Idflieg authorities and asked whether the firm would receive any orders for aircraft. The Idflieg's Lieutenant Kersten replied that "it had been decided only IFA would be awarded contracts."[67] As the conversation continued, it became clear that the Idflieg favored the cause of its creation rather than the original firm. When Spaleck asked about the status of an experimental order placed with ICO for five new aircraft, another official, Captain Schwarzberger, replied that "IFA was created for the purpose of taking over [ICO] aircraft factory."[68] When Spaleck responded by noting that the founding protocol of IFA allowed for the continued production of aircraft by ICO, Schwarzenberger replied that that was a private matter. Spaleck retorted that supposedly the founding of IFA had also been a private matter, although everyone knew that Idflieg had been the catalyst. Concluding the report, Spaleck noted that the Idflieg officials chose to hide behind each other by claiming that none of them individually held the power to grant orders, although Major Wagenführ had done so for years.[69]

Fortunately for Junkers, contingent circumstances intervened to break the impasse. By the middle of 1918, the German Empire was in crisis. Aware of the spring offensive's failure in the West, the High Command chose to focus on the victory in the East to deflect public awareness of the imminent collapse. On the western front, German pilots faced their Allied adversaries, now joined by US pilots and planes, with fewer numbers and inferior machines. The "America Program" failed to deliver two thousand planes per month, and soon Idflieg began to look throughout Germany for facilities to produce more aircraft.[70] ICO, dismissed from earlier calculations, reappeared as a possible choice. Development of aircraft continued there despite the absence of military orders and IFA's best efforts. In September 1917, the duralumin J-7 prototype appeared, only to be seriously damaged by Fokker's "accident" in January 1918. A successor, the J-9, flew in April 1918, and in early May, Idflieg gave verbal approval for an order of twenty of the new aircraft, six to be delivered in June and the rest in July.[71] Although supplies of duralumin initially proved difficult to obtain, an agreement with the Düren firm, which possessed a temporary surplus due to a lessening of demand from the Zeppelin Works, produced the required amounts, and production began immediately.[72] Junkers, surely aware of the bittersweet irony of this official volte-face, noted the wastage of time and resources by army officials in his diary on May 23 and cynically summarized the official stance of officials like Major Wagenführ: "They said to Junkers: 'Yes, your ideas are very valuable, but before we support you, before we compensate you for your work, you must bring proof that your construction has proved itself in practice, that is at the Front. Go to Capitalists and *ask them for money upfront!* And then at the same time search for a clever practical man who can make your theoretical things practical. When you have made your craft front-ready, then we will take advantage of you by providing you with large orders and reasonable prices, out of which you can support all your costs and efforts.'"[73]

Work on the new planes proceeded slowly throughout the summer of 1918. Labor and raw material shortages meant that only three were ready by the beginning of August, and complaints from Idflieg over construction delays further soured relations between officials and the firm.[74] By the war's end, only twelve J-9s had been delivered.[75]

While construction continued, Junkers began charting the course of his eventual independence. In a personal inventory tabulated on July 28, 1918, he estimated the value of his companies with the aim of presenting a prospectus to creditors in order to raise enough capital to buy Fokker out.[76] Two months later, he reiterated this aim in a letter to his Berlin agent, Major Seitz: "My concept and my plan . . . is to immediately obtain the money and buy Fokker out, the sooner the better, *without the help or knowledge* of the Treasury or the War Ministry."[77] Once again, however, events interceded, making Junkers's plan unnecessary.

In July 1918, *Kogenluft*, the Office of the Commanding General of the German Air Forces, decided to reorganize the Idflieg in a last-ditch effort to maximize production and win the war.[78] With this reorganization came new priorities and attitudes, particularly the official stance toward Junkers and his aviation research. On August 17, Major Seitz wrote to Junkers in Dessau and informed him of the new atmosphere: "Today the War Minister spoke warmly and hopefully about the state of our affairs. . . . He said: 'Send only one aircraft for proofing; the Prince will support Professor Junkers at the Front.'"[79] The following day Seitz wrote again, informing Junkers that Dr. Archenhold, a new member of the Inspectorate, "was dead keen on Junkers, the research institute and everything that you do. . . . In the future he will control valuable connections."[80] Seitz also noticed the changed attitude of the Idflieg's now-promoted Lieutenant-Colonel Siegert: "Siegert is again warmly supporting our achievements and goals. . . . He said, 'Please arrange for Junkers to come see me and tell me his troubles immediately!' . . . Of Fokker, Siegert said that he had knowingly enriched himself by copying the intellectual property of others. . . . I explained the fundamental difference between the superficial, cost-driven work of Fokker and the solid, high quality achievements of Junkers to Dr. Archenhold. [Archenhold] enjoys close relations with Kogenluft, and he will try to set up a meeting between his Excellency von Höppner and myself."[81]

Events moved quickly. Seitz wrote again on September 26 with even better news: "Major Wagenführ has officially declared that he wishes to help us in every way. We may expect with certainty an order for approximately 150 aircraft. He could not commit to a higher number, but in any case an order of so many aircraft will give us a sufficient advance to buy out Fokker as a shareholder. . . . I believe that we may count on the assistance of Major Wagenführ and think that his influence on Fokker will succeed. . . . Our relationship to the Inspectorate experiences a complete turn for the better. . . . Lieutenant Sporleder, adjutant of Lieutenant-Colonel Siegert, who for many weeks spoke of a 'fantastical inventor' and wholly supported our opponent, now speaks with great confidence about the imminent upswing of the Junkers concerns."[82]

Unfortunately for Junkers, these reversals of fortune occurred against a rapidly fragmenting and chaotic background. Germany's military and political situation deteriorated as its allies dropped out of the war. By September 1918, the High Command realized that defeat was inevitable. The army, retreating back toward the German frontier, began to break down as supply lines disintegrated and conscripts deserted or refused to leave Germany. Germans, fueled by expectations of imminent victory through the military-controlled press, were shocked to learn that their government had secretly transmitted an armistice offer to the Allies on October 3. On October 26, "literally and figuratively at his wit's end," Erich Ludendorff resigned as chief quartermaster general of the German armed forces.[83] On November 4, the sailors at Kiel mutinied after learning their officers planned to lead them into an honorable but suicidal *Todeskampf* (death struggle).[84] The revolution spread quickly throughout Germany, as soldiers and sailors disarmed their officers and formed councils. One week later, on November 11, hostilities ended. Military and imperial rule collapsed, and the German Republic began.

In Dessau, where the revolution occurred relatively quietly, Junkers conducted negotiations with Fokker and contemplated the future of his firms. Fokker, now very interested in leaving Germany after narrowly escaping from an angry workers' council in Schwerin, learned of Junkers's change of fortunes in Berlin.[85] Realizing his opportunity to recoup funds from IFA might be slipping away, Fokker wrote to Major Seitz on November 13 with his terms; estimating his share of IFA to be worth 1,595,000 marks, plus 200,000 more that he expected to receive as profit for production during 1918, Fokker declared his willingness to reach agreement for 1,800,000 marks.[86] Seitz replied with his own figures, arguing that under current circumstances, Fokker's share of the firm amounted to only 1,465,000 marks and noted that this figure represented the highest amount he could offer under the circumstances.[87] Fokker responded the next day, arguing that Seitz's numbers, which included the contentious issue of the 500,000 mark nonrefundable license, were too low. Regarding the license fee, Fokker argued that this was a separate issue, irrelevant to current negotiations. Fokker set his revised price at 1,740,000 marks.[88] Seitz replied immediately again, reiterating his offer of the previous day and informing Fokker that his inclusion of an estimate of profits from IFA for the year 1918 ran counter to reality; IFA would, in fact, incur a loss for 1918. Seitz also noted that with the current chaotic political situation, it could not be assumed that the army still possessed the power to honor its price agreements.[89] Fokker responded, arguing that the figures would be available to determine whether IFA made a loss or profit for 1918 within a few days and that once these figures became available, both parties could agree on a settlement sum.

Seitz, armed with IFA's figures for 1918, replied three days later. Calculating that IFA's losses for 1918 totaled 354,638 marks, he pushed for a compromise. Perhaps aware of Fokker's increasingly precarious situation at Schwerin, where revolutionary guards now controlled the Fokker factory, Seitz pressed Fokker to settle, warning that if an agreement could not be reached, the military authorities would be notified of Fokker's intransigence. Cleverly, Seitz followed up his threat with an incentive—an increase of Junkers's offer to 1,600,000 marks and the promise of immediate payment.[90] Fokker declined to accept the offer immediately, but as his circumstances worsened throughout December 1918 and January 1919, he became more receptive. On November 27, 1918, Seitz wrote to Junkers informing him that the Idflieg had approved his plan to unite IFA and ICO and would be granting him an advance of 2,600,000 marks for this purpose.[91] On December 5, official approval came, and the Idflieg also awarded all existing raw material stocks then present at Dessau to Junkers.[92] On December 9, Seitz authorized the transfer of 1,490,000 marks to Fokker.[93] Although the partnership was not formally dissolved until April 24, 1919, Fokker's involvement in IFA came to an end, and Junkers renamed the firm Junkers Flugzeugwerke AG, retaining the IFA acronym.[94] Escaping to Holland in February 1919, Fokker faced Junkers in the courts over patent disputes for twenty more years; the cases continued even after the deaths of both men.[95]

Through these developments, Junkers emerged out of the war in a strong financial position. He now owned the new facilities of IFA and regained his control of all aspects of the firm. Although Junkers only delivered 210 aircraft out of an official total of 47,931 produced by all German manufacturers up to November 1918, the characteristics of the Junkers aircraft design system—rugged reliability and strength—assured him of a strong position in the postwar market, where the focus would shift to civilian designs for general aviation, transport, and ultimately passenger configurations.[96]

Junkers also recognized that changing circumstances required the firm to move toward self-sufficient peacetime production in October 1918. In a conference on October 15, Junkers and other executives outlined a course of action for both ICO and IFA. Recognizing that the resumption of work undertaken by the firm before the war would be insufficient to fully utilize the now massively enlarged plant facilities, they outlined new strategies for keeping both concerns afloat in the coming peacetime. For ICO, four possibilities existed: development of gas motors for use in submarines, aircraft, and automobiles; restart of heavy motor development for maritime use; resumption of boiler production at maximum capacity; and further development of gas water heaters. For IFA, prospects seemed less certain, as no further large orders of military aircraft could be expected. Junkers counseled careful consideration of IFA's future, as no designs for civilian aircraft existed, and months would be needed to develop these designs.[97] After deliberation, Junkers resolved to continue aircraft development. On November 11, 1918, the day of the Armistice, he gathered his engineers and aircraft personnel together and told them all work on military designs would cease and that IFA would now focus on developing aircraft for civilian use. He suggested two ways forward: conversion of existing aircraft types for civilian use and development of new designs for passenger use and air transport.[98]

Following this plan also meant breaking away from state support for IFA, an aim long desired by Junkers personally. On November 18, one week after the end of the war, Junkers Director Paul Spaleck assessed the contemporary situation in the German aircraft industry:

> It is known that the current military authorities plan to award peacetime contracts to firms for the purpose of faster and safer transition to peacetime operations. . . . Considerable private and economic considerations stand in the way of such a tempting arrangement. . . . Our Sales departments of the past peacetime were eliminated and most personnel dismissed. We now rely only on our Representatives. Dependence

on a single contractor [the state] for prosperity endangers our development, we have had enough of that during the war for a lifetime.

Just as in wartime, one would be encouraged by the authorities
to calculate profit bureaucratically, with minute price and accounting
checks being the result. A structured leveling of the sales price will be
striven for and thus the free development of technical innovation will
be inhibited.[99]

This memorandum clearly outlined and reflected Junkers's intentions.
Just two days earlier, he himself commented on political developments
and set a course for himself for the future.

(1) The developments of the political situation have struck all of
us like a bolt of lightning. But after the deafening thunder has
passed, it appears to me that from the storm that has broken out
over us, only a cleansing, refreshing and *invigorating*, not deadly,
effect is expected.

(2) Admittedly we are not lying in a bed of roses. Hard, difficult times
stand before us. Great demands will be placed on us. Is it right to
hang one's head and throw in the towel? No, now is the time to
show that we are men worthy of great tasks that await us, tasks
that will only weaken the weak, but *strengthen the strong*. . . . The
greater the pressure, the stronger our counter pressure. . . . The war
has taught us what a man can achieve when he has to and wants
to.[100]

These statements, remarkable given their proximity to the war's end, illustrate the tenacity of Junkers in the face of adversity. Tenacity would
both help and hinder him in the coming years, as peace promised neither
stability nor prosperity for Germany generally and the German aircraft
industry in particular.

Despite its hardships, the war served Junkers well. His aircraft production facilities at Dessau grew from a small section of one of the ICO
buildings to manufacturing plants covering over 20,000 square meters
(60,000 square feet). The workforce expanded from fifteen in 1915 to
over two thousand by November 1918.[101] A new plant financed by IFA
now lay at his disposal, and with the state-enforced union with Fokker

dissolved, he once again directed all aspects of the Junkers Works. The crucible of war had vindicated his design principles, and all-metal Junkers airplanes had not only flown, but acquitted themselves admirably in frontline combat and conditions. A new, all-metal era of aviation had begun, beginning with the first successful flight of the J-1. More wary than ever of external involvement in his affairs, Junkers also sought to end his reliance on state contracts and create a new market for his aircraft in the civilian arena. He criticized the state's wartime aviation policies in a note drafted just before the war's end, where he remarked that the support of the state throughout the war had been "one-sided and insufficient." By focusing on granting large orders for front-proven designs, the state disadvantaged itself by not realizing the latent potential of research and development over a longer period. He characterized state programs such as the "Hindenburg Program" as wasteful and inefficient—if the war really was total, as the High Command argued, then why was more effort not put into assuring that the state had the best and most modern weapons available? These actions, Junkers wrote, precluded the possibility of success; the state, by focusing on quantity rather than quality through its policies and actions, failed to provide the conditions necessary for victory.[102] Although these conclusions involved considerable self-exculpation on the part of Junkers himself, they were merited at least in part by the war's outcome.

For their part, military officials concluded that Junkers had prioritized his own agenda, focused on development and perfection of a system of metal aircraft manufacture over urgent state requirements. His stubborn refusal to compromise construction techniques and material composition of his aircraft during the critical years of 1917 and 1918 seemed to support this assertion. Junkers aircraft required four times as many workers to manufacture as did wooden aircraft and took longer to complete.[103] The Fokker merger, seen by Junkers as a heavy-handed decree "from above," made good sense from the state's perspective, as Junkers possessed neither the means nor the facilities to undertake large-scale production of aircraft urgently needed at the front. Junkers's facilities and workforce grew strongly through state assistance during the war, and all surviving evidence shows that many Idflieg officials, such as Major Felix Wagenführ, although desperately overworked and faced with enormous and constantly changing responsibilities, did all they could to assist

Junkers while still pursuing the empire's primary interest—production of as many frontline aircraft as possible with existing resources.[104]

Junkers emerged from World War I as the German Empire perished. A relatively small player in the wartime aircraft industry, Junkers had managed to avoid high levels of official scrutiny and had ridden the wave of rapid expansion that total war had offered. These circumstances changed dramatically as his position in Germany's aviation industry rose during the interwar years. The war had changed aviation in far-reaching and permanent ways, both in terms of the lethality, precision, and perceived strategic potential of military aviation, as well as dramatically accelerating the technological rate of change within aviation more generally. This "hothouse evolution" suited the aims and ambitions of Junkers perfectly. He was the first among his peers to see global opportunities emerging from the war in general and commercial aviation that transcended the narrow vistas above the battlefields, and promised the development of a new, interconnected aerial future that would shrink the world. He would dedicate the rest of his life toward realizing this vision, a quest that would consume both himself and his firm.

The Russian Affair, 1918–1924

Chaos, anxiety, and uncertainty marked the end of Germany's Great War. The imperial system in place since 1871 evaporated, and German speakers across the empire's former territories awoke to find themselves residents of a broken world. The postwar vacuum encompassed all areas of German political, bureaucratic, and social life, rendering old certainties irrelevant. For German business and industry, transformed by four years of war, the peace brought equal measures of trepidation and optimism. Overwhelmingly export-oriented, the German economy stood to benefit from a reopening of global trade. However, dangerous obstacles stood in the way of a return to pre-1914 trade patterns; vengeful victors, above all France, sought to emasculate German military and industrial strength through the erection of a punitive postwar framework that permanently limited Germany's military and financial capabilities. The Treaty of Versailles in 1919 did just that, placing responsibility on Germany for the war's outbreak—therefore holding Germany financially accountable for its costs—and prohibiting the embryonic German Republic from possessing or developing many areas of cutting-edge military activity and technology, such as submarines and, most crucially for Hugo Junkers, aircraft.

Cut off from domestic opportunities and facing increased global competition elsewhere, Junkers decided to participate in a top secret venture in Bolshevik Russia, part of a larger attempt by Europe's two postwar pariah states to circumvent the military and technical embargoes of the Treaty of Versailles. This project, hampered from the outset by misunderstandings and unrealistic expectations, ended in failure and mutual acrimony, but not before creating a foundational framework for Soviet aviation that would persist for decades. Junkers designers and technicians would help train the USSR's first generation of aviation experts, and Junkers design principles would remain visible in Soviet aircraft until the end of the Cold War.

On November 11, 1918, the Junkers aircraft firm refocused its energies on civilian designs.[1] This move began Junkers's attempts to create a civilian transportation "system" based on his all-metal aircraft, an objective mentioned both in his prewar patent applications and during the latter years of the war.[2] Junkers correctly discerned that with the war's end all military contracts would soon cease, and the entire aircraft industry, created and nurtured by the state, faced the possibility of collapse. Convinced his technological edge gave his firm a crucial advantage, Junkers and his designers began work on an entirely new type of aircraft in January 1919. This all-metal design, incorporating an enclosed cabin for four passengers, reflected the advances made in aircraft development by the firm during the war. It would become the F-13, the world's most advanced aircraft for the next five years. The F-13 was a revolutionary aircraft that would usher in the modern era of all-metal aviation. Modern commercial, freight, and executive aviation also began with the F-13, which would fly all over the world until the 1970s.

On February 10, 1919, the Junkers representative Major Seitz and chief designer Otto Mader met with Idflieg officials in Berlin to discuss the new design and the future of German civil aviation. Major Felix Wagenführ noted that the future boded well for aircraft, particularly for postal transport, then later for passenger and freight use. Army officers spoke glowingly about the new design, noting that "security for the distinguished businessman is the primary concern."[3] Major Wagenführ also observed that with the demobilization of the air force airfields would be placed at private industry's disposal and that export possibilities for the new aircraft, at present only wished for, needed to be pursued aggressively.[4]

Junkers's fears about the industry's future proved well founded. The chaos surrounding the kaiser's abdication and the empire's collapse permeated all areas of German life. In Berlin the Idflieg, despite being renamed the German Air Office by its new civilian masters, continued work under its old name and staff, and promised to honor all current contracts with aircraft manufacturers. At the same time, however, it informed the industry that no further contracts could be expected and, under instructions from the demobilization office, payment for existing contracts included no profit margin.[5] Idflieg officers strongly encouraged aircraft firms to pursue business from the private sector and convert their plant facilities for production of peacetime items such as furniture or saddlery. While Idflieg officials provided this advice, local soldiers' and workers' councils issued contrary orders, often shutting down factories entirely.

Another problem surfaced with the appointment of August Euler, one of Germany's aviation pioneers, as the head of the new Reich Air Office on November 26, 1918. Euler, long an advocate of civil aviation and an ardent opponent of the Prussian Army, viewed his role in expansive terms—as the overseer of the liquidation of military aviation and the conversion of the industry to a smaller, peacetime structure. A power struggle ensued between Euler and the Idflieg as the former sought to end the army's control of the aircraft industry. Aircraft firms themselves, caught in the middle of the bureaucratic and political melee, frightened by the prospect of Bolshevism and forced in many cases by local workers' and soldiers' councils to maintain their workforce despite a lack of contracts, became increasingly desperate. Euler's recommendation that the industry accept the "inevitability of drastic contraction" provided little comfort, and one by one, the largest wartime manufacturers began to leave the industry.[6] Anthony Fokker, threatened with execution by the local council near his Schwerin plant, left Germany for Holland with as much of his wealth and resources as he could carry.[7] The gigantic Siemens Schuckert Works shut down its aircraft facilities, and other firms struggled to survive through production conversion or through sales in the glutted market of converted military aircraft.[8] Between January and May 1919, the industry generally limped along, hoping circumstances would change. In May, circumstances did indeed change, but for the worse.

In marked contrast to his fellow manufacturers, Junkers's firm weathered the first six months of peace extremely well. Settlements negotiated between Junkers, Fokker, and the Idflieg at the war's end left the Dessau complex with modern plant facilities, raw material supplies, and a welcome infusion of capital. With the separation from Fokker finalized in April 1919, Junkers sought to expand the profile of the firm internationally with the introduction of his new design, the F-13. The new aircraft first flew on June 25, 1919, and immediately caused a sensation. Vastly superior in design and performance to any domestic or foreign airplane, the F-13 ushered in the modern age of passenger aircraft in dramatic fashion, setting an unofficial world altitude record with eight people on board on September 13, 1919.[9] Junkers's aim of attracting global attention through targeted publicity and spectacular feats paid off. Foreign firms and governments immediately began discussions with Junkers's representatives regarding production and sales of the F-13.

Additionally, the concern received an extra capital infusion from the German government. In the summer of 1919, Junkers presented a claim for compensation to the Idflieg. He argued that during the war relaxations of patent rights led to a loss of license revenue from other manufacturers using Junkers's patented design characteristics, such as the use of the "thick-wing" profile and the storage of fuel tanks in wing cells. Junkers initially demanded a license fee of 5 percent for every aircraft produced that incorporated his patent technology, a figure of almost 15 million marks.[10] In July 1920, both parties reached agreement; Junkers received a license fee of 2 percent of all aircraft produced, totaling 2 million marks. Additionally, he received an interest-free credit of 5 million marks, not due for repayment until 1926. Even before Junkers received these sums, he began an extensive program of workshop construction and equipment purchase for series production of the F-13.[11] The future, and Junkers's prospects, appeared infinitely bright. This optimism faded under the harsh restrictions of the Treaty of Versailles.

German demobilization's slow, unwilling pace had not escaped the attention of Allied representatives placed in Germany to oversee enforcement of the terms. Concerning the surrender of German aircraft, the Allied Armistice Commission reported on December 12, 1918, that only 730 out of a required 1,700 aircraft had been received from the

German Army. Continued stalling by the German authorities over the next several months only increased Allied anger, and concern over Germany's technological prowess, represented by the final generation of frontline fighter designs such as the Fokker D-7, encouraged a harsh response in the final peace treaty.[12]

The release of the Treaty of Versailles's peace terms on May 8, 1919, dealt a shattering blow to the German aircraft industry. Five articles of the treaty, 198 through 202, dealt specifically with aviation. Article 198 forbade all military and naval aviation. Article 199 ordered the demobilization of the air force. Article 200 exclusively gave Allied aircraft free passage through Germany and landing rights at German airfields. The next two articles directly affected aircraft producers: Article 201 banned aircraft and aircraft parts manufacturing for six months after the signing of the treaty, and 202 ordered the surrender of all military and naval aviation matériel to Allied and associated governments within three months. A new body established under Article 210, the Inter-Allied Surveillance Commission, would ensure adherence to the terms.[13] Over the next several months, industry, army, and government officials discussed the treaty's conditions, hoping in vain that the Allied stance would soften. Behind these discussions, the struggle continued between the army and civil agencies for control of German aviation, as the army sought to create a military postal service in competition with embryonic civilian airlines. These actions only further aroused the anger of the Allies, who reiterated the binding nature of the peace treaty and resolved to follow Articles 198–202 to the letter. After a stormy political debate, the German government signed the peace treaty on June 28, 1919, with its provisions effective as of January 10, 1920. Within six months, nearly all of the major wartime aircraft producers closed their doors.[14]

Within this darkening storm, Junkers's position appeared to strengthen. The success of the F-13 and the attention surrounding its debut brought a succession of foreign visitors to the Dessau factory, including representatives of the Dutch, Belgian, Japanese, and Czechoslovakian governments as well as Finnish and US businessmen, in particular John Larsen, a Swedish-born entrepreneur.[15] Larsen, who before the war operated as the Curtiss Aeroplane and Motor Corporation's European representative, immediately grasped the importance of the F-13 and traveled to Dessau to view the plane.[16] Junkers, ever suspicious of outside involvement, realized the potential market for the F-13 in the United States and rebuffed Larsen's initial request for a license agreement to produce the F-13. Larsen, undaunted, offered to buy one hundred F-13s from Junkers in the first year and erect a factory to produce one hundred more F-13s in the United States the following year. After unsuccessfully trying to talk directly to US government officials, Junkers agreed, and a contract appeared on November 27, 1919.[17] To increase publicity and encourage sales, Junkers immediately provided two "propaganda aircraft," both of which Larsen then employed in a series of record-breaking flights across the United States and Canada throughout 1920 and 1921.[18]

Three circumstances precluded the ultimate success of the Junkers-Larsen venture. First, Junkers increasingly distrusted Larsen. Aware of both the F-13's positive reception in the United States and the increasing inflation of the US dollar, Junkers sought to increase the unit sales price of the aircraft in an attempt to stave off currency fluctuations and increasing domestic production costs. Larsen's refusal to consider this proposal led to a series of written accusations back and forth across the Atlantic and a permanent damaging of relations between the two men.

Second, Junkers insisted on sole control of the F-13's characteristics. Fiercely protective of his design, and surely still with memories of Fokker in his mind, Junkers refused to allow Larsen to modify the craft in any way once it reached the United States, a stance that proved disastrous. After an initial order by the US Postal Service of eight F-13's, a series of mysterious crashes plagued the aircraft between August 1920 and February 1921. Investigations revealed the source of the problem to be US-produced benzine, which unlike the European benzine mix, ate through the rubber seal connecting the fuel line to the motor, resulting in a fuel leak into the engine cowling. Press coverage of F-13 accidents proved devastating to the Junkers-Larsen venture, as prospective buyers shunned the craft for less flammable designs.[19] Media publicity proved a double-edged sword, especially in the crucial US market.

Third, the Treaty of Versailles, Articles 201 and 202, which came into force on January 10, 1920, ended exports of the F-13 to the United States. Initially, officials of the Allied oversight body, renamed the Inter-

Allied Control Commission, tacitly accepted the Junkers firm's description of the F-13 as a civilian aircraft, allowing the first exports to Larsen to proceed. On May 4, the commission informed Junkers that the F-13 had officially received "classification as a civilian device."[20] However, efforts by the German aircraft industry to evade the Treaty of Versailles restrictions throughout the first months of 1920, principally continued aircraft manufacturing in contravention of Article 201 and deliberate avoidance of Article 202, elicited a strong Allied response at the Ambassadors' Conference in London in June of that year. At the conference, members voted to extend the ban on aircraft manufacture in Germany until the Inter-Allied Control Commission deemed that Germany had completely fulfilled all disarmament provisions.[21] When this measure failed to stop infractions, the Allies went further. At the Boulogne Conference later that month, Allied officials declared that Article 201 would henceforth be more liberally interpreted to include all German aircraft, not just those designed for military use. German vows to ignore this new interpretation meant little, as both sides knew Germany possessed neither the means nor the will to prolong the struggle.[22]

Technological considerations also played a role in this new Allied stance. A report by the French undersecretary of state for aeronautics in January 1921 underscored Allied apprehension over rapid advances made by Junkers and other German designers in aircraft design. Seeking to protect their own domestic industries, the Allies strove to prevent the appearance of advanced German designs such as the F-13, which the report dubbed "the craft of the future," on the international aviation market. The report accepted the technological superiority of the Junkers design, and Allied representatives in Germany aimed to protect their perceived national interests.[23]

Commission officials made the first move. In August 1920, commission leader Air-Commodore Masterman offered Junkers the chance to produce twenty F-13s for export in exchange for delivery of one F-13, without payment, to each of the five Allied nations.[24] When Junkers refused, in October the commission confiscated eleven F-13s in Hamburg packaged for delivery to Larsen in the United States. Junkers later estimated the losses incurred by the firm through the confiscation at 19 million marks.[25]

Junkers now found himself in serious financial straits. Expecting large orders from the United States, he had invested much of his liquid capital in new workshop construction, materials, and workforce maintenance. With the US market closed to him, at least for the time being, and Allied restrictions on production extended indefinitely, Junkers faced a frustratingly uncertain future. The year 1920 represented the greatest year for the concern in terms of technological achievement and autonomous action. Ironically, circumstances forced Junkers back into the relationship he strove most to avoid—close contact with the German state. In May 1920, before difficulties arose, Junkers wrote in his diary about the risks of state support:

1. We now need no help from the government. This was the case before the war, at the start of the war, and later, when the first aircraft appeared ready.
2. When the government gives help, it is not substantial, and it requires proof of worthiness, which lies not in the past, or in conversations, or in mere prospects for the future. The state dislikes these circumstances in normal times, and particularly now, when it finds itself in great financial need. No official dares give up or ask for something for nothing.
3. Government assistance requires the expenditure of endless effort, time, and money, and abandonment of other more promising tasks.
4. State preference for a single concern causes jealousy in others, which ends up being costly both for the state and the preferred.
5. The state sees weakness in assistance requests and is easily disposed to infer that the requester lacks maturity. The result is that the state sees itself as obligated to provide further help or rectify committed mistakes. (This is the main argument behind why Junkers received no (wartime) orders for aircraft.)
6. The state attaches conditions to the type of use of the assistance that are extremely irritating, for example state control, etc.[26]

Junkers, aware of the pitfalls of involvement with state organs, particularly the military, nevertheless enjoyed few private financial prospects by 1921. Still shackled by the Allied manufacture ban and with the West closed, but refusing to give up his aim of establishing an air transportation system, he turned east, toward the vast expanses of Eastern Europe and European Russia. This movement dovetailed precisely with the aims of the new German Army, the *Reichswehr*, whose new leader, General Hans von Seeckt, favored the creation of an economic and military alliance with the other international pariah state, Bolshevik Russia.

Although the Treaty of Versailles expressly ordered the abolition of the old imperial general staff and the Prussian Army—a circumstance supposedly reinforced by the creation of the Reichswehr under the Weimar Constitution—contingent political circumstances prevented significant internal reform of the armed services. Forced to call on the army to defend it from internal strife, the Weimar Republic allowed the army to conduct its own affairs behind the convenient illusion of the services being "above politics." For its part, the army encouraged this belief and developed its own ethos of loyalty to an abstract ideal of the state rather than to the Republic itself—a suitable compromise that encouraged continuity in traditions and, more importantly, personnel, even after the Kapp Putsch of 1920 demonstrated the questionable loyalty of the army to the Republic. When Hans von Seeckt assumed command of the Reichswehr in March 1920, he began to move German military policy toward the East in an attempt to circumvent the restrictions of the Treaty of Versailles with the long-term aim of restoring Germany's 1914 borders. Administrative reforms in the wake of the Kapp Putsch gave von Seeckt control of both central departments of the Reichswehr, the *Truppenamt* (Personnel Office) and the *Waffenamt* (Weapons Office), removing them from the jurisdiction of the defense minister.[27]

These reforms gave von Seeckt freedom of action to pursue military policy without civilian oversight. A political realist, von Seeckt accepted the status quo on Germany's western frontier and turned east, where the newly created state of Poland fought a desperate battle for survival against the Red Army. Von Seeckt, who served on the Eastern Front during the war and respected his former adversaries, sought to establish closer ties with Russia. The Russians, too, had reason to encourage closer ties. Faced with war in Poland, a continuing civil war, and foreign troops occupying Russian ports, Lenin and Trotsky approved the courting of

German armaments producers and military officials, both for short-term reasons of necessity and long-term plans for the use of German expertise to create an indigenous weapons industry. Lenin's move away from War Communism and toward the adoption of the New Economic Policy provided further impetus to these negotiations, as did mutual dislike of the Western Powers.

Negotiations began unofficially through third parties. Karl Radek, the Bolshevik expert on German affairs, remained in prison in Berlin after the war's end. In the summer of 1919, von Seeckt established contact with Radek through a mutual friend, Enver Pasha, the former Turkish minister of war.[28] In October 1919, Pasha flew from Germany to Moscow in an F-13 prototype, carrying a letter from von Seeckt proposing the establishment of a relationship between the Reichswehr and Soviet Russia.[29] At the same time, Victor Kopp, the semiofficial Russian representative in Berlin, began his tenure in Germany. Kopp contacted several German armaments producers, including Krupp, the submarine firm Blohm and Voss, and the Albatros Works, the largest producer of aircraft during the war, about establishing production facilities in Bolshevik Russia. All three firms expressed interest but also voiced reservations concerning Russia's uncertain political and economic climate.[30]

Lutz Budrass notes the choice of Albatros made sense during initial negotiations, before the effects of the Treaty of Versailles really took hold, and also from the Reichswehr's perspective, as Albatros's compliant stance toward official control during the war and its experience in efficient mass production made it the first choice for the Russian venture. However by 1921, when more official negotiations took place, Albatros's circumstances had worsened considerably, and the Russians, interested above all in technology transfer and the creation of their own indigenous industry, pressed for the involvement of the Junkers firm.[31] All these negotiations occurred against the backdrop of the Russo-Polish War and internal unrest in the former German provinces of East Silesia, where German volunteer troops, the *Freikorps*, resisted the Polish takeover. At a critical time for both nations, hatred of a common enemy encouraged expansive promises. Junkers soon found himself in the center of these circumstances.

From a personal perspective, Junkers enjoyed a long relationship with Russia. As a young man, he had traveled extensively throughout European Russia and had pondered the possibilities and needs of this vast region with little modern infrastructure. In 1914, he established a relationship with the Nobel munitions firm in Russia and its owner, Emanuel Nobel. Writing to Nobel in 1921, he observed, "Recognition of the importance of aircraft as a means of transport grows every day. . . . Air transport is certainly destined to play a large role in Russia's reconstruction."[32] By this time, Junkers needed no further encouragement to pursue possibilities in Russia. In January 1920, Major Wagenführ informed Junkers's Major Seitz that German steel magnate Hugo Stinnes planned to erect a large air transport network throughout Scandinavia.[33] In April 1920, Junkers received a report from Gotthard Sachsenberg, a former Marine pilot who flew Junkers aircraft during the war.[34] Sachsenberg at that time ran a volunteer fighter group that operated throughout East Prussia and the Baltic States; his report outlined the opportunities for Junkers in the region and noted that "the airplane as means of transport, as it requires neither roads nor tracks, will play an important role in opening up former Russian regions. . . . This [circumstance] brings the possibility of a huge sales area for the German aircraft industry, in particular airline companies supplied by a Junkers factory in Russia."[35]

Later in September 1920, an emigré Russian colonel, Michel Dolukhanov, offered to involve Junkers in an airline network between Stockholm and Danzig (now Gdansk), via the Baltic States, with financial backing provided by the Russian petroleum magnate Lianosov and support from his old friend Emanuel Nobel. Junkers maintained interest in this proposal, which would take effect "after the fall of the Soviet Government," until the defeat of General Wrangel's White Russian army in November.[36] Unable to reach sales markets in the West, Junkers considered moving the company out of Germany but found the costs of relocation prohibitive. Frustrated, Junkers appealed to federal and state government officials, emphasizing the national and local importance of his enterprise and asking for financial help. Writing to the mayor of Dessau, Junkers asserted that he would be received "with open arms" in England or America.[37] In a country where aircraft manufacture remained forbidden, however, no government could easily justify subsidizing aircraft producers, and Junkers's pleas made little headway. With few sales, the aircraft factory workforce declined by half between November 1920 and April 1921.[38] Forced into alternative production to remain solvent, the firm produced silverware, ice skates, yachts, and cookware.

Fortunately for Junkers, negotiations between the German and Soviet governments continued throughout 1921. In April, Victor Kopp returned to Moscow and reported to Trotsky that several German firms were willing to establish factories in Russia and that a group of German technical experts would come to Russia to discuss the terms.[39] Trotsky and Lenin agreed, and in the summer of 1921, a German delegation led by Major Oskar von Niedermayer traveled secretly to Moscow.[40] Prior to leaving for Russia, Niedermayer contacted Erich Offerman at the Junkers office in Berlin and informed him that plans existed for the creation of a munitions industry in Russia supported by the German government. During the meetings that followed, Russian representatives expressed their desire for the inclusion of Junkers in the plans. Returning from Moscow, Niedermayer again contacted the Junkers Berlin office and received confirmation that Junkers would participate in the venture.

At the same time, secret negotiations between the Reichswehr and the Bolshevik government intensified. The two parties met secretly in the Berlin apartment of Major Kurt von Schleicher, a location chosen for its proximity to the Foreign Ministry.[41] Colonel Otto Hasse of the Truppenamt on the German side and Leonid Krasin, chairman of the Council for Foreign Trade, on the Russian side sought to reach agreement on the proposed military and economic cooperation. In the wake of the recent Red Army defeat outside Warsaw, the Russians sought assurances of German military support if the war in Poland resumed. Von Seeckt, informed of the negotiations by Hasse, declined to make any concrete assurances as he believed that such action would prompt an immediate invasion of Germany by Czechoslovakia and France. By November, the two sides reached a basic agreement that German firms would be allowed to operate in Russia, with the German government providing financial support for the venture. Crucially, however, a precise definition of the level of this financial support was never quantified. This uncertainty led to enormous subsequent problems. General von

Seeckt sought to keep the negotiations with the Russians secret—few people within the Defense Ministry knew of the talks, and for funding purposes, von Seeckt informed only Chancellor Joseph Wirth, previously the finance minister, within the government. President Friedrich Ebert, known to be an opponent of von Seeckt's Eastern policy, was not informed.

While negotiations continued in Berlin, Junkers considered his options. After receiving a report from Major Seitz on the Berlin talks, it was clear to him that both governments intended to produce military aircraft in Russia for their own ends. Yet Junkers also could derive advantages from the arrangement; four possibilities presented themselves: first, a chance to circumvent the domestic ban on production; second, the possibility of creating an airline network from Sweden across European Russia to Persia, with the erection of production and maintenance facilities at both ends; third, the ability to produce military and civilian aircraft for the international market in Russia, free from Allied restrictions; and finally, the use of capital generated in Russia to fund further research and development.[42] At the same time, in preparation for the Russian venture, Junkers hired Sachsenberg and his pilots as employees.[43] Sachsenberg, who realized his position in the company depended on success in Russia, began preparing for negotiations with both the German and Russian authorities.[44] He did not have to wait long.

Initial Reichswehr plans called for a series of German companies to begin working in Russia, apparently independent of any official support or encouragement—an early example of "plausible deniability." Speaking with Russian officials early in 1921, Oskar von Niedermayer outlined a massive plan for the expansion of the Bolshevik Russian Air Force to between five and ten thousand aircraft, a force larger than the combined forces of the French, British, Polish, and Czech air arms. Not surprisingly given the ongoing Russo-Polish tensions, these plans attracted considerable interest from the Russian side. Niedermayer estimated Junkers would be called on to build at least two thousand aircraft. Due to Russia's uncertain political circumstances, the government could only provide a guarantee against losses through initial subsidies from the Deutsche Bank. Niedermayer apparently also promised funds for the procurement of raw materials and motors, as well as governmental responsibility for the risk of the venture.[45] Tragically for all concerned, Niedermayer made these promises without consulting or informing his superiors. For his part, Junkers entered negotiations with the Reichswehr assuming Niedermayer's claims reflected a general consensus.[46]

On November 21, 1921, Reichswehr officers traveled to Dessau to conduct official negotiations. Reflecting the project's importance, two of the army's three leaders, Waffenamt commander General Ludwig Wurtzbacher and Truppenamt commander Colonel Otto Hasse, headed the military negotiating team. The ensuing discussions set in motion a series of misunderstandings that plagued Junkers's subsequent involvement in Russia. Wurtzbacher and Hasse pursued an agreement with Junkers that focused on political and military objectives outlined by their superior, von Seeckt—establishment of German military presence on Russian soil to circumvent the Treaty of Versailles and strengthened military relations with the Bolshevik Russians against their common enemy, Poland. Only tangentially interested in economic issues, the Reichswehr negotiators sought a quick agreement, and little else.

Junkers and Sachsenberg, representing the firm, arrived at the table with fundamentally different concerns. Aware of the difficult economic conditions in Russia, both men desired assurances of support from the German government that this project, initiated and driven by government interests, received a corresponding amount of government assistance, in particular financial support. Junkers noted that high production costs in Russia ruled out competitive sales prices for his aircraft on the world market and that the entire operation stood little chance of economic solvency for several years after production began. Most notably, Junkers stressed that his firm on its own lacked sufficient capital either to begin the project or to sustain it for any length of time.

Wurtzbacher and Hasse sidestepped Junkers's financial inquiries and stressed the need for both secrecy and haste. When Junkers persisted, the Reichswehr leaders called for further negotiations and advised Junkers to pass the costs onto the Soviets, adding that "if this fails, then the client will undertake a guarantee for the invested capital, or provide it themselves in some form."[47] This evasive response revealed the Reichswehr's lack of interest and expertise in financial issues surrounding the project.

However Junkers, driven by necessity and also perhaps wishful thinking, chose to accept the Reichswehr's statements and, crucially, also failed to keep a written record of the negotiations.[48] Reichswehr leaders also stated that the army assumed all existent risks surrounding the establishment of production in Russia, a statement directed toward political risk but which Junkers assumed meant all risks, including financial.[49] Both parties therefore emerged from the negotiations without clarifying the financial parameters of the project, a situation amenable to Wurtzbacher and Hasse, who returned to Berlin and confirmed Junkers's involvement to von Seeckt. Junkers, clearly still enamored with the expansive promises of Niedermayer, hoped to formalize the financial arrangements at the next round of negotiations.

In December 1921, the Reichswehr created a secret department, Special Section "R," responsible for all activities in Russia. Later that month, another German delegation led by Niedermayer traveled secretly to Moscow; Sachsenberg and Director Paul Spaleck represented the Junkers firm. Only von Seeckt and a few others knew of the meetings; the Foreign Office and the civilian government were not informed. During the ensuing negotiations, astonished Junkers representatives heard of the plan for aircraft production in Russia. The plan envisaged two stages of production, both centered on the automobile factory facilities at Fili, outside of Moscow, formerly used for the production of the gigantic Sikorsky Ilya Muromets aircraft during the war.[50] Stage One called for the refitting of the Fili factory both for the production of a small number of metal aircraft and aero-engines and for use as a repair facility for wooden aircraft. Stage Two called for an expansion of the Fili facility and the erection of a sister plant near St. Petersburg in the event of a European war, increasing the production capacity of both sites to one hundred aircraft per month. For the completion of Stage One, Reichswehr officials allocated 150 million paper marks, for the more ambitious Stage Two, 600 million marks.[51]

While talks continued between German and Russian military officials, Bolshevik War Commissar Leon Trotsky asked Junkers representatives for cost estimates for the successful completion of the two programs. Junkers officials calculated Stage One required 350 million extra marks to complete, for Stage Two between 500 and 600 million extra marks. Writing to

Director Spaleck from Dessau, Junkers outlined some of his demands in return for involvement at Fili:

1. Airline route concessions, especially the Moscow–Kovno (Kaunas) route, the essential connection route to Germany.
2. A majority holding in case of government involvement.
3. Oil concessions connected to our motor production.
4. Government funds provisional construction costs.
5. Payment of a premium for every motor and aircraft produced under our direction during provisional phase. Possibly our development costs during this time also funded by government.
6. The government involves itself in our concern through contributions in the form of factories, land, and equipment.
7. Free provision of living quarters for our personnel.
8. Our directors retain the right to speak directly with the highest authorities.[52]

Although Trotsky chose not to accept any of these demands, on February 6 he oversaw an initial agreement between the Russian government and the Junkers firm—signed by both Junkers representatives—that committed Junkers to both the smaller and the larger programs. Importantly, Oskar von Niedermeyer also signed this document, lending the appearance of Reichswehr support. Once again, misunderstandings grew out of this provisional agreement. For Junkers and the Russians, Niedermayer's signature conveyed the Reichswehr's acceptance of the cost estimates for both stages submitted by the Junkers representatives. However, in a secret annex to the agreement unknown to Junkers, Niedermayer made no reference to these estimates and repeated the figures of December 1921 for each stage, namely 150 million and 600 million paper marks. This difference ensured that from February 1922 Junkers and the Reichswehr operated under vastly different assumptions of the latter's financial commitment to the Fili project.[53]

Each side's assumptions surfaced three weeks later on March 15, 1922, when Junkers and the Reichswehr drafted a preliminary contract outlining their respective obligations. Junkers committed his firm to the Fili project and agreed to begin preparations for production once the

Russian government signed a final contract. In return, the Reichswehr committed 140 million paper marks—40 million to cover losses and costs of the venture, and 100 million for working capital to cover purchases of aluminum, factory fittings, and equipment.[54] This secret provisional contract, referred to subsequently by both sides as the "March Agreement," only became legally binding when the firm completed a final concession agreement with the Russians. Interestingly, however, the Reichswehr agreed to begin disbursing funds to Junkers *before* the firm signed a contract with the Russians. Payments commenced on March 27, 1922, followed by further installments on May 12, July 10, and December 8.[55]

Junkers's personal doubts about the Fili operation first appeared in his diaries in early 1922. On January 17, he considered the problem of raw material supplies, noting that orders needed to be placed three months in advance for essential elements such as aluminum, steel, and glue. These conditions ruled out a swift start for production.[56] Reports from Russia describing the dilapidated state of the Fili site increased his concerns. Russian promises of modern facilities and equipment proved illusory. Transport infrastructure was nonexistent with no railway terminus linking the factory to the Moscow lines. Another source of anxiety lay in the apparently changed stance of the Reichswehr regarding funding for the project. During the March Agreement talks, General Hasse stunned the Junkers officials, at this point still unaware of Niedermayer's secret addition to the Trotsky Agreement, when he stressed that no further funds beyond 140 million marks would be available.[57] Hasse's announcement rendered the Trotsky Agreement moot and also signaled that the proposed Stage Two, discussed in December 1921, was already a dead letter.

Despite these serious problems, Junkers declared himself ready to proceed and accepted the terms of the provisional contract. Clearly, he believed that Russia's vast expanses provided tremendous possibilities for transport and commercial aviation and that any firm that established itself first in Russia stood to reap the most benefits. Production of military aircraft also appeared lucrative, given the absence of any domestic Russian competitors, the ongoing tensions with Poland, and the Reichswehr's apparent interest. With the final contract with the

Russians still under negotiation, Junkers set aside his doubts and began preparations for production in Russia.

Several complications appeared immediately. At the same time Junkers concluded the March Agreement with the Reichswehr, he learned an affiliate of Deutscher Aero-Lloyd (DAL), his largest domestic airline competitor, had received an exclusive license for the provision of air transport services between Moscow and Königsberg, capital of East Prussia.[58] Excluded from the most direct route between Germany and Russia, Junkers's airline aspirations in Russia suffered a serious setback. Reichswehr attitudes toward Junkers also shifted negatively. As previously noted, Junkers's involvement in the Russian project stemmed primarily from Russian rather than German interest. Reichswehr officials, fully aware of the difficulties between the firm and the army during the war, viewed the firm ambivalently, at best, and when Junkers sought to include a 10 percent license fee for each aircraft produced at Fili within the terms of the March Agreement, army representatives threatened to approach Fokker, Junkers's "old Dutch friend," and exclude Junkers entirely.[59]

All these events took place against the backdrop of intense negotiations between the German and Bolshevik Russian governments that resulted in the Treaty of Rapallo on April 16, 1922. Rapallo established formal diplomatic ties between the two countries and encouraged closer economic cooperation between Germany and Russia. Immediately the Bolshevik government renounced all claims to German reparations nominally due under the Treaty of Versailles and refused to cooperate with Western European proposals for the economic restructuring of Europe at the International Economic Conference in nearby Genoa. Rapallo also unconsciously reinforced the Reichswehr's Russian policy, and it now moved toward a formal military protocol with the Russians without the knowledge of the Foreign Office or Reich President Ebert, in direct violation of the German constitution.[60] On July 29, 1922, Colonel Hasse and the Russian negotiator Rosenblatt signed a preliminary treaty approving German-Russian military collaboration. Two weeks later, Major Veit Fischer, head of Special Section R, concluded the military convention in Moscow.[61] Simultaneously a holding company appeared, the innocuously titled Gesellschaft zur Förderung gewerblicher

Unternehmungen (Society for the Furthering of Commercial Enterprises, or GEFU), with offices in Berlin and Moscow. This agency linked Special Section R and the German firms in Russia, providing funds with no direct connection to either the Reichswehr, the German embassy in Russia, or the German government. GEFU therefore added another layer of plausible deniability to the enterprise.

For Junkers, concession negotiations with the Russians progressed slowly. Russian officials, incensed with the Reichswehr's abandonment of its earlier funding promises and lacking funds of their own, sought to limit their own liability for the Fili project. Reichswehr officials further outraged the Russians by leaving the negotiations for three months, only returning in July. Junkers, informed of the slow progress in Moscow, noted his frustration in his diary, "The Russians imagined they could build a great fleet of aircraft. They counted on (a) Great German interest in Russia and the Russian air force (b) German money (c) German know-how (cheap or completely free.)"[62] In June he added, "The Russians are dominated by boundless suspicion. They see everyone as an exploiter, hindering and impeding actions that can and will help them. They wish things achieved through paragraphs and legal compulsion rather than good will. These actions cripple productive work."[63]

Junkers's concerns rested on sound foundations. Preparations for production at Fili began immediately after the conclusion of the March Agreement. Granted priority above all other projects in the research and construction departments, Junkers workers began designing new types of military aircraft and equipment for the Russian project.[64] In Russia, work proceeded slowly, hampered by inadequate infrastructure. In his diary, Junkers remarked on unsatisfactory storage facilities for raw materials, shortages of laboratory supplies, and the poor performance of Russian foremen.[65] With his principal resources devoted entirely to the Fili operation, Junkers pressed for a quick end to negotiations. Increasing German inflation throughout 1922 encouraged Junkers's stance. The mark's value dropped alarmingly against the US dollar over the summer, and the funds transferred to Junkers by the Reichswehr lost two-thirds of their value between March and October.[66] The currency crisis affected all the Reichswehr's Russian projects as its financial resources evaporated. Knowing this, Junkers sought to insulate himself by gaining concessions from the Russians. This strategy appeared to succeed when the Russians agreed to pay a 50 percent deposit for any aircraft orders from the Fili factory, a step Junkers believed would provide the necessary capital to sustain the operation. Unfortunately, this belief relied on the factory receiving a steady stream of orders from both German and Russian authorities.

Finally on November 26, 1922, both sides reached an agreement. In a contract extending over fifty-nine paragraphs, Junkers received three concessions from the Russian government. The first awarded Junkers the right to produce aircraft in Russia for thirty years. The second granted Junkers rights to airline routes between Sweden and Persia over Russian territory. The third awarded Junkers a contract for an aerial survey of Russia.[67] The first concession obligated Junkers to construct an aircraft factory at Fili "of the highest technical quality," which from March 1924 possessed the capacity to produce 300 aircraft and 450 aero-engines per year.[68] Junkers also agreed to provide stocks of aluminum and other raw materials sufficient for the production of 750 aircraft and 1,150 engines within six months of the contract's commencement. Additionally, Junkers agreed to employ substantial numbers of Russian workers at Fili, 50 percent of the workers and 10 percent of the managers over the first five years, increasing to ratios of 70 percent and 50 percent thereafter.[69]

Caveats within the contract placed further responsibility on the firm. Article 3 assigned responsibility for all improvements at the Fili complex to Junkers, including the construction of a railway line and terminus. Article 5(a) indicated the Russians only guaranteed a purchase of 20 percent of the firm's annual production, a mere sixty aircraft out of three hundred. Article 15 required Junkers to sign a final contract for the manufacture of aluminum in Russia within six months. As the firm possessed no previous experience in aluminum production, this seemed a tall order.[70] Clearly the Russians got the better of the bargain, but Junkers, faced with mounting financial pressures, encouraged by Reichswehr officials to proceed, and still personally convinced of the project's long-term viability, accepted the terms. Russian officials placed an initial order for 100 two-seat military aircraft on December 4, 1922, and on January 29, 1923, the new Soviet Council of People's Commissars drafted the contract into law.

Problems arose immediately. Factory refitting consumed far more capital than the Reichswehr provided, forcing Junkers to fund these improvements from other areas of the firm. On May 13, 1923, Junkers noted the critical and draining influence of the Fili operation on the entire Junkers concern, forcing the postponement of all important company decisions.[71] With poor Russian transport infrastructure delaying the arrival of required machine tools and specialized equipment, Junkers decided to build the planes in Dessau, ship them to Russia, and reassemble them at Fili until the factory came online. This decision bought the firm time, but also more problems. Dividing assembly tasks between Dessau and Fili resulted in an increasingly complicated construction process. In November, Junkers noted that ski production for the J-21 took place in Dessau, where the task depleted valuable manpower, rather than in Russia, where excess labor existed.[72] Soon after construction began, external events interceded again.

On January 11, 1923, the French government, tired of German intransigence toward reparations payments, took matters into its own hands and occupied the Ruhr Valley, Germany's industrial heartland, with the aim of obtaining reparations in kind, principally coal. The effects of the Ruhr occupation paralyzed German industry, as the French took control of the German transport system and banned all trade between the occupied zone and the rest of Germany.[73] The Ruhr crisis hit Junkers particularly hard, as the Düren Metal Works, Junkers's supplier of duralumin, lay within the occupied zone and could not deliver the raw materials needed for the Russian order. Unable to procure duralumin from any other source, work at Dessau and Fili ground to a halt.

Although no active German resistance occurred during the Ruhr occupation, contingency plans existed for military action if the French advanced deeper into Germany. The new German chancellor, Wilhelm Cuno, enjoyed a close friendship with General Seeckt, and the two men cooperated in a series of measures in preparation for this possibility. Chancellor Cuno secretly authorized the transfer of government funds into a "Ruhr Fund" to purchase weapons for national defense.[74] German army units most urgently needed modern fighter aircraft. General Hasse contacted Major Wilhelm Schubert, director of the Fili factory, and asked whether the factory was ready to produce one hundred fighters.

Schubert, who later argued he misunderstood Hasse's inquiry, replied no, and the Reichswehr purchased the aircraft from Fokker.[75] When Junkers heard of the Fokker purchase he became enraged and threatened to reveal the Fili project to the press. He now also realized the Reichswehr sought to undermine rather than strengthen his involvement in Russia. General Hasse, wary of the consequences of public disclosure, mollified Junkers in October 1923 by justifying the Fokker order as a "misunderstanding" and placed an order for one hundred aircraft and engines at Fili.[76] Further salve arrived from GEFU in the form of an interest-free loan of US$500,000 for this order on November 5, which doubled to US$1 million in February 1924.[77]

Other reasons lay behind the purchase of Fokker aircraft over those of Junkers. Budrass notes that the Fokker D-13 far outperformed the Junkers J-21 and J-22 designs destined for production at Fili. Too slow and heavy for effective use against French fighters, the J-21 and J-22, described as Schulflugzeuge (training aircraft) in Reichswehr reports, lacked the performance characteristics to attract large German orders even before production began. The Fokker fighters not used in Germany ended up at the new German flying school in Lipetsk, Russia. Unfortunately for Junkers, the Soviet Air Force drew the same conclusions as the Reichswehr and between 1923 and 1926 purchased 324 single-seat fighter aircraft from Fokker.[78]

Russian concerns over Fili gradually mounted during 1923. The slow pace of production at the factory was no secret. Transferring specialized equipment machine tools from Dessau to Fili took months, and the extensive repairs required at Fili swallowed up all funds sent from Dessau. Ignoring these problems, the Russians increased pressure on Junkers to speed up production. Caught in a liquidity crisis, Junkers could only continue to assemble aircraft at Fili rather than build them there, a situation the Russians justifiably argued violated the terms of the concession contract. Adding to the firm's troubles, the J-22 design experienced significant performance problems, forcing Junkers into modifying the J-21 design as a substitute. By December 1924, the Russians received only seventy-three of the one hundred aircraft ordered, and all of those delivered failed to meet the performance parameters established in the December 1922 contract.[79]

Differences over aero-engine production aroused further friction between all three parties. In October 1923, Reichswehr representatives visited the Fili factory and confirmed that few facilities existed for engine production, although the production of engines formed a core part of the contract between Junkers and the Russian government. Seeking to speed up the process, bring in outside capital, and remove Junkers from control of the entire facility, Captain Vogt of Special Section R recommended that another firm, the Bayerische Motor Werke (BMW), be approached and asked to begin production in Russia.[80] Junkers had just reestablished his engine facilities in Germany and endured a long history of conflict with BMW over license and patent rights. He refused to consider the Bavarian firm's inclusion. Officially, he justified his stance patriotically, noting that BMW's largest shareholder, Camilio Castiglioni, as an Austrian citizen, could not be included in a task of such secret, national importance. Personal interest played the most important role, however, as Junkers sought a production outlet for his new engine firm. Junkers's refusal to allow BMW's involvement at Fili worsened relations between the Reichswehr and the firm considerably and led to Special Section R's decision to cancel its November 5 order.[81]

German domestic politics again exerted influence on Junkers's fortunes. In August 1923, the Cuno government fell under the pressure of hyperinflation, and his successor Gustav Stresemann began implementing a markedly new foreign policy. Convinced the only way forward for Germany lay in reaching accords with its Western neighbors, Stresemann implemented policies designed to break Germany's political isolation by ending resistance to reparations and opening dialogue with Germany's former enemies, above all, France. France's change of leadership, with Aristide Briand replacing the Germanophobe Raymond Poincaré as French prime minister, ushered in a new era in German-French relations culminating in the Treaty of Locarno in October 1925. Stresemann's plans encouraged a profound change in military policy, particularly toward the secret programs in Russia. Even though Stresemann's tenure as chancellor ended in November 1923, he remained as foreign minister and directed German foreign policy until his death in 1929.

By March 1924, Junkers's financial position forced him to inform the Reichswehr that without further financial help the Fili factory faced immediate closure. On March 25, Sachsenberg wrote to the Waffenamt, outlining the firm's financial position and proposing a solution. In his letter, excerpted below, Sachsenberg noted:

> Facts
>
> Throughout early 1924 we reckoned on receiving the following contracts:
>
> From the Special Section
> (a) 100 aircraft at $27,000=$2,700,000 with down payment of 50%
>   = $1,350,000
>   100 engines at $17,000=$1,700,000 with down payment of 75%
>   = $1,275,000
>
> From the Russians
>   60 aircraft at $27,000=$1,620,000 with down payment of 50%
>   = $810,000
>   140 engines at $17,000=$2,380,000 with down payment of 50%
>   =$1,765,000
>
> Total down payments = $4,625,000
>
> With the recent reduction of the Special Section order and the decision of the Russian government to temporarily grant no orders whatsoever, we now only expect with the Special Section's order of 50 aircraft and 50 engines a down payment of $1,312,000. Irrespective of how we respond to the Russian Government's breaches of contract, we must for the time being expect a budget shortfall of $3,300,000. . . Our labor costs will remain the same, and the material supplies for the original orders continue to arrive.[82]

Sachsenberg proposed the Reichswehr pay the full price for its order in advance, decreasing the shortfall significantly. He argued that the money would even out if and when the Reichswehr decided to reinstate its original order. He also pushed for a further credit of US$2 million to erase the budget shortfall, which Junkers would repay with "products of the Moscow factory."[83] Receiving no response, Sachsenberg wrote again on April 15, noting that the firm allowed Colonel Thomsen of the Special Section to examine its books, and gave him an account of

Junkers's expenditure on the Fili project from its inception, a sum totaling US$1.5 million. Sachsenberg claimed this amount exceeded the combined subsidies provided by the German and Russian governments and that Junkers's financial resources were now exhausted. Without immediate assistance, the Fili factory would close, precipitating the collapse of the entire firm. More positively, Sachsenberg observed that the plant's reconstruction and outfitting approached completion, and full production could begin by the end of 1924. He asked for an immediate transfer of $600,000 as an advance against subsequent orders to cover the factory's operating costs, "absolutely before Easter."[84] When the Reichswehr failed to respond, Junkers implemented another, more aggressive, plan.

Aware the Reichswehr had deliberately withheld information from the German Foreign Office about the Fili project, and that Russian Ambassador Ulrich von Brockdorff-Rantzau hated General von Seeckt, Junkers sought to play the two state organs against one another. On April 27, 1924, Sachsenberg met with Ago von Maltzan, state secretary of the German Foreign Office. Sachsenberg gave von Maltzan a thorough description of the history and circumstances of the Fili project, noting,

> We stand before the danger of not only giving up the Russian enterprise because of a lack of economic viability, but also of losing the German factories due to a draining of our strength—this is an immediate danger. . . . At the end of the day the German firm's well-being is more important than the maintenance of the Russian project. . . . Junkers is therefore not only entitled, but obliged to see to it that the German core firm is not endangered. This can only happen when the Special Section fully acknowledges its great responsibility and makes the appropriate decisions to continue what it began without endangering or destroying the existing enterprise. That Junkers and the Special Section pursued political rather than economic goals must be considered. Should the state, for whatever reason, decide to abandon these goals, the appropriate economic consequences must be drawn.[85]

Junkers's strategy paid immediate dividends. On May 5, 1924, under the combined pressure of the Foreign Office, Junkers, and Foreign Minister Stresemann, the Reichswehr agreed to consider all previous disbursements totaling 4 million goldmarks as subsidies and provide a further 4 million goldmarks to support the Fili factory. In exchange, Junkers agreed to finance the remaining amount for completion of the firm's contractual obligations, 12 million goldmarks, through loans or credits.[86]

This new agreement appeared to give Junkers a great victory over the Reichswehr. However, both sides knew otherwise; the Reichswehr, fully aware of the Junkers concern's precarious financial position, realized Junkers stood little chance of gaining the credit he needed from private sources. Germany's financial climate remained extremely unstable despite the end of hyperinflation, and on April 5, 1924, Hjalmar Schacht, the new president of the Reichsbank, took the extraordinary step of curtailing credit. With credit restricted to those businesses who could show anticipated benefits to the German domestic economy, Junkers found banks unwilling to grant him loans for an uncertain and, for security reasons, largely unknown foreign venture.[87]

The tone between Junkers and the Reichswehr now changed markedly. Until this point, the two parties negotiated on more or less equal terms, but the conclusion of the new agreement left no doubt surrounding the new power relationship. The Reichswehr presented its offer in the form of an ultimatum, and Junkers, faced with bankruptcy, was forced to accept the position he hated most, a state client forced to adhere to its commands.[88] Meanwhile the Russians, who watched the battle between Junkers and the Reichswehr closely, realized their objectives regarding technology transfer were almost complete and resolved to continue their stance of playing the German sides off each other. With friction between themselves and Poland abating, along with a steady supply of Fokker's high performance aircraft, the Russians now no longer needed Junkers, whose efforts had already outfitted the factory complex and trained many of their designers. They resolved to continue withholding large orders and bide their time, convinced the firm would eventually default on its contractual obligations and give them sole control of Fili.

Between May and July 1924, Junkers visited the United States, where he toured the Ford Motor Company and met Henry and Edsel Ford. Impressed by the scale and magnitude of the Detroit factories, Junkers attempted to canvas financial support from US investors. Junkers carried with him plans for a transatlantic airline network, supplied with a fleet of huge flying-winged aircraft, the Junkers R-1.[89] He approached Henry Ford with his plans, but the American, amazed by the projected sums necessary to begin the project, responded coolly. Junkers returned to Germany impressed by American industrial potential but opposed to American methods, claiming in his dairy that Ford's techniques represented the antithesis of his own work ethic, "Quality versus quantity, Junkers versus Ford."[90]

In a stroke of bitter irony, the Fili complex came online just as both of its official benefactors, the German and Russian governments, finally lost interest in its products. For Junkers, the lack of orders from both sides gave him little choice; he continued seeking credit from the Reichswehr and from private banks. Frustrated with the Special Section and GEFU, Junkers wrote to General Seeckt himself on July 22, 1924. Within the letter, Junkers noted that "despite the difficult economic situation over 4000 men work in my enterprises in Russia and Germany, yet . . . hindrances . . . exist that endanger not only my enterprises, but in the same or perhaps stronger ways other German firms."[91] Specifically Junkers complained about "naïve" GEFU representatives, who, he argued, "irresponsibly played with the vital interests of German companies." Junkers claimed that GEFU officials undermined his chances of receiving private credit by informing commercial banks that "the state would have nothing more to do" with the firm. Junkers urged von Seeckt to "take care of the matter to avert incalculable damage not only in Russia, but also in Germany."[92]

Junkers's letter evoked a strong response from von Seeckt, who followed the Russian projects very closely. Von Seeckt first countered that Junkers's complaints "contained unjustified conclusions," then moved onto the offensive, arguing that Junkers officials attempted to extract credit from private sources through misrepresentation of the financial arrangements between the firm and GEFU. Von Seeckt accused Junkers of seeking to pressure the Reichswehr into further payments by divulging information about Fili to private citizens, a practice he described as "inexcusably thoughtless." The Reichswehr chief dismissed Junkers's claims, noting that the firm's past history of "inappropriate behavior invalidated your complaints." He also noted that Junkers willingly accepted involvement in the Fili project "for more than purely national reasons" and that Junkers officials "were fully informed of the material risks involved and chose to sign the contract." Subsequent claims from the firm alleging no acceptance of the financial and economic risks surrounding the venture, von Seeckt argued, were therefore "distortions of the truth." Von Seeckt continued to attack Junkers's demands for further assistance by noting that during the negotiations over the agreement of May 5, 1924, General Hasse "repeatedly stressed that further sums would not be available, and there was no hope whatsoever of the firm receiving more money. You yourself assured General Hasse that you completely understood this." Von Seeckt's letter concluded with a threat, reminding Junkers of the power relationship between the two parties: "I cannot conclude, Professor, without once again expressing confidence and the certain expectation that you, just as you have previously, will continue to pursue and work toward new avenues that you may dislike, but the necessities of state require."[93] Junkers responded to von Seeckt on October 22 and asked for "impartial" arbitration to settle the differences between the two parties. Such arbitration, Junkers argued, would "clarify the material aspects of the differences between my firm and the Waffenamt regarding the GEFU payments."[94] One month later, von Seeckt responded by refusing Junkers's request for arbitration on "military and political grounds."[95]

Von Seeckt's refusal effectively ended the involvement of both Junkers and the Reichswehr at Fili—although the factory would continue to produce Junkers aircraft until December 1926, when the Soviet Union purchased the factory for 6 million marks. Fili became the core of the new Soviet aircraft industry, as designers such as Andrei Tupolev began producing all-metal aircraft for the Soviet Air Force. Experience gained by Tupolev and others at the Fili complex, staffed by Junkers's best designers between 1923 and 1926, proved invaluable, and subsequent Russian aircraft reflected Junkers design characteristics for decades. Fili's effects resonated throughout the Soviet Union, as indigenous aluminum factories appeared to supply the new aircraft industry. The Fili factory continued to expand, and when a German aircraft industry delegation visited there in 1941, they saw a massive complex employing over twelve thousand men.[96] Junkers's position as the founder of the Soviet Union's aircraft industry represents arguably one of the professor's greatest achievements; however, he received little contemporary or subsequent recognition.

Throughout the course of the Fili project, Junkers's autonomy and freedom of action fundamentally declined. The Reichswehr and Russian authorities, pursuing different agendas, successfully outmaneuvered Junkers by withholding orders and establishing unrealistic goals. The Reichswehr, never vitally interested in the Fili factory, achieved its objectives in other areas in Russia and sought to end its involvement at Fili as soon as possible thereafter. For their part, the Russians desired the modernization of the factory and training of the Russian workforce, goals they quickly realized they could attain by pitting the two German sides against one another. For Junkers, initial optimism quickly faded as he recognized neither of his objectives—the creation of an airline network linking Europe and Asia, nor the establishment of production facilities independent of both Allied and German control—matched those of his clients. He continued the project regardless, initially out of determination and later out of necessity as his financial resources dwindled. With few European sales and mounting debts from his airline operations, Junkers employed indirect financing to use funds earmarked for Fili to support the Dessau factory, an action that set in motion a series of events that ultimately led to his expulsion from Dessau and the loss of his companies.[97] For Junkers, the Fili project realized his worst fears and became "the stillborn child that returned to strangle its mother."[98]

Junkers's personal responsibility for his subsequent difficulties must therefore be assessed in light of his actions. Although external circumstances gave him little choice but to pursue the Russian venture, his perception, encouraged by Sachsenberg, that Russia provided a great business opportunity clouded his judgment and encouraged him to ignore the project's obvious political and financial risks. Junkers overrated his own technical achievements and his role within his patrons' agendas and underestimated the relative power of the Reichswehr and the Russian government within the relationship. The Reichswehr's vague promises of support and financial assistance, as well as its increasingly hostile actions, demonstrate its great share of responsibility for the project's failure, but do not exculpate Junkers. Fili provided one catalyst for Junkers's subsequent problems but did not do so alone. His other ventures, particularly the creation of airlines throughout Europe, increased his financial vulnerability at a critical point, leaving him without sufficient capital resources to withdraw from Fili independently. The next chapter charts Junkers's involvement in German and European air transport between 1921 and 1925 and analyzes the connections between this involvement and the Fili project.

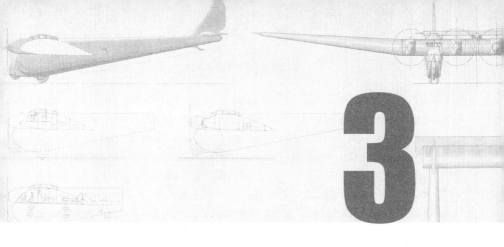

Diverging Paths, 1921–1926

Civil aviation in Germany entered the twentieth century with distinctly militaristic overtones, as Count Ferdinand von Zeppelin's creations loomed over Europe, creating sensations of wonder and dread. Within Germans themselves, the Zeppelins inspired feelings of enormous pride in their technical abilities, and Peter Fritzsche argues the cigar-shaped dirigibles awakened a potent popular nationalism.[1] The Zeppelins' public displays across Germany also demonstrated that the new century offered new transportation opportunities. Formal airship services began in 1910 under the control of the Deutsche Luftschiffahrts AG (German Airship Company) and, by August 1914, carried over thirty-seven thousand passengers.[2] When aircraft overtook the Zeppelin in performance and then proved their capability during the war, army officials began to view aircraft both as weapons and as transport vehicles for post, freight, and ultimately passengers, particularly in regions where no terrestrial infrastructure existed.

Serious contemplation of civil and general aviation began in military circles in 1917, when General Erich Ludendorff nominated Kogenluft, the commanding general of the German Air Forces, as the military representative for air transport. Morrow notes that Ludendorff's move sought to ensure military direction and control of civil aviation after the war's end and also advocated military subsidies to preserve competition within the

aircraft industry.[3] Ludendorff's stance reflected both continuity in military perceptions of the industry and recognition of the aircraft's growing
importance as an instrument of state interests; as the state had created
and nurtured the industry throughout the war and controlled the path of
technological progress to suit its own aims, Ludendorff saw no reason to
change the existing arrangement. This position already held sway within
the Prussian War Ministry, who responded to a request by an Austrian air
transport company for flight permits in April 1917: "The extent to which
the airplane can be permitted to serve as a means of transportation de-
pends upon the results of the discussion of a proposed air transport law.
It does not seem proper to make any concession to a private company at
a time when it is impossible to determine the extent of the restrictions
on non-military air transportation, because the private company could
derive rights and demands from such concessions that would harm state
interests."[4] This statement clearly defined the War Ministry's position regarding aviation and encouraged the creation and expansion of courier
mail units within the army throughout 1917 and 1918. These services
appeared both in Germany and in the occupied regions of Russia in 1918,
as the army pursued experience in the nascent field of air transport.[5]

At the same time, private industry began to explore postwar possibilities for air transport. Discussions between the Postal Ministry and the
Deutsche Bank in 1917 resulted in a trial aerial postal service between
Berlin and Cologne throughout the year. The Deutsche Bank's chairman, Emil Georg von Stauss, who participated in these discussions with
the postmaster general, also spoke with other figures in private industry, including Walter Rathenau.[6] Rathenau, president of electricity and
manufacturing giant AEG, hoped to ensure the solvency of his firm's
aircraft manufacturing division in peacetime and employed Walter
Mackenthun, one of Germany's earliest military pilots, to draft a study
entitled, "The Expected Development of Air Transport after the War."[7]
Mackenthun reached positive conclusions, and the study recommended
the establishment of a trial air transport company. Rathenau concurred,
and on December 13, 1917, AEG converted its rubber factory at Ober-
spree into the headquarters for the new firm, the Deutsche Luftreederei GmbH (German Air Shipping Company, Pty. Ltd.).[8] The demands
of war and the chaos following the revolution meant that little prog-

ress occurred during 1918, with one important exception: A transport company founded by Dr. Joseph Sablatnig, a small aircraft producer, played a crucial role during the earliest phase of the November revolution. Employed by Gustav Noske, later the Weimar Republic's first defense minister, the Sablatnig Air Company transported large sums of money from Berlin to Kiel on November 11, 1918, back payments for the mutinous sailors of the Imperial Navy.[9]

As noted in the previous chapter, the end of the war ushered in a prolonged battle for control of Germany's air transport networks between August Euler, the undersecretary for aviation, and the military authorities.[10] Already angered by the characterization of his office, the *Reichsluftamt* (State Air Office) as an "air travel bureau" by army authorities, Euler responded sharply to the War Ministry's creation of a new air courier service in a letter to the National Assembly in Weimar on February 25, 1919:

> At the same time that a civilian air transport service emerges under the leadership of the Reichsluftamt, the military authorities have begun a courier service allegedly for the National Assembly but really for military purposes. I protest strongly against this action and believe the corrupting effects of such an air service act contrary to the national interest. The military lacks all qualifications for the establishment of a safe, reliable air service. Military matériel would be used for purely civilian purposes without creating the necessary budgetary foundations. The military would also create enormous costs that bear little relation to their minimal effect without approval from the representatives of the people. At the same time emerging civilian companies would be stifled by the military competition. The use of military equipment in the airline area is completely disorganized and a waste of resources. Also the Entente, whom this militarily inspired air transport service cannot be concealed from, will perceive its creation as a violation of the Armistice and the commitment to demobilization.[11]

Throughout 1919, Euler sought to ensure German civil aviation's independence from both state and military control. In June, he advocated the creation of a united air transport organization funded by and staffed with officials from federal and state governments and the founding of air transport companies under the overall leadership of an independent management official.[12] Euler's position regarding military involvement in civilian aviation received support from the victorious Allies, who demanded an end to military involvement in Germany's aircraft industry. Unfortunately for Euler, they also intended to remove all German aircraft from the skies.

With the activation of the Treaty of Versailles regulations on January 10, 1920, all German aircraft production became technically illegal. Use of aircraft by various German forces in "police actions" throughout 1920 hardened the Allied stance, leading to a ban of these "police units" on November 8, 1920. Restrictions on all manufacture tightened, and German aircraft were banned west of the Rhine River, cutting Germany out of Western European air transport networks. The German government reacted angrily to these developments, particularly in the Reichstag, where members passed a bill to compensate domestic producers for their losses during the production ban. However, weakness ultimately tempered German defiance. The production ban finally came to an end in February 1922, when Allied officials deemed themselves satisfied that Germany had both complied with Article 202 of the Treaty of Versailles and that all military matériel had been destroyed or confiscated. However, in order to ensure Germany could not rearm, all military aviation remained prohibited, and a series of *Begriffsbestimmungen* (Articles) appeared, limiting the performance of civilian aircraft designs.[13] Although these restrictions purported to prevent German rearmament, in reality they also acted to protect Allied aircraft manufacturers against their technologically superior German competitors in domestic and international markets.

Aware of this, the German government formulated a clever response. Germany, knowing that Allied civilian aircraft possessed landing and flyover rights to German airspace under the Treaty of Versailles, now declared that any foreign aircraft with performance characteristics superior to those outlined in the Articles that landed in Germany would be considered a military aircraft subject to confiscation. Tension between Germany and her neighbors over air transport rights only eased after ratification of the Locarno Treaty in 1925, when German aircraft were again allowed to enter Western European airspace unmolested.[14] Effects of the Articles persisted far longer, however, particularly in the field of engine design.

Between the war's end and the enforcement in May 1920 of the Treaty of Versailles, many small air transport firms appeared to use converted military aircraft. These firms often disappeared quickly, as the routes they flew between local towns and cities possessed no profit potential. Once the Versailles restrictions on aircraft manufacture and airline routes over Germany took effect, most of the firms soon collapsed or merged with stronger competitors, with only those fortunate enough to possess extensive financial support able to survive. By 1923, two firms dominated German civil aviation, each embodying a vastly different corporate structure and approach. The first, DAL, founded on February 6, 1923, represented established transport and financial interests in the new air transport field. Based on Germany's first airline, Deutsche Luftreederei (DLR), which merged into an airline group, the Aero-Union AG, in 1921, DAL's shareholders included the Deutsche Bank, the Hamburg-America Shipping Company (HAPAG), the Norddeutsche Lloyd Shipping Line (NDL), and the Zeppelin Aircraft Works.[15]

DAL represented a strong amalgamation of capital, airline companies, and marketing offices, with services throughout Germany and through partner airlines between Germany and the rest of Europe.[16] Purely a transport organization, DAL maintained a diverse collection of aircraft that both provided overland transport services and served as adjuncts to the shipping services provided by DAL's parent companies. DAL distributed air routes among its airline partners, with service provided from a common pool of aircraft. The financial strength and established marketing apparatus of DAL's shareholders gave the firm a solid foundation from which to conduct operations in the turbulent and unprofitable arena of air transport and allowed it to undercut competitors without the possibility of financial collapse.

Both within Germany and throughout Eastern Europe, the Junkers Luftverkehr AG (Junkers Air Transport Company, or ILAG) competed fiercely with DAL. For Junkers, development of civilian uses for his aircraft remained a constant goal throughout his career as an aircraft manufacturer. The successful unveiling in 1919 of the F-13, the world's first modern airliner, provided Junkers with an advanced transport design; however, few airline firms existed to operate the aircraft. In contrast to DAL and its ancestors, who as purely transport firms established themselves first and procured aircraft second, Junkers formulated an alternative business model that stressed close and exclusive cooperation between the manufacturer and the airline. Within this model, IFA provided aircraft as working capital in exchange for a stake in the airline.

For Junkers, the advantages included guaranteed sales markets, ongoing returns through maintenance for aircraft and provision of flight personnel and mechanics, and the ability to influence airline policy without substantial capital outlays. The technological dominance of the F-13 appeared to support the plan's viability. However, within Germany the contingent environment severely limited air transport's possibilities. Undaunted, Junkers struck out eastwards in October 1920 and established the Lloyd-Ostflug GmbH in partnership with NDL, the Albatros firm, and the Ostdeutsche Landwerkstätten GmbH (OLA), an airline company newly established by Gotthard Sachsenberg out of the remnants of his wartime fighter squadron. In 1921, Lloyd and Albatros left the partnership and established the Lloyd Luftdienst GmbH, one of DAL's ancestors. The partnership between Junkers and OLA solidified later that year as OLA merged into the Junkers firm, and an air transport department, Abteilung Luftverkehr, appeared under Sachsenberg's leadership in January 1922.[17]

Abteilung Luftverkehr began work immediately by pursuing avenues for airlines both within Germany and throughout the world. A series of aeronautical expeditions set out in North and South America, both to publicize the F-13 and investigate future airline routes.[18] Concurrently, Sachsenberg pursued connections with new airline firms throughout Eastern Europe and Asia, as these areas remained unaffected by the Versailles provisions. This strategy bore fruit rapidly, and airlines supported by Junkers and flying Junkers aircraft appeared in Switzerland, the Free City of Danzig, Sweden, Austria, Finland, Hungary, Latvia, and Italy by 1923.[19]

Within Germany, a similar approach followed, particularly after the lifting of the production ban in 1922. German states and cities desired their own airline services, both as symbols of prestige and self-importance as well as for commerce. Many areas already possessed usable airfields left over from the war; therefore, the largest and most expensive piece of infrastructure already existed, making it appear that airlines were a relatively inexpensive investment. In reality this seldom held true, as state, city, and municipal governments bore the costs of funding local airlines and supported these air services through subsidies. Air transport remained dependent on financial assistance for survival throughout the decade. A typical example is the foundation of the Schlesischen Luftverkehrs AG (Silesian Air Transport Corporation), on January 31, 1925. Junkers contributed four aircraft, two motors, and spare parts to the company, worth a total of 384,000 marks. In return, Junkers received a quarter of the company's shares, one hundred shares worth 1,000 marks each, and 284,000 marks in cash. Junkers also pledged to provide future aircraft at a significant discount.[20]

As Junkers became involved in more airline companies, rivalry between the Junkers concern and DAL increased in intensity and bitterness, as both sides fought to control German airspace. Soon their domestic routes overlapped between the largest cities, creating an excess of capacity and services not matched by customer needs. Both airlines also refused to allow each other to use their infrastructure, creating absurd situations for travelers that involved traveling between two airfields within the same city or town to make connections. Duplication led to a drain of public subsidies and an increasingly negative public perception of air transport.

Internal problems combined with two important external circumstances: Germany's inflation crisis and perceptions of air travel as both unsafe and expensive. The inflation crisis of 1923 threw all facets of German life into turmoil. Effects of inflation precipitated a drop in airline revenues, as many people lacked the resources to travel at all, least of all in an aircraft. Regarding aircraft security and comfort, while Junkers could proudly demonstrate a near-perfect safety record, suspicions lingered, and the narrow, cramped confines of most passenger aircraft combined with droning engine noise and long flight times to further discourage air travel as a mass transit alternative.[21] Kurt Weigelt, future chairman of Lufthansa and one of the most ardent supporters of civil aviation, nevertheless described air travel in the 1920s as "terribly monotonous," and in 1925, aircraft only traveled roughly twice as fast as trains. Fare prices averaged between four and five times more than first-class train tickets over the same route. For freight, the prices were ten to twelve times more expensive than ground shipping. Technical considerations also influenced consumer choice; night flying only became practical at the end of the decade, and relative distances, particularly in Europe, offset the speed advantages of the airplane.[22] These factors combined to temper the public's affection for air travel throughout Junkers's career. Like so many before and after him, Hugo Junkers sought to bring the future into the present, only to find that the present was not ready.

As the currency crisis abated, both Junkers Luftverkehr and DAL consolidated their hold on the air transport market through expansion and mergers. For Junkers, characteristically ambitious, this meant aiming well beyond a united domestic or even regional air transport network toward the world's first international airline system. His plan envisaged two steps. The first was to combine all existing Junkers-affiliated airlines into "unions" that shared a common marketing strategy, repair and maintenance network, and aircraft pool along international and major regional routes. Abteilung Luftverkehr encouraged this process by tightening connections between existing airlines and creating new ones in European countries not served by Junkers, such as Norway, Italy, Spain, Bulgaria, and Portugal. This process approached completion by the end of 1924. Second, these two regional unions—the "Trans-Europa Union," which was founded in May 1923 and included Germany, Switzerland, Austria, and Hungary, and the "Ost Europa Union," which was founded in October 1923 and included Danzig, East Prussia, Lithuania, Latvia, Estonia, Sweden, Finland, and Russia—would merge and form a new entity, the "Europa Union," with a network of connected routes stretching from England to the Caucasus and beyond.[23] Once completed, the Europa Union, with a market capitalization of 10 million marks, would give Junkers the ability to resist hostile attacks from competitors and usher in the possibility of even more grand designs, such as that proposed by Junkers in a letter to government authorities in January 1924: a merger with DAL to form a united corporation, funded by the state to the tune of 18 million goldmarks, which would dominate world air transport and commerce, restore Germany to world prominence, and offset the lack of a military air force.[24]

By 1924, the two unions involved over twenty-five airline firms, and Junkers controlled the largest air transport network in the world. Forty percent of all global air traffic traveled on Junkers aircraft in 1924. Passenger numbers increased from 2,230 in 1921, to 11,005 in 1922, to 26,509 in 1923, and finally to 40,298 in 1924. Postal freight increased from 2 tons to 146 tons over the same period, with the number of aircraft increasing from eleven to seventy-eight.[25] Junkers aircraft flew throughout the world, from Bolivia to Japan. Once again, Junkers appeared to have broken free of state intervention in his affairs; the multinational component of the proposed "Europa Union" ensured that no one nation could control its activities—indeed only Junkers himself held enough power within the union's intended corporate structure to direct policy.[26] Once again, however, external circumstances combined with a recurring problem, capital scarcity, to prevent Junkers from consolidating his position within world aviation.

The Junkers concern's corporate structure contributed significantly to the financial difficulties of the aircraft factory. By 1925, eight separate firms existed in three different nations, producing a range of products from hot water heaters to aero-engines.[27] Although a central office, the Hauptbüro, existed in Dessau to supposedly coordinate all areas of company policy, in reality Junkers, largely out of necessity, chose to delegate control of the operations of each component of the firm to trusted subordinates. These delegations removed direct management oversight and created an environment where no overall plan existed for the concern's future other than vague notions of market dominance. Nowhere is this process clearer than in the evolution of Junkers Luftverkehr, the air transport division. Technically a department of the aircraft factory until 1924, the air transport division grew rapidly as its domestic and foreign partnerships expanded. This growth came at a price, as the aircraft factory found itself producing aircraft to supply to the new "partners," but the nature of the partnership meant that returns fell far below those of sales on the open market. Also, the agreements obliged Junkers to provide future aircraft at a significant discount, cutting into IFA's future profits in an uncertain economic environment. Junkers himself noted concerns about Abteilung Luftverkehr's growth as early as 1922: "Air Transport has already taken on such dimensions that it endangers the entire concern if it is not economically operated."[28] Junkers's concerns reflected his growing unease over the airline division's financial situation. Such unease proved justified when the leader of the airline department, Gotthard Sachsenberg, failed to provide transparent information on its fiscal health.

Gotthard Sachsenberg entered Junkers's employ on the recommendation of his brother, Hans Sachsenberg. Terms of fusion between Junkers and Gotthard Sachsenberg's airline company, OLA, proved extremely advantageous for Sachsenberg, whom Junkers entrusted with full power over the direction of the firm's airline policy. Sachsenberg brought with him wartime associates such as Erhard Milch and Dr. Gottfried Kaumann, who formed a core of staff within the Junkers firm primarily loyal to Sachsenberg rather than to Junkers.[29] These "old comrades" also controlled personnel allocation and management and possessed wide financial power. Sachsenberg himself drew his own monthly income directly out of company funds without any oversight until 1925.[30] Coming straight out of military service into the new field of air transport, Sachsenberg and his comrades knew little of sound budgetary methods or accounting practices.

Acting on Junkers's directive to expand air transport connections to provide sales opportunities, Sachsenberg entered partnerships between IFA and other airlines without regard for immediate viability or even a healthy prospect of returns. Until 1924, no cost estimates existed for airline operations, and the financial official responsible for bookkeeping between Sachsenberg and Junkers, Dr. Ernst Körner, later revealed himself loyal to Sachsenberg and helped disguise the whereabouts of large sums allocated to airline operations.[31] Possibly Junkers never counted on having to bear the entire costs of the operation himself; yet by June 1923, the spiraling costs incurred by Sachsenberg's air transport division forced Junkers to confront Sachsenberg openly:

> During the last conference I pointed out the need for an exact financial overview of the entire concern. . . . With dismay I have learned that the Air Transport Division received a subsidy of $80,000 in one year, and invested about one million dollars over the same period; this greatly exceeds any allowable limit. My anxiety increased when I requested the necessary documents in order to get an idea of where these enormous

sums are, and came to the frightening realization that no bookkeeping records exist. Based on your profitability calculations, there has to be a profit yielded. How is it that instead a giant loss occurred? When I consider that you use your wide powers of authority, granted to you by me, like they are nothing, that worries me so much that I have to say: The fate (of the department, and by extension the entire concern) rests in hands like those on the wheel of a joyriding car hurtling along un-known roads, until they are smashed to pieces. ... Various observations strengthen my growing apprehension, for example (1) the manner in which, at the end of a several-hour conference, you so casually asked for approval of a $40,000 advance for Russian airline development without any explanation or documentation, like it was nothing; (2) the manner in which the entire affair was handled through protocol, with my earnest admonishments and warnings entirely omitted and in con-trast the necessity of generously founding the enterprise stressed, and where further the $40,000 advance became $70,000.[32]

Junkers demanded sweeping changes to the Air Transport Department's accounting methods as the "highest priority," including filing of regular account records showing supply stocks, earnings, and costs; monthly balance sheets showing profit and loss calculations; and much closer collaboration with both IFA and central administration at the Haupt-büro.[33] He continued: "I am all the more surprised over the miserable economic results as I have repeatedly pointed out that we must develop airlines economically. . . . I am not convinced that those involved are sufficiently aware that borrowed money funds the airlines, and that this money not only accrues interest payments, but soon acts as a huge loss."[34]

Günter Schmitt argues, "Unfortunately Junkers, through faulty char-acter judgment, surrounded himself with a wide circle of people who considered the Junkers institutions more as a place of lucrative sine-cure than a place of important work."[35] Mounting costs from the firm's airline operations encouraged Junkers to remove Abteilung Luftverkehr from IFA's corporate structure, leading to the establishment of ILAG in August 1924. By severing the connection between the firm's air trans-port operations and its aircraft production facilities, Junkers hoped to place emphasis on better management through enforced austerity and accountability.

By 1924, Junkers found himself faced with mounting debts in three areas of the Junkers Works: the Research Institute, the Fili operation, and airline operations. With little chance of securing outside credit due to the country's currency crisis, the firm had little choice other than to steady the course, hoping that state funds from two sources—the army for Fili and the Reichsverkehrministerium (Reich Transport Ministry, or RVM) for airline subsidies—would be sufficient. Reliance on these sources meant, however, that Junkers remained hostage to the prolonged goodwill of the two state agencies providing the funds. Unfortunately for him, changing agendas within these agencies meant an end to their financial support.

The Reichswehr's new stance reflected both frustration with Junkers over the Fili Affair and a broader change in covert rearmament strategy.[36] The Ruhr Occupation dealt a severe blow to the external strategy championed by General von Seeckt by demonstrating that such a strategy provided no security for the homeland in the event of foreign incursion. The costly and unsuccessful nature of the Fili operation also convinced many officers that "camouflaged" foreign ventures were wasteful, inefficient, and militarily useless, as none of the aircraft produced by Junkers at Fili matched army performance expectations.[37] A new direction, supported by officers in both the Supply and the Aviation Departments of the Army Command, advocated the return of covert rearmament within German borders, where planning and procurement contingencies could be developed in close cooperation with industry.

Additionally, the new plans advocated developing Germany's potential to mass-produce military matériel rapidly after the outbreak of war, an aim that involved analyzing existing firms within certain key industries, such as aircraft and engine manufacture, and then encouraging these industries to maintain a latent rearmament potential through standardization of parts and manufacturing techniques. Not only would this new direction improve efficiency, it also required far less expenditure. The currency crisis severely affected the Reichswehr and reduced its secret funds dramatically; by reorganizing covert rearmament along these lines, Reichswehr planners sought a detailed, cost-effective overview of Germany's latent rearmament capability.

For the aircraft industry, this meant identifying key firms as core components of a new "rational" rearmament program. With most of the old wartime firms gone from the industry, and dissatisfied with Junkers, Reichswehr planners focused their efforts on several small new firms that appeared in the wake of the currency crisis. These firms, such as the Rohrbach Metallflugzeugbau GmbH, the Dornier Metallflugzeugbau GmbH, and the Ernst Heinkel Flugzeugwerke GmbH, shared several common traits that made them attractive to close contact with Reichswehr authorities. By 1924, all three firms possessed aircraft that technologically rivaled those of Junkers, all welcomed collaboration with the military, and all accepted the primacy of the military's requirements in the state-industry relationship.[38] Despite the appearance of these new firms, however, Reichswehr authorities knew that no effective rearmament plans could afford to omit Junkers, Germany's largest aircraft producer. Junkers's history of opposition to military oversight ruled out harmonious collaboration and encouraged the pursuit of alternative means to assure his firm's involvement in rearmament plans. By the middle of the decade, the firm's increasing financial difficulties offered such an opportunity.

Within the RVM, a similar stance developed toward the Junkers firm, although from different origins. For some time, both federal and government officials watched the process of consolidation within the domestic air transport market with considerable unease. Increasingly bitter struggles between Junkers and DAL for control of German air transport routes spilled over into both the political and public arenas, resulting in increasingly loud calls to regulate an industry widely perceived as pursuing its own interests to the detriment of the German public.[39] As both enterprises relied on state subsidies for survival and showed little interest in reform due to the absence of any possible rivals, critics pointed to wasteful practices within the two firms as evidence of callous use of taxpayer funds. One obvious example was the duplication of services along popular routes; with the two firms and their affiliates providing more seats along these routes than necessary, and with the state funding both of them through subsidies, air transport in Germany fell into disrepute. In Junkers's case, Reich officials became increasingly aware of the firm's reliance on state airline subsidies for financial solvency, particularly by 1924 when the combined obligations of operating the Fili plant and supporting the expansion of the regional airline unions stretched the Dessau firm's financial resources to the limit.[40]

Junkers's development of airline unions posed particular problems for the RVM. Operating both within Germany's borders and abroad, the unions allowed Junkers to obtain subsidies from both Germany and foreign nations, a circumstance that satisfied the Dessau firm but contravened the agenda of the German state, which sought to use the domestic airline network for covert military purposes. The head of the RVM's aviation department, Ernst Brandenburg, originally appointed at the request of General von Seeckt, faithfully pursued this aim throughout his tenure and worked closely with Reichswehr officials in formulating a plan to nationalize the airline industry, merging ILAG and DAL into a new national airline completely under government control.[41] Three advantages were obvious: immediate reductions in subsidy expenditure; more efficient use of infrastructure and equipment; and the ability to closely tailor airline policy to covert military requirements.

Germany's desire for closer connections between civil and military aviation reflected not only particular needs due to Versailles restrictions but also wider contemporary thinking concerning the use of aircraft as instruments of state. Peter Fritzsche notes, "The airstream represented a vast arena for renewed national competition. Not only did most political observers expect states to scramble for economically and militarily vital positions and routes in the 'air ocean' but they also agreed that governments would have to promote aviation at home in order to remain great powers in the coming air future. . . . Aviation would not alter the struggle for hegemony among the great powers; a smaller world was not a friendlier world. To speak about an embrasive world 'state above all states' or global federation showed insufficient racial pride and excessive idealism."[42]

Junkers, already concerned by the Reichswehr's stance regarding Fili, became aware of these movements against him in early 1924. Initially he believed the major threat came from his corporate opposition rather than from the state. In his diary, he noted the need for "proof, whether perhaps Gessler [then Reichswehr minister], von Cuno [director Of HAPAG, formerly chancellor of Germany] and the other members of Aero-Lloyd seek to force Junkers to merge with Aero-Lloyd through the withholding of Special Section payments."[43] By March 1924, convinced of an imminent hostile takeover, Junkers outlined a defensive strategy: "Seek external financial involvement first in Germany, then in England, then America! Fully exploit the political side in Germany for the reduction of difficulties with the Russians and the Special Section, also Postal subsidies (the more financially independent Junkers is, the more protected state interests are), and stress to Ebert [Friedrich Ebert, president of Germany] the importance of the organization of the Aviation Office for this great project."[44]

However, Junkers's trip to the United States during the summer of 1924 yielded no tangible results, and he returned to Dessau in August without any promises of foreign investment.[45] As the year progressed, capital reserves declined, and General von Seeckt's refusal to allow independent arbitration for state security reasons forced Junkers into merger discussions with DAL representatives by December 1924. Junkers, now increasingly surrounded by debt, turned to one of his greatest adversaries, finance capital, to save him from the other, the state.[46] Not surprisingly, the talks came to nothing, as Junkers refused to give up a controlling interest in the firm. Junkers earlier described his views of DAL's executives in his diary: "(1) These gentlemen operate with totally different methods and principles. (2) They sit on high horses and recognize only their own opinions, methods and principles as right, and demand that others follow them. (That is the capitalist method) I hold fundamentally different views."[47]

He also noted that the failure of talks meant an increase in pressure from DAL as they attempted to drive ILAG out of the market: "Aero-Lloyd wishes to wear us down through disruptive acts; they make offers that are practically unfeasible to hurt us. Colsman, [Dr. Albert Colsmann, managing director of the Luftschiffbau Zeppelin GmbH, a shareholder of DAL] has said in our presence . . . that he wants to force us into a merger."[48]

Despite these increasing financial woes, Junkers's aircraft divisions continued to expand throughout 1925. Aware that sales of transport aircraft such as the F-13 and the new, larger G-24 lacked the power to correct the firm's financial situation, Sachsenberg persuaded Junkers to embark on a new course—construction of "fabrication centers" in foreign nations. Sachsenberg argued that these new centers, based on the example of the Fili plant and located in Sweden and Turkey, would provide not only a "sales organization backbone" when international demand increased but could also produce military aircraft for customers not interested in civil aircraft. These new plants also neatly encompassed both ends of an envisaged airline route linking Scandinavia, through Russia, to Asia and beyond, and thus they could serve as maintenance and modification centers for the Junkers aircraft flying these routes.[49] These new plants possessed the added advantage of location; outside Germany, Versailles restrictions held no power, and the firm would be free to develop aircraft whose performance exceeded that mandated by the Articles of April 1922. Junkers agreed, and in March 1925, the firm AB Flygindustri appeared with its base at Limhamm, near Malmo, Sweden.[50] In June of that year, another satellite firm appeared in Turkey, the Türkische Motoren-und Flugzeugbau-Aktiengesellschaft (Turkish Motor and Aircraft Corporation), a firm owned jointly by Junkers and the Turkish government.[51] While these expansions seemed to lay a foundation for future success and, in the Turkish case, provided badly needed capital that helped keep the firm afloat, neither of them solved the firm's immediate financial problems.

Rising production costs magnified Junkers's troubles. His reliance on skilled labor rather than diluted or mass production techniques resulted in a reduced profit margin for aircraft sales; by 1924, production costs for an F-13 rose to two-thirds of the sales price, primarily through rising material costs and increased salaries for employees, particularly within the Hauptbüro.[52] As Junkers sold relatively few aircraft on the open market—most of those produced were used as capital in airline ventures—this problem became critical by 1925.[53] Competitor aircraft, such as the Dornier Komet II, sold for US$11,000 in 1924, which was US$2,000 less than the Junkers F-13.[54] With the international sales market remaining depressed throughout 1923 and 1924, the produc-

tion of F-13s at both Dessau and Fili led to a surplus of forty-four unsold aircraft, whose value corresponded to half the capitalization of
the aircraft factory.[55] Additionally, by November 1925, monthly wage
and salary obligations throughout the Junkers Works totaled 998,000
marks.[56] Junkers also faced the maturation of several loans and credits
granted by state agencies and private banks, valued at a total of 12 million marks by January 1926. An initial payment of 600,000 marks came
due on October 6, 1925, followed a week later by a further payment of
900,000 marks.[57]

These various financial constraints placed an insurmountable burden
on the firm's resources by the end of September 1925. On October 1,
the concern stopped payment of employee wages.[58] With private banks
refusing to extend loans, only immediate state assistance would avert
bankruptcy. This assistance ultimately arrived, but at a high price. When
RVM grants totaling 1,300,000 marks that were meant to cover expenses
through July 1925 failed to turn the financial tide, Brandenburg took
matters into his own hands. As Sachsenberg met with Brandenburg on
October 7, 1925, to discuss the firm's financial situation, Brandenburg
presented him with an ultimatum: further credit depended upon the
ceding of a controlling interest in ILAG to the RVM.

Brandenburg's October 7 announcement culminated several months
of secret planning between the RVM and the Reichswehr. In May 1925,
due to the imminent Locarno Treaty negotiations, the Reichswehr
transferred oversight control of the Fili project to the RVM. Additionally, contact between Brandenburg and Reichswehr officials increased as
Brandenburg became aware of the Reichswehr's new covert rearmament
plans. State control of Germany's civil aviation network formed a crucial
part of these plans, and Brandenburg saw Junkers's financial woes as
an opportunity to solve several problems at once. By forming a unified
national airline out of ILAG and DAL, state aviation subsidies could be
both significantly reduced and more tightly supervised, the Reichswehr's
plans accommodated, and IFA's covert rearmament potential fully and
economically developed. In August 1925, Brandenburg wrote to Captain
Vogt in the Reichswehr's Waffenamt and proposed a "general examination of Junkers, with the aim of not only assuring the correct use of
state funds, but also before all else, to establish a decisive influence on

the leadership of the firm in order to make it profitable."[59] Vogt replied positively and assured Reichswehr support. Budrass notes Brandenburg assumed that once placed under official oversight, and with substantial managerial changes, the firm would return to profitability within three months.[60] Under Brandenburg's plan, the RVM assumed control of the Fili plant, with Junkers reduced to a minority partner. With few alterations, Brandenburg relayed these demands to Sachsenberg.

Sachsenberg in turn relayed the RVM's demands to Junkers. The conditions were devastating for both men. In exchange for a one-time advance of 655,000 marks to cover existing debt, Junkers ceded 80 percent of ILAG's shares to the RVM and agreed to accept the creation of a new company to control the Fili operation, with ownership divided in a ratio of three to two, to the state's advantage.[61] Furthermore, the RVM demanded Junkers sell his stake in the Russian factory for 5 million marks, although it later retracted this condition. Junkers, faced with bankruptcy, angrily accepted these conditions the following day, although not without making his feelings known. On the afternoon of October 7, he responded to the conditions in a letter to Brandenburg:

> I confirm that I received a summary of today's meeting in your Ministry, during which you outlined the conditions that the Junkers Aircraft factory must satisfy for an advance of 655,000 marks. Regarding these conditions I make the following remarks:
>
> Re (1) I refuse to accept the unconditional handing over of 80% of the Junkers Luftverkehr shares, as they will eventually end up in the hands of the banks which will lead to a fundamental change in the only possible principle that lies in the state's interest, the free development of air transport. To me it seems impermissible to force me into action that I feel fundamentally undercuts state interests.
>
> Re (2) I declare that the Reichswehr Ministry is fully aware that I have expended far more of my own money and time in the Russian enterprise than they have. Therefore I regard the share quota of 2:3 as unjust.
>
> Re (3) I declare that the demand I cede my share in the Russian factory for 5 million, although it is known that I invested about double

that amount at the instigation of and in the interests of the state, is unreasonable. . . .

Finally allow me to remark further, that I consider it improper . . . to use the financial crisis of the aircraft factory that I cannot accept responsibility for to gain concessions from me, as the financial difficulties that I have struggled against from month to month lead back to expenditures made at the state's instigation and in the state's interest for the Russian factory.

I find myself obliged to hold you responsible for the immensely difficult consequences of the corporate supervision that I must request tomorrow.[62]

The following week, the RVM provided a further 900,000 marks to clear outstanding ILAG debts, with strict instructions for the money's use and a threat that "any deviation from the payment plan would result in unpleasant consequences."[63] Angered by the settlement's terms yet powerless to oppose them, Junkers recorded his feelings in his diary: "Difficult times to go through, nationalization or corporate oversight. (I have the choice between Scylla and Charybdis). . . . It is heartbreaking that the enormous waste of effort and the shortage of capital that characterized the Russian venture affected us directly and indirectly. . . . However we are ready to increase our production significantly, and I hope that in the not too distant future we can emerge from our financial misery and ward off the danger that our latent worth, our promising research, will go under the hammer and be lost to us and the public at large."[64]

As part of the terms accepted by Junkers, external experts appeared at Dessau to examine the firms' books. These experts included Bruno Heck, director of the Continental-Gas Gesellschaft of Dessau, and Moritz von der Porten, director of the Vereinigten Aluminium Werke (United Aluminum Works). By the middle of October, their investigations revealed stunning levels of debt throughout the Junkers group of firms; to rectify the aircraft factory's problems alone would cost 17.5 million marks.[65] Armed with this information, the RVM presented three additional demands to Junkers. The first was to, with state funds overseen by a trustee, raise IFA's share value through additional issues of common stock from 3.5 million to 7 million marks. These shares would then be held in trust, overseen by a state-appointed trustee. The second was to link the debts of the engine factory, Junkers Motorenbau (JUMO), to IFA, and the final demand was to conclude a contract agreement between Junkers and IFA concerning further patent use. With fulfillment of these terms, the RVM agreed to provide the necessary credits to fund additional IFA shares.[66] On October 20, 1925, Gotthard Sachsenberg and Hermann Schliessing, representing the firm, accepted the RVM's terms. Writing the next day in his diary, Junkers likened the reorganization efforts of RVM officials to an "incorrect diagnosis of a doctor that mandates confinement, restriction and death rather than freedom, light and movement."[67]

Acceptance of the terms ended Junkers's involvement in German air transport. It also ended the Europa Union, which had been scheduled to commence operations in the winter of 1925. At the edge of his greatest success in air transport, Junkers found himself frozen out of the European market, as his former associates abandoned the Europa Union and sought connections with the new, nationalized airline, Deutsche Lufthansa, incorporated on January 6, 1926.[68] Under the terms of the October 20 agreement, the new airline took over all ILAG's assets, including aircraft, equipment, and personnel. From now on, Junkers participated in European air transport only as an aircraft supplier. Interestingly, although the RVM took control of ILAG after October 20, 1925, Deutsche Lufthansa's board included a former ILAG employee, Erhard Milch. Milch, later described as an "opportunist" by contemporaries, chose to leave Junkers's employ and enter state service.[69] Junkers regarded Milch's actions as treasonous and vowed to oppose the new airline in every possible way.

At the same time, however, an unlikely opportunity presented itself. Sachsenberg, who realized his position in the firm was increasingly precarious given the Fili debacle, ILAG's takeover, and the emnity of the firm's new official overseers toward him, sought to resurrect his career and Junkers's independence at the last moment. During the October negotiations with the RVM, Sachsenberg claimed that the state owed Junkers 12 million marks previously promised to IFA by the Reichswehr in August 1924 to support the Fili factory. Not surprisingly, this claim, although undocumented, caused a considerable stir, especially when experts valued IFA's total debt at the same figure. Budrass notes that Sachsenberg's claims held a deeper motive: an implicit threat to publicly reveal the covert rearmament programs in Russia.[70]

Sachsenberg's timing proved impeccable; the RVM's role in Deutsche Lufthansa's birth received wide attention in the press. Reports questioned the state's role in the new monopoly, particularly the amount of public funds used in the takeover.[71] Meanwhile, negotiations taking place in Paris over Germany's admittance into the Western European airline network, an offshoot of the Locarno Treaty, had entered their final phase, and the government sought to contain any potentially damaging information until after negotiations ended. For its part, the Reichswehr, up to this point soundly opposed to Junkers's repeated requests for arbitration of the Fili Affair, recognized Sachsenberg's threat and sought to prevent "unauthorized circles" from gaining knowledge of its Russian projects, many of which were still in operation.[72] In December 1925, General Hasse offered Sachsenberg a compromise: instead of public arbitration proceedings, the two sides would present legal briefs privately to a third party, Reich Court President Dr. Walter Simons, in January 1926. Sachsenberg accepted the Reichswehr's proposal, and both sides began to gather evidence that supported their claims.

Sachsenberg's actions seemed futile to Junkers, who questioned how an attack on the Reichswehr would assist the firm in its struggle against the RVM. During preparation of the firm's legal brief, Junkers stressed the need for a balanced, dispassionate argument:

(a) The composition should be as carefully worded as possible in order to prevent harm through provocation of the opposing side.
(b) Several trumps will be saved for later negotiations. This will increase the importance of Simons' judgment once it becomes known that several important documents were held back.

II. It is particularly important that the brief's sections describing the personal involvement of Junkers closely correspond with his personal recollections. For this purpose:

(a) Examine the diaries of Fall 1921–1922.

(b) Check whether written evidence of these events is available.

(c) Subsequent examination of the existing files of the period. . . .

IV. It is crucial that Simons gains a direct impression from the personal experiences of Junkers. There is no doubt whatsoever, that he (Junkers) conveys these experiences best in oral negotiations, and that this is Junkers's best trump card. . . . The central theme of "trust" should extend throughout the entire brief.[73]

Junkers reiterated his views at a meeting the following day:

> Yesterday I expressed my thoughts over whether I considered it right to send the arbitrator a manufactured case. I have now further crystallized this train of thought. I believe that this course is not the correct one, although it is most common in legal actions. I would like to think that we can find a completely different method to reach our goal. . . . Our goal is to move towards a new kind of collaboration. We want to achieve this with the least expenditure. . . . The intended legal means lead only to conflict that engenders enormous work and bequeaths very unpleasant consequences. . . . Simons will help us regardless . . . therefore we don't quarrel with the others. This is a waste of time that serves neither party.[74]

Prolonged legal maneuvering now commenced. In their initial briefs, both sides presented broadly the same evidence and focused on the same central issue: whether the verbal promises made by Reichswehr authorities to Junkers between November 1921 and April 1922 amounted to financial responsibility for the entire project.[75] With neither side possessing written memoranda of these meetings, the arguments devolved into mutual accusations, with Junkers accusing the Reichswehr of recalcitrance, and the Reichswehr accusing Junkers of entering into the project fully aware of the financial risks. Simons received both submissions and retired to consider his verdict.

While the arbitration process continued, the IFA's trustees examined their options. Directed by Brandenburg to return the firm to profitability within three months, the members of the Finance Committee of the Supervisory Board soon realized that this objective was unattainable. The nature of Deutsche Lufthansa's creation, with its takeover of ILAG's and DAL's fleets, led to immediate declines in demand for new aircraft.[76] In January 1926, the Finance Committee also learned of financial obligations due both in Russia and Turkey worth 2,650,000 marks. Faced with these additional expenses, the committee saw no other option but to cut production, a move that precipitated a drastic reduction in the firm's workforce. Between December 1925 and April 1926, the workforce at IFA and JUMO declined from 4,300 to 3,000.[77] Junkers, still a member of IFA's board, complained about these measures to the head of IFA's Finance Committee, former Finance Minister von Schlieben:

> The responsibility that I carry as a member of the Board of Directors requires me to inform you that I fear the worst[,] that all your commendable efforts . . . will not lead to success.
>
> My long years of experience support my conviction that the firm will be irretrievably ruined if, as was expressed as a matter of principle at the last meeting, production cuts follow the current lack of orders. Our aircraft factory only operates effectively on a large scale. A certain production level is essential to achieve profitability. . . . If you decide to act contrary to my advice, I must leave the fate of the firm in your hands. . . . I feel myself obliged to retain my position as a member of the Supervisory Board not only because in reality the Finance Committee controls the Board, but more so because I will not suffer the outward appearance that the strikingly trenchant measures taken meet my approval.[78]

Junkers's protests fell on deaf ears, however, and the firm continued to shed workers throughout the first half of 1926 until by June only 650 remained; still the firm's financial woes continued. Without orders, losses continued to mount, running at over 500,000 marks a month. The Finance Committee calculated that the combined costs of honoring IFA's outstanding financial commitments, completing existing orders, and developing new aircraft types throughout 1926 added a further loss of

2,900,000 marks. On May 4, the Finance Committee recommended three possible plans to Transport Minister von Schlieben, who then presented these findings in a full Reich Cabinet meeting the following day.[79] Finance Ministry officials charged with funding IFA's "restructuring" argued for liquidation, while the RVM, concerned with the firm's financial tailspin but aware of the need to maintain its production potential for the future, advocated radical cutbacks, but not bankruptcy. On May 5, the Marx Cabinet agreed with the RVM and voted against liquidation. Additionally, the cabinet passed a resolution that further credits required approval from the Reichstag Budgetary Committee, a decision that proved crucial for the firm's future.[80]

Arbitration continued. Junkers, removed from the pressures of day-to-day control of the firm, continued to refine his strategy. Preparations had begun nearly five months earlier. On January 28, 1926, Simons sent a letter to Junkers that asked what he hoped the arbitration process would achieve. Junkers and his senior advisors outlined their response during a series of meetings throughout February: "Ultimately we hope (a) that the hostilities that we are exposed to are rendered harmless, (b) that the Junkers Works faces no more obstacles in the pursuit of its future plans. *Pioneering work must be free.* . . . We have been weakened in the worst way and our name dragged through the mud. . . . Our defense, only verbally alleged, is not obvious from the outside. Therefore the preparation of a memorandum is required to demonstrate the correctness of our methods and the irreparable public damage our destruction would cause. Through the necessity for secrecy, the Russian part of the memorandum will be publicly restricted."[81]

At a subsequent meeting on February 12, Junkers returned to the planned memorandum, which he viewed as a vehicle for the expression of his views regarding the Fili Affair:

1. Purpose of the Memorandum
   (a) The Judge shall see that the adversary (the state) acted improperly through its oppression of Junkers.
   (b) Simons shall become aware that our goals match state interests rather than oppose them.

(c) Simons shall have the opportunity to compare the standard of our views with our adversary's opinions.

(d) The memorandum shall support our damage claims.

2. Reasons for temporary withholding of memorandum
   (a) Wait and see how our adversary acts further.
   (b) Hold to our earlier plan to not give out everything too early. Keep hold of our trumps.[82]

Junkers's strategy proved well founded. On March 30, 1926, Simons presented his findings before Junkers, other representatives of the firm, and a Reichswehr lieutenant. Few people, least of all the Reichswehr, expected what then occurred. Simons ruled in favor of Junkers and declared that the state's actions led to Junkers's financial collapse; therefore the state assumed responsibility for Junkers's current financial situation—a stunning victory for Junkers. Simons then announced a three-part settlement proposal: first, the shares of ILAG should be returned to Junkers; second, Junkers shall regain full control of the Dessau factories, with all outstanding state debts written off; third, the state shall provide an initial credit to enable Junkers to resume his business activities.[83] The Reichswehr, stunned and angered by the judgment, refused to accept this decision, withdrew from arbitration in May 1926, and declared Simons biased.[84] Relations between the two sides soured further during this period; in a ministerial meeting discussing the firm's future, the Reichswehr declared that it "no longer had any interest in maintaining the firm from the standpoint of national defence" and advocated reducing the Junkers concern "to the level of a research institute."[85] At the same time, it presented the Marx Cabinet with figures showing the large sums poured into the Fili venture. Aghast at these amounts, and with the Locarno negotiations completed, the Marx Cabinet felt sufficiently secure to ignore the Simons judgment, declared it "unavailable for consideration," and advised Junkers to pursue further legal action through the court system.[86]

Junkers, prepared for the government's response, now took the offensive. For several years the Junkers Works, aware of the need to maintain good relations with politicians at all levels of government, had cultivated relationships across the political spectrum, particularly with members of the permanent Reichstag Transport Committee, whose members established subsidies for German air transport.[87] The concern employed several methods of cultivation, including the use of Junkers aircraft for special flights, feted trips to the Dessau factories, and, more discreetly, financial contributions.[88] These actions gave Junkers direct access into the byzantine world of Weimar parliamentary democracy and established connections that proved crucial to the firm's reemergence. Junkers, also conscious of the media's power in the Weimar Republic, employed similar methods with prominent journalists by giving them free air travel in exchange for positive press coverage. In 1926, these relationships bore fruit, as Junkers now used this reservoir of established goodwill to promote his cause both in the press and the Reichstag.[89]

Junkers, aware that the Reichswehr and the RVM wished to keep detailed knowledge of the Fili venture from both the Reichstag and the public, and realizing after the rejection of the arbitration decision this was his last real chance to regain control of his firm, turned up the pressure. Through Reichstag member Kuhlenkampff, also a longtime member of IFA's board of directors, Junkers fired the first salvo. In letters to both Foreign Minister Gustav Stresemann and Reich Chancellor Hans Luther, Kuhlenkampff indicated that Junkers was prepared to initiate legal proceedings against the government that would involve public disclosure of the Fili Affair.[90]

Stresemann, by now angrily aware of the broad parameters of the Reichswehr's Russian engagements and the consistent attempts of army officials to keep him in ignorance, took an increasingly hard line against demands from the Finance Ministry and the Reichswehr to liquidate the firm's assets.[91] These demands increased throughout 1926 as it became clear that Brandenburg's prediction of returning the firm to profitability within three months had been a grave miscalculation. Brandenburg's clever manipulation of Junkers's financial difficulty in the creation of Deutsche Lufthansa ignored one vital point: the nature of the connection between ILAG and IFA. By April 1926, this connection's importance for the parent firm's sales capabilities became obvious, as the fusion of

ILAG into Deutsche Lufthansa left IFA without an established sales organization and increasing inventories. On April 20, 1926, IFA Director Friedrich Janssen reported to Junkers that IFA debts already amounted to over 17 million marks.[92] These numbers were all the more damaging now that the state controlled the firm's operations.

Few could deny that the firm's financial situation had worsened since the state's takeover, a situation that supported Junkers's claims that his business acumen surpassed that of the RVM.[93] Debt totals now exceeded funds allocated by the RVM for the firm's reconstruction. In response, the Marx Cabinet decided to involve the Reichstag in allocation of further support. This decision represented both a belated acknowledgment of the republic's constitutional structure and an implicit recognition that Brandenburg's policy had failed. Responsibility for the firm's fate now shifted to the Reichstag Budgetary Committee.

Junkers now realized events were moving in his favor. Characteristically, he returned to the offensive. Earlier in 1926, Junkers had considered relocating the firm to Sweden. He now increased pressure on the RVM by declaring this intention publicly. The RVM now faced being forced to bankroll the firm's massive losses to prevent possible relocation.[94] At the same time, he responded to the government's rejection of Simons's arbitration award by pursuing legal action against the state through the courts and arranging for an expert examination of his damage claims. Research at IFA also ground to a halt, as Junkers now refused to work with the firm's government supervisors.

The professor now also played his "trump card." On May 1, aware that the government had rejected demands from the Reichstag Budgetary Committee for a complete disclosure of events surrounding the Fili Affair, Junkers distributed more than one hundred copies of a brief outlining his own perspective of these events to government ministers and senior officials.[95] After reading a copy of this brief, Brandenburg exclaimed, "I have never received such a sycophantically mendacious pamphlet."[96] Despite the omission of names and actors in the brief, it revealed the principal role of the Reichswehr in the affair, and many Reichstag deputies, angered by the Reichswehr's arrogant pursuit of independent foreign policy, began to call for a full inquiry. On May

20 and June 7, Junkers also wrote to Chancellor Marx and asked for cabinet intervention.[97] When the government refused to budge, a second brief appeared on June 25, 1926. The June brief was distributed to the members of the Budgetary Committee and prominent opposition politicians, particularly those of the SPD (Social Democratic Party).[98]

Incensed by Junkers's publications, Reichswehr Ministry and Finance Ministry officials pushed for IFA's immediate liquidation. Publication on July 9 of Junkers's losses for the previous fiscal year bolstered these claims and provided ammunition for the Reichswehr and RVM against Junkers's assertions of financial stability prior to state takeover.[99] On August 13, the Reichswehr continued its counterattack when it produced a response to Junkers's June 25 brief that reiterated both its rejection of responsibility for Junkers's financial crisis and the Reichswehr contention that Junkers's sales policies led to the firm's downfall.[100] Both parties took their arguments to a meeting at the RVM in Berlin on August 15.

Despite the Reichswehr's countermoves, the meeting's participants emphasized the shift in momentum toward Junkers. Three members of the Reichstag Budgetary Committee, Privy Councilor Reinhold Quaatz and Representatives Wieland and Kuhlenkampff, joined the opposing parties and other involved government ministries. In a meeting characterized by suspicion and counterclaims, the power of the Budgetary Committee as final arbiter became clear as Kuhlenkampff defended Junkers against the Reichswehr's attacks and Quaatz called for "further examination of both parties' claims."[101]

By August 1926, IFA's monthly losses exceeded 1 million marks. The RVM now sought to end involvement with IFA at the earliest possible opportunity. Attempts to transfer IFA's shares to a third party failed, as Junkers refused to cooperate with such a venture, and liquidation, despite the arguments of the Finance and Reichswehr Ministries, created more problems than it solved as patented Junkers equipment would appear on the open market without legal approval for its use.[102] The RVM also found itself under pressure from the Foreign Office, who argued against liquidation both for reasons of "national prestige" and also over concern for its investment in Turkey.[103] Within this environment, Brandenburg enjoyed little room for maneuver and grudgingly accepted

Privy Councilor Quaatz's offer of mediation between the two parties. Negotiations began in September 1926.

Meanwhile, Junkers continued to examine his options. In a meeting at the firm's Berlin office on September 9, Junkers stressed the need to continue several actions concurrently, as no one tactic could be counted on to succeed. He noted the following moves already underway:

1. Parliamentary through Quaatz,
2. Pressure on the Foreign Office and Stresemann personally (foreign policy reasons for removal of the state from IFA),
3. Concern of the Reichswehr Ministry over public legal actions or discussions, in particular those regarding GEFU,
4. IFA's difficulties (Lack of capital, Personnel)
5. Possibility of a nullity suit. . . . These options by themselves cannot achieve our goals, it must be the sum of the pressures. We must strive to simultaneously strengthen these various pressures. . . . Tactically, regarding the clash with the state, time works for us by making the difficulties on the other side grow from month to month, with the consequence that resistance from reluctant state officials against a decent agreement with Junkers automatically lessens. . . . The trend towards a change of the current situation must be systematically strengthened.

Consider the following:

1. Attainment of more expert reports to further reinforce the basis of the invalidity of the October Contract. . . . This invalidity not only helps our legal case but also the anxiety created in maintaining this invalidity constantly weakens the RVM.
2. RVM officials, especially the would-be Minister Brandenburg, must be concerned about having to deal with the Parliament and the public in embarrassing ways. The closer the re-assembly of the Reichstag draws, the worse this anxiety must become. We must prepare action for this opportunity. Our relationship with the SPD will play a special role.

3. IFA's financial difficulties worsen daily. We have no interest in
diminishing these difficulties through procurement of orders.
The difficulties will soon be so great that the RVM will face two
alternatives, a new radical contraction of the firm, or petitioning
the Reichstag for more funds. The RVM will shy away from both
these options. The workers' press will complain about a new
contraction—the funds request will lead to unpleasant Reichstag discussions. . . . Nobody will enter IFA as a third party without Junkers's agreement, particularly as long as the questionable
October Contract hangs over like the Sword of Damocles. . . . We
must also take steps to increase the anxiety of the Reichswehr
Ministry. Perhaps we should pursue this with several more reports about the Russian enterprise. However it appears necessary to show the RWM that if required their strongest political
enemy, the SPD, will take an interest in the matter. . . . We need
not worry about the discretion and national loyalty of the SPD
politicians. . . . All large plans must be put off until von Schlieben
[IFA's supervisor] is removed and Stresemann returns.[104]

Even with all these efforts, little changed throughout September 1926.
On September 18, Transport Minister von Krohne wrote to Junkers and
declared he and the Reichswehr minister would "leave the resolution of
the claims to the discretion of the legal authorities;" therefore, no action
would be taken in the near future to change the status quo.[105] Behind
the scenes, however, pressure began to increase for a final resolution of
the whole affair.

Circumstances changed abruptly the following month. On October
6, Reichswehr Minister Otto Gessler dismissed General von Seeckt from
his post as head of the army. Gessler's action, prompted officially by the
involvement of a member of the former royal family in a military pa-
rade, ended an era and temporarily reduced the Reichswehr's political
power.[106] Von Seeckt's demise spelled the end of independent military
policy, as Social Democrats led an attack on the "Chinese Wall" erected
by von Seeckt around the army and demanded the military be brought
under civilian control. His dismissal also meant the army's commander
no longer possessed any personal interest in the Junkers Affair. At an

interministerial meeting on October 27, the Finance Ministry abruptly refused to provide further funds for IFA's support.[107]

The RVM now found itself faced with two unpleasant choices: either begin bankruptcy proceedings or proceed with an immediate liquidation of the firm's assets. Either choice seemed certain to arouse a storm of controversy, particularly from the political Left whose members already stood opposed to the firm's closure. Importantly also, either decision meant that the state stood to recoup virtually nothing for its massive investment in IFA since October 1925. Faced with this reality, Brandenburg continued to negotiate with Privy Councilor Quaatz in the hope that a better solution might appear. Junkers's stubborn refusal to consider the involvement of any third party in settlement negotiations paid dividends, as the political climate shifted more in his favor throughout November and December 1926.

Gradually, Junkers's plans matured. After a prolonged investigation, a team of experts hired by Junkers under the leadership of attorney Dr. Erwin Loewenfeld published their preliminary findings on Junkers's damage claims.[108] Ominously for the RVM, these findings noted that no liquidation of IFA was possible under German law without a three-quarters majority holding, an unreachable figure given Junkers's minority stake. Additionally, the findings raised doubts surrounding the legal force of the October 1925 contract. Armed with this information, Junkers reinforced his position and refused to accept any outcome other than the return of IFA to his control. Cleverly, however, he offered to renounce any further claims for state funding and promised to efficiently manage the firm's finances in the future. He also agreed to accept the proposal of Privy Councilor Quaatz that all other damage claims, such as those arising out of Fili, would be abandoned with an agreement.[109] Slowly but surely, the two sides drifted closer.

Public disclosure of the Fili Affair accelerated the negotiations between Junkers and the RVM. On December 3, 1926, the *Manchester Guardian* broke the story by publishing an article, entitled "Cargoes of Munitions from Russia to Germany: Secret Plan between Reichswehr Officers and Soviet."[110] The article unleashed a storm of criticism against the German government, both domestically and from abroad. Three days later, the *Guardian* printed a follow-up story, entitled "Berlin

Military Transactions," that broadly outlined Junkers's Russian activities. Importantly for Junkers, the article placed the blame for the firm's financial woes firmly on the Reichswehr, and both articles appeared in the Socialist daily *Vorwärts* (Forwards) later that week.[111]

Junkers followed these developments closely and used the furor created in the press to propose a settlement. On December 10, Junkers formulated a preliminary proposal. He agreed to abandon any further claims against the state in return for the withdrawal of the state supervision of IFA and the return of all IFA shares. Junkers also requested the state provide IFA with the ability to gather private credit so that the firm could rebuild itself. If the RVM accepted these conditions, Junkers committed to renouncing state assistance for three years.[112] On the same day, Loewenfeld conveyed these proposals in a letter to Privy Councilor Quaatz, who then presented them to the RVM.[113] On December 18, the Reich Cabinet accepted Privy Councilor Quaatz's proposals and directed the RVM to conclude a formal agreement with Junkers.[114]

Brandenburg, facing a barrage of accusations surrounding the recent press releases and now resigned to agreement with Junkers, sought to minimize damage to the RVM's prestige by exacting a price for Junkers's resumption of sole leadership of IFA. On December 19, 1926, three days after Philip Scheidemann, the "father" of the Weimar Republic, attacked the state's military policies in the Reichstag, the RVM conveyed its "unalterable" terms to Privy Councilor Quaatz.[115] The RVM declared it would dissolve the October 1925 contract and transfer its majority shareholding in IFA to Junkers. The RVM also agreed to write off all the firm's state debts, totaling some 15 million marks. In return, Junkers had to pay the RVM 1 million marks in cash by December 31, 1926, agree to provide 3,700,000 marks worth of equipment from existing IFA stocks to the National Research Institute and the Air Transport Flight School, and furnish four large aircraft of the state's choosing for Deutsche Lufthansa, with deliveries to begin on May 1, 1927. As security, the state retained possession of twelve completed Junkers aircraft until these provisions were satisfied. Additionally, Junkers was required to transfer his remaining 20 percent stake in ILAG, now part of Deutsche Lufthansa, to the state and permanently renounce all claims "of any

type" against the Reich concerning the Russian enterprise or other connections.[116] The next day, Junkers accepted the RVM's terms and on
December 23, 1926, signed the agreement granting him sole ownership
of IFA.[117] On December 30, Junkers wrote to Simons, thanking him for
his help and hoping that the new year would be "a year of work after a
year of conflict."[118] The following day, in accordance with the December 24 agreement, the RVM officially wrote off IFA's debts, an amount
totaling 26,450,000 marks.[119]

Once again, Junkers had engineered a stunning comeback and
emerged victorious from state supervision. His victory appeared almost
total; within the agreement, designed by Quaatz to consolidate all conflicts between Junkers and various state agencies, the RVM, the Reichswehr, and the Foreign Office renounced all claims to ownership of IFA's
foreign ventures in Russia and Turkey. Junkers once again possessed sole
ownership of these ventures and, by March 1927, managed to transfer 8 million marks back into IFA's coffers through both the sale of Fili
to the Russian government and, in Turkey, through indirect financing
procedures similar to those employed earlier in Russia.[120] This capital
injection rendered outside financial assistance unnecessary and allowed
IFA to increase production and pursue an independent research agenda
throughout 1927 and beyond.

However, these positive results concealed the long-term repercussions for the Junkers Works, particularly in its relationship with state
representatives and ministries. The Reichswehr, disgusted with the outcome of events, resolved to have no further contact with the Junkers
concern and excluded it from subsequent rearmament plans, all the
while waiting for the next financial crisis to engulf Junkers and provide
an opportunity for revenge. The RVM, whose use of Junkers aircraft
in Deutsche Lufthansa's fleet required it to maintain relations with the
firm, resolved to place the minimum number of orders possible in future.[121]

Junkers's financial reputation also sustained lasting damage from
the state bailout and reinforced the conviction in banking circles that
Junkers lacked the financial expertise necessary to run the firm profit-
ably. Such convictions boded ill for the future, as capital generated by the
Fili sale and creative accounting methods would not last forever. Most

significantly, Junkers now found himself excluded from involvement in European air transport networks, a development that cut off potential sales markets closest to the Dessau factory and forced the firm to search further afield for markets in regions that lacked established transport infrastructure. These markets required heavy initial capital investment and possessed few prospects for short- or medium-term profitability.

The conflict between Junkers and state agencies between 1922 and 1926, initially with the Reichswehr and later with the RVM, underscored the increasing divergence of both parties' aims for German aviation over this period. While Junkers continued to manufacture military aircraft in Sweden, Russia, and Turkey, he came to the conclusion that the best use of aircraft within Germany would be peaceful and that German air transport networks should be created and supported to offset the lack of a military air force. Within this view, expressed by Junkers in letters to Reich President Ebert and successive German chancellors, Germany would regain her place as one of the world's leading nations through peaceful and commercial means.[122] Junkers noted that aircraft transcended the terrestrial divisions of the German nation wrought by the Treaty of Versailles and possessed vast potential for the furthering of German commercial aims throughout Europe and beyond. Naturally, of course, Junkers's products would form an integral part of this process. However, Junkers's proposals ignored his precarious financial situation and state agencies' contrary air transport agendas.

More than any other aviation pioneer, by the early 1920s, Junkers had recognized the almost unlimited potential of a vertically and horizontally integrated global air travel, mail, and freight network. Seeking to develop this framework before his competitors, Junkers overleveraged, creating serious financial liabilities that exposed him to external criticism and eventual takeover. He also delegated too much authority and autonomy to his subordinates, who proceeded to operate his airlines without any regard for risk or budget. When the winds turned against him, he could not continue independently, and he lost the ability to influence the formation of the German national airline. Frozen out of its center, the Junkers airline network lost crucial access to profitable air routes and could not easily disperse its production facilities in response. Tragically, this era would also be the only time Junkers aircraft designs, including the F-13, held a competitive technological edge. Dozens of F-13's fanned out across the world, flying long-distance routes, usually for the first time, across every inhabited continent. F-13's also set dozens of distance and endurance records, creating worldwide press attention for Junkers aircraft that translated into commercial opportunities, as air networks began to expand and develop regionally, nationally, and internationally.

Unfortunately for Junkers, powerful interests at home, including many government officials and military officers, remained committed to a different vision of Germany's future. Within aviation, this vision coalesced by 1925 into a blueprint for the covert rebuilding of the state's military air capabilities that incorporated close connections between state-controlled research, planning, and production centers.[123] Key officials within the RVM, such as Brandenburg, joined forces with Junkers's competitors and opponents to remove him from control of civilian aviation in Germany, a move that halted Junkers's airline ventures at their widest reach.[124] With state oversight of civil aviation established, covert military aviation operations within Germany's borders commenced, a move that ended the pro-Russian policy of von Seeckt and began a new phase of strategic planning that continued into the Third Reich. Junkers, weakened by the Fili debacle, lacked the means to resist or influence these actions, and his December 1926 victory merely reinforced the state's conviction to pursue aviation policies firmly bound to narrow perceptions of national interest and military utility.

Although external forces and agendas exerted a considerable influence on the events of 1922–26, Junkers's actions and corporate practices contributed equally to his troubles during this period. Junkers's characteristic decision to grant Gotthard Sachsenberg autonomy in the air transport department of the Junkers firm returned to haunt him as Sachsenberg showed little interest in accounting or budgetary procedures. Sachsenberg, nicknamed the "Napoleon of Dessau," preferred instead to interpret the professor's directive to expand the firm's airline partnerships as carte blanche for action without regard for cost or subsequent profitability.

Sachsenberg's expansion policies must therefore be evaluated against contemporary air transport funding arrangements. As ILAG's viability rested on the provision of state subsidies, the decision to pursue the creation of international union networks supported by subsidies from numerous nations meant that national interests took second place, a situation the RVM could not possibly bear. While evidence exists that plans existed in government circles to unite ILAG and DAL before the state took control of IFA, nevertheless Junkers's announcement of the planned Europa Union in May 1925 tipped the state's hand.

Junkers's strident cries against state control during 1926 obscured both his deliberate incognizance of the RVM's accountability within the Weimar Republic and his own responsibility for his circumstances. With losses mounting from both the Fili factory and air transport from the beginning of 1924, he found himself caught burning the candle at both ends; the flames came together in October 1925, and only two years of state intervention saved the firm from liquidation. When difficulties again enveloped his companies, Junkers found himself forced to reap the bitter harvest of 1926. The next chapter traces the course of events from 1927 to 1932.

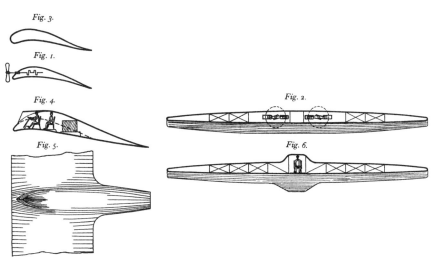

Image of the 1910 patent awarded to Hugo Junkers by the Reich Patent Office for his design of a flying wing, based on extensive wind tunnel testing at the facility he built at the University of Aachen. Modern flying wing designs such as the Northrop B-2 possess similar profiles. (Courtesy Deutsches Museum, Munich)

As part of strength tests for the J-1, Junkers workers stand on a wing prototype, 1915. (Courtesy Deutsches Museum, Munich)

The Junkers J-1, ready for takeoff, 1915. A new era of aviation was about to begin. (Courtesy Deutsches Museum, Munich)

This photograph shows the Junkers J-1 in flight, October 1915. The J-1 was the world's first all-metal monoplane aircraft. (Courtesy Deutsches Museum, Munich)

Work on the J-2 at the Junkers factory, Dessau, May 1916. Note the hand-intensive production methods. (Courtesy Deutsches Museum, Munich)

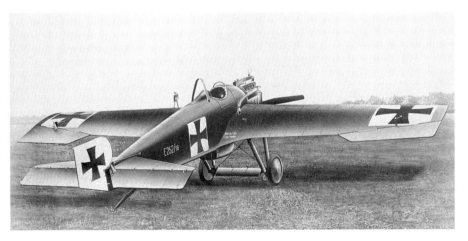

The J-2 in German colors, 1916. (Courtesy Deutsches Museum, Munich)

The J-4, a ground-attack design that proved highly successful due to its armor "bathtub" that protected the pilot and gunner. Grateful crew sent letters to the Junkers factory thanking the designers and engineers for saving their lives. (Courtesy Deutsches Museum, Munich)

The J-7, the best of World War I designs produced by Junkers, crashed by rival Anthony Fokker in controversial circumstances at a military competition late in 1917. (Courtesy Deutsches Museum, Munich)

Prefiguring a new era in aviation, Junkers produced the F-13, a purpose-designed luxury passenger and commercial freight aircraft, in 1919. The F-13 would soon fly all over the world, opening up general and commercial aviation opportunities in Europe, Asia, and Latin America. (Courtesy Deutsches Museum, Munich)

Demonstrating its advanced capabilities, the F-13 achieved several distance and speed records in 1919 and 1920 that Junkers employed as global marketing assets. This photograph
shows the pilots and crew of the F-13 "Annelise," named after Hugo Junkers's daughter, in
September 1919. (Courtesy Deutsches Museum, Munich)

F-13 in Latin America. Crew of an amphibious F-13 in the Bay of Botafogo, near Rio de Janeiro, Brazil, in 1921. F-13s would be the first aircraft to fly the routes that would later form the Central and South American air network. (Courtesy Deutsches Museum, Munich)

F-13 equipped with ski package in Russia, 1922. Demonstrating its ruggedness and durability in a variety of conditions was an important selling point for Junkers aircraft, and also led to the ill-fated partnership between Junkers, Weimar Germany's military and the Soviet Union. Unfortunately for Junkers, unscrupulous state partners, technical flaws, and cost overruns doomed his Russian dreams, and his market opportunities fell to others. (Courtesy Deutsches Museum, Munich)

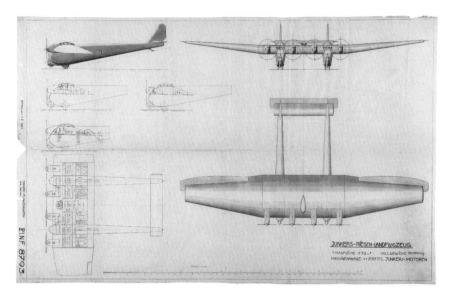

This image shows a blueprint design for a huge four-engine transport aircraft project, the Junkers R-1, which first appeared in 1921. The R-1's design features, including passenger sleeping and dining facilities embedded within the aircraft's massive flying-wing fuselage, envision a global aviation capability only achieved decades later, primarily due to engine performance limitations. (Courtesy Deutsches Museum, Munich)

A three-engine Junkers G-24, in flight in Lufthansa service, 1926. Junkers's defeat at the hands of his former employees at Lufthansa would tremendously weaken his global airline ambitions. (Courtesy Deutsches Museum, Munich)

This image shows the Junkers Works in Dessau, 1920s. Technikmuseum Hugo Junkers, Dessau, 2013. (From author's collection)

Junkers aircraft were designed to be durable, multipurpose designs, useful for both civilian and military applications. Here a Junkers W-34 sits on the tarmac in National Socialist insignia. First introduced in 1926, the W-33 and W-34 designs stayed in service for over a decade. (Courtesy Deutsches Museum, Munich)

A Junkers G-31 in flight. The G-31 represented an intermediate step between the smaller designs of the early 1920s and the far larger aircraft produced by the company later in the decade. (Courtesy Deutsches Museum, Munich)

Inside a G-31 cabin as lunch is served during the 1920s. Commercial air travel, then and now, shares many remarkable similarities. (Courtesy Deutsches Museum, Munich)

This image shows an artist's rendition of the J-1000, another huge passenger aircraft concept designed by Junkers engineers to operate amphibiously as a recognition of the limits of engine performance during the 1920s and 1930s. The J-1000 "Super Duck," which appeared in 1931, was featured in a December 1931 article in *Popular Mechanics* as the future of aviation. True transoceanic travel only became feasible with jet engines. (Courtesy Deutsches Museum, Munich)

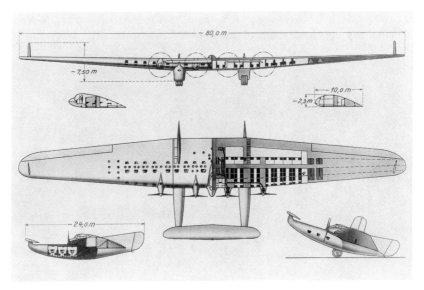

This blueprint shows the enormous size and futuristic cutaway features of the J-1000, many of which would not look out of place today. (Courtesy Deutsches Museum, Munich)

Junkers's largest passenger aircraft was the enormous four-engine G-38, first introduced just as the global depression savaged global aviation markets. A marketing failure, only a handful were produced. This aircraft, the "Field Marshal Von Hindenburg," was used by Lufthansa. (Courtesy Deutsches Museum, Munich)

Until the end of his tenure at the company, Hugo Junkers remained committed to pushing the boundaries of aviation research and challenging technological limits. This image shows a high-altitude research design, the Ju-49, which set several high-altitude records in the early 1930s. (Courtesy Deutsches Museum, Munich)

The most famous of all Junkers aircraft designed under its founder was the Ju-52, or "Tante Ju" (Aunty Ju), a rugged multipurpose transport and passenger design that went on to serve throughout World War II in a myriad of roles. This image shows the Lufthansa Ju-52 "Werner Voss." (Courtesy Deutsches Museum, Munich)

This image shows Hugo Junkers (fifth from right), his wife, Therese Junkers (fifth from left) and their daughter, Annelise (center), with other company and aviation officials in front of several F-13s in Dessau. (Courtesy Deutsches Museum, Munich)

Today, what remains of the Junkers factory complex, including a museum dedicated to the company and its founder, is contained within a light industrial zone outside of Dessau. This image shows the remains of a wind tunnel, with an abandoned corporate building in the background. June 2013. (From author's collection)

This image taken in June 2013 shows the front of the museum dedicated to Hugo Junkers, the Technikmuseum Hugo Junkers, founded and staffed by former Junkers employees and other local supporters. The company's famous flying man image can be seen on the building's exterior. (From author's collection)

This poster includes portraits of the famous Anhalters honored in the state's 800th anniversary celebrations in 2012. Hugo Junkers and Kurt Weill were the only twentieth-century luminaries to make the list. The bottom caption reads, "Idea rich and strong as a bear." (From author's collection)

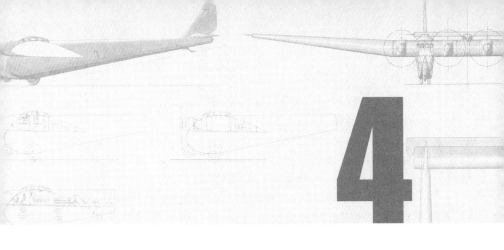

On the Edge, 1927–1932

As 1927 began, Junkers's optimism returned. The struggles of the previous two years lay behind him, and once again, he directed the firm's operations without state oversight. The sale of his remaining stake in the Fili plant provided the firm with a fresh injection of capital, a financial base further strengthened through the transfer of funds from Turkey back to Dessau. Characteristically, he began work on two new ambitious designs, each one dramatically different in scale. The first design, the huge four-engine G-38, represented the culmination of his efforts to design a large thick-winged aircraft that contained both engines and passenger space within the wing cavity, an aim pursued by Junkers since registering his first aviation patent in 1910.[1] With a wing thickness of over 6 feet, the G-38 also utilized engines from JUMO, Junkers's engine division, fulfilling Junkers's aim of unity between engine and airframe design. More than any other design, the aircraft realized Junkers's corporate vision, which had long envisaged a united and harmonious interaction of research, development, and horizontal integration of airframe and aero-engine production.

When it first flew on November 9, 1929, the G-38 was the largest land-based passenger aircraft in the world and would remain the largest until after 1945.[2] Unfortunately, the appearance of the G-38 could not have come at a worse time, and although the craft proved that Junkers's vision was technically feasible, contemporary economic conditions combined with poor economies of scale to render the G-38 an impressive white elephant. Significantly, the G-38 design also demonstrated circumstances that boded ill for Junkers's future in aviation. The craft's relatively low maximum speed and poor fuel economy, even equipped with the best current aero-engine technology, indicated that Junkers's design characteristics were now clearly obsolete. Only two were built, both eventually purchased by Deutsche Lufthansa.[3] It was clear to all in the aviation industry that the future lay not in larger, thick-winged designs, but in smaller, thin-winged aircraft that could fly faster and with better fuel economy, such as those produced by Junkers's rival, Ernst Heinkel. Junkers's technical advantage over his competitors, long his best trump card, had disappeared.

The second design differed drastically from the G-38. In response to Junkers's perception that air travel would soon become a mass transport option similar to the automobile, work began on a small single-seat design, the A-50, also known as the "Junkers Junior." In a significant departure from previous designs, Junkers planned to mass-produce the A-50 for the upper class and market the aircraft through automobile dealerships.[4] Behind this strategy lay the hope that large sales of the A-50 would relieve the increasing financial pressure on the firm. Although Junkers hoped for sales of over five thousand, fewer than fifty of the craft were sold, and the crash of 1929 ended any hope for a mass market. Like the G-38, the A-50 project demonstrated that technical viability failed to guarantee economic success, and although IFA managed to absorb the losses from the A-50 project, the Junkers Works entered the worldwide economic depression without substantial cash reserves.[5]

Internal and external problems further complicated Junkers's position. State intervention in and subsequent bailout of IFA restored its immediate financial solvency but failed to solve two crucial long-term problems. First, Deutsche Lufthansa's takeover of Junkers's air transport operations removed the aircraft factory's primary customer, and the new airline's aircraft surplus, a result of the merger of ILAG's and DAL's fleets, meant that significant orders could not be expected within the foreseeable future. Internationally, sales prospects also appeared less than promising; the satellite factory at Limhamm in Sweden continued to operate at a loss due to a lack of orders, the firm's operations in the Soviet Union had concluded the previous year, and the Turkish facilities struggled to remain afloat.[6]

While sales opportunities remained elusive, internal production costs continued to rise. Budrass notes that the effects of wage inflation, endemic within the Weimar Republic between 1925 and 1929, exercised an increasingly restrictive effect on Junkers's financial freedom of movement.[7] Aircraft production costs rose significantly, while competition within the industry kept sales prices static. Additionally, research and development costs continued to rise, particularly within JUMO.[8] Despite these warning signs, Junkers continued to believe that the German and world economic situation, relatively stable between 1927 and 1929, supported continued growth in the aviation market. This viewpoint, despite contrary evidence, clearly illuminates the combination of determined optimism and speculative risk-taking so characteristic of Hugo Junkers. Unfortunately, this attitude proved counterproductive, as it precluded any consolidation of the group's financial and corporate structure at a crucial juncture.

Second, relations with the RVM and the Reichswehr, the only possible remaining sources of contracts for Junkers aircraft in significant numbers, remained poor.[9] The events of 1925 and 1926 had been a major public scandal, revealing to the German public and the world that Germany's armed forces had not only deliberately defied the Versailles restrictions but also misled their own government. Following assurances from Defense Minister Otto Gessler that all future military plans would receive full parliamentary scrutiny, officials within the Reichswehr and the RVM learned from the Junkers fiasco and adjusted their rearmament plans accordingly.[10]

As before 1926, two primary aims underlay the strategy of the RVM-Reichswehr alliance—controlling the path of the rearmament program through the responsible ministerial apparatus and limiting knowledge of rearmament within the Reichstag. After Allied restrictions on German civil aviation ended, the creation of Deutsche Lufthansa facilitated the return of secret military aviation development within German borders.[11] This reorientation offered the crucial advantage of allowing the RVM and the Reichswehr to closely supervise and coordinate the activities of the aircraft industry. The Junkers Affair accelerated this process by illustrating the need for central coordination of aviation policy and rearmament objectives. Given the limited funds available, this meant that the number of firms participating in covert rearmament would have to be small. However, limited resources also offered their own advantages. By limiting the size and scope of the rearmament program, other ministries with competing agendas such as the Finance and Foreign Ministries could be removed from informed circles. Even more importantly, unwanted parliamentary oversight could be avoided entirely.

Both the RVM and the Reichswehr pursued these general aims over the next two years. Central to the process of tighter coordination were two connected initiatives: a drive for standardization within the German aircraft industry and the creation of a system of subsidies for aircraft orders linked to both military procurement priorities and industry efficiency and profitability. To oversee these procedures, new organizations appeared from within the Waffenamt, and overall aviation policy—hitherto disjointed due to the division of responsibilities between the two Reichswehr branches—became centralized and more closely coordinated with the RVM.[12] In 1926, the Waffenamt created two civilian holding companies, Fertigungs GmbH (Production Pty. Ltd.) and the Stahl- und Maschinenbau GmbH (Steel and Machine Construction Pty. Ltd., or STAMAG).

Fertigungs GmbH appeared to coordinate technical aspects of the covert rearmament program and to assist the aircraft industry in its transition from "individualized hand-crafted production to continuous-flow production."[13] Underlying this initiative lay the assumption that the next war would only be won through mass-production of war matériel, which would not be possible in the aircraft industry without standardization. Virtually no standardization existed within the industry at this time. Edward Homze notes that "Fertigungs GmbH found the aircraft industry in a chaotic condition, without common industrial techniques, drawings, engineering standards, or even numbering systems. . . . The magnitude of the task can be seen from the fact that one light aircraft . . . required an average of 32,000 parts and 50,000 rivets."[14]

For their part, firms resisted Fertigungs GmbH's incursions just as they resisted sharing trade secrets with rival manufacturers. Fertigungs GmbH officials considered this knowledge transfer essential for licensed production—in their view, the only means of producing large numbers of aircraft during an emergency. Industry resistance was understandable—although design firms were required to release technical data and information to their licensing affiliates as mandated by Fertigungs GmbH, financial and political circumstances meant that little chance existed that these designs would actually be manufactured. Nor, as Homze observes, did firms wish to invest in "jigs, machines and labor training without assurance of an immediate return on their investment."[15] As long as no large-scale guaranteed orders appeared—that is, until 1933—tension remained between the Reichswehr and industry concerning these standardization priorities.

STAMAG appeared to coordinate and supervise the financial relationship between the Reichswehr and the aircraft industry. The need for secrecy due to the Versailles ban on military aviation development meant that funds could not be transmitted directly from the Reichswehr to firms, but instead they had to pass through an apparently unconnected civilian intermediary. Precedent existed for this type of holding company; during the Fili operations, Junkers received funds through GEFU.[16] With covert rearmament now based within Germany, it was a logical and proven measure. Significantly, STAMAG also assumed additional roles such as assessing firms' financial health and participating in restructuring efforts when necessary, such as the restructuring of the Rohrbach firm between 1926 and 1927.[17] The experience of the Junkers Affair, which had been directed primarily by the RVM and had been characterized by vaguely defined aims regarding guarantees of the firms' future financial health, encouraged the creation and utilization of STAMAG by the Reichswehr as an active participant in the aircraft industry's coordination.

The appearance of Fertigungs GmbH and STAMAG signaled the emergence of the Waffenamt as a principal and autonomous actor in rearmament policy.[18] Importantly, the active role of STAMAG in the Rohrbach restructuring also served as a blueprint for future relationships between the Waffenamt and the aircraft industry, in general. No longer would firms possess complete independence in their design and economic strategies where these strategies intersected with covert rearmament priorities; the events of 1926 marked a decisive break with the past. In all sectors of aviation, from research through development and production into training and personnel recruitment, the Reichswehr and the RVM now pursued a single unified policy: the development of covert rearmament characterized by close state supervision and coordination of private industry.[19] Budrass likens this new coordination to the formation of an aviation rearmament cartel.[20] Junkers noted these changes and expressed his thoughts in a memorandum entitled "The Situation on July 9":

> Over the last three years, the erection of a state-controlled aviation trust monopoly has been consistently prepared and is now almost complete. Beginning with the technical Research Institute [Deutsche Versuchsanstalt Luftfahrt, or DVL] and the various production centers [Dornier, Rohrbach, etc.] through to the flying schools, Deutsche Lufthansa including its transport policy, and coordination of all circles and means through whom the public attitude toward aviation is influenced, . . . this immense creation constitutes a powerful Aviation Trust, like that first organized in Russia. There can no longer be the slightest doubt that the German state authorities have decided on this organizational form for aviation. In this development one sees not only the various circles of the RVM, which desire an increase in size and influence, . . . but also the Reichswehrministerium, which due to the lack of a military air force desires the permanent economic mobilization and maintenance of civil aviation.[21]

A change in the Reich Cabinet during February 1927 brought new leadership to the RVM and gave Junkers some hope for improvement in the concern's strained relationship with it.[22] Privately however, the professor exhibited little optimism. He expressed his frustration in his diary throughout April 1927. On April 6, he noted, "German aviation interests are safeguarded by the [RVM] Air Office, which strictly speaking possesses the viewpoint that civil aviation must directly support military requirements."[23] Nine days later he expanded his viewpoint:

Particularly for we Germans there is a question of especially great importance: (a) the military.

1. Through the connection of civil aircraft to the military the development and utilization of the airplane will be severely restricted. It is already outrageous that the Versailles Treaty has forbidden Germany to possess even the smallest air force, not even for police purposes. Now in addition we wish to also undermine the development of civil aviation and the airplane ourselves.

2. In Germany things are especially bad, because here the entire development of civil aviation lies in the hands of the state, which has monopolized the aircraft industry as well as civil aviation— not directly and officially, but indirectly and covertly, through the use of the following instruments of power:

    a) the universal authority of the state
    b) its decisive influence through enactment of laws and decrees, through negotiations with foreign countries, for example over the opening up of civil aviation . . .
    c) through immense funds, which Parliament grants through petition, and the discretion of the Air Office, which respective Transport Ministers more or less defer to
    d) through secret involvement in the aircraft industry, which to the greatest extent possible can only exist because of state subsidies and therefore is completely dependent on the authorities. Granting of large sums to the dependent industry, for large aircraft, etc.
    e) through the maintenance (at least 90 per cent) of an immense research institute, the DVL, with 300 engineers and employees, which oversees the inspection of aircraft. Not surprisingly, this enterprise operates completely uneconomically.[24]

Junkers's derisive view of his domestic competitors was no secret, and many of these men, particularly the Dornier firm's director, Dr. Albert Colsmann, sought to use the Junkers Group's financial difficulties during 1925 and 1926 to remove it from its preeminent position in German

aviation.[25] When these attempts failed, Dornier and other firms attempted to isolate Junkers by forming an industry association that deliberately
excluded IFA and JUMO. The Reichsverband der Deutschen Luftfahrt-
Industrie (National Association of the German Aviation Industry, or
RDLI) appeared on April 1, 1927, whose principal function revolved
around an "organized boycott of Junkers."[26] Significantly, the RDLI also
placed itself at the state's disposal and pledged its support of the covert
rearmament program. Junkers's isolation now deepened, as the firms of
the RDLI, particularly Dornier and Heinkel, forged close connections
with the Reichswehr. For these two firms in particular, this connection
provided crucial insurance during the coming world economic crisis.

Increased Reichswehr involvement within German aviation boded ill
for Junkers, as the fallout from the Fili Affair continued to permeate relations between the two sides. Faced with little hope of attracting military
work, Junkers concentrated on the civilian sector, hoping that continued
economic stability and the growth of international aviation would provide sales outlets for the firm's products. As well as passenger aircraft such
as the G-38, the firm expanded into freight-carrying designs, beginning
with the W-33, a streamlined offshoot of the highly successful F-13, and
culminating in 1930 in the Ju-52, a hybrid design incorporating both passenger and freight conversions. Additionally, he expanded his research
and development efforts, particularly in aero-engines, in an attempt to
realize his long-term aim of developing a viable diesel aero-engine. Diesel presented several advantages over benzine: lower flammability, greater
reliability, and significantly better fuel economy, particularly over longer
distances.[27] Reflecting this effort, JUMO's workforce expanded to over
1,800 employees in 1927.[28]

For the next five years, Junkers harnessed motor and airframe research
and development with two objectives: first, to reinforce horizontal integration between IFA and JUMO, with JUMO providing the benzine L-5
and the anticipated diesel JUMO 4 for Junkers aircraft, and second, to
address the crucial lack of indigenous engines within the German aircraft industry.[29] Junkers intended to overcome his domestic problems
through aggressive international marketing, building on the firm's excellent reputation abroad established by the F-13, and opening up new
markets through a series of highly publicized endurance flights. Between

1927 and 1930, Junkers aircraft achieved thirty-one world records of varying types.[30]

It was not a German, however, but a US pilot, Charles Lindbergh, who transformed the aviation world in 1927. Lindbergh's nonstop flight from New York to Paris across the Atlantic Ocean in the *Spirit of St. Louis* on May 20–21 revealed to the world that aviation had entered a new phase; transoceanic air travel moved from fiction to plausible reality. At the same time, Lindbergh's success ushered in a state of anxiety in Europe, particularly in Germany, where aviation policy rested on the belief that German technical superiority, long thought unassailable, offset the lack of a military air force.[31] This assumption died in May 1927, and the RVM redirected civil aviation policy toward the development of aircraft types suitable for the emerging transatlantic market.

Characteristically, Junkers saw Lindbergh's success as a challenge and an opportunity. He began two parallel efforts, one international, the other domestic. First in spring of 1927, the concern initiated an attempt to supersede Lindbergh's feat by successfully crossing the Atlantic from east to west. Junkers authorized two separate projects. One involved a seaplane conversion of a G-24 crossing the Atlantic from Portugal via the Azores. The second, more ambitious attempt envisaged a direct land-to-land crossing from Europe to the United States. Two Junkers W-33s were converted into long-range endurance aircraft, complete with extra fuel tanks in the wing cells. Junkers's "thick-wing" design perfectly suited this modification. A successful crossing guaranteed positive publicity for the firm, not only in terms of aircraft design but also significantly in the aero-engine field, as Junkers decided to use the Atlantic flight to prove the capabilities of JUMO's L-5. NDL provided financial support through its public relations manager, Baron Ehrenfried Günther von Hünefeld, and Deutsche Lufthansa's night flying expert, Hermann Köhl, contributed technical assistance.

The Atlantic flight program gathered increased momentum.[32] In preparation, Junkers insisted that endurance flights take place over land to ensure the L-5's reliability. On August 3, 1927, two aircraft, whose names, *Europa* and *Bremen*, reflected NDL's involvement, began an attempt on the world endurance record over a course between Dessau and Leipzig.[33] Although the *Bremen* made an emergency landing due to engine trouble shortly into the flight, the *Europa* successfully broke the world endurance record, remaining aloft for over fifty-two hours.[34] This success encouraged an attempt on the Atlantic crossing. On August 14, 1927, both aircraft took off from Dessau. Prior to their departure, Junkers gave a speech defining his hopes for the outcome of a successful transatlantic crossing: "What we must expect from aviation is *not merely the building* of aircraft of many different types, but also the fulfillment of *political and economic tasks*. We must utilize aircraft to bring peoples closer together; my highest goal is through productive struggle to bring both material and cultural prosperity to mankind. This transoceanic flight should help this goal come true. Air transport should not only be *free from politics* within Germany, but also without. Instead of aircraft being instruments of war, we will make *them weapons of Freedom and of Mankind*. This Junkers aircraft, when it touches down on US soil, will be a *messenger of Peace*, and we hope that other nations will join us as one in this great mission."[35] Weather conditions forced both planes to abandon their attempts. The *Europa* crashed at an airfield near the city of Bremen, while the city's namesake returned to Dessau. Poor weather conditions and the onset of winter prevented any further attempts throughout 1927.

Public opinion now also turned against further attempts, following a series of deaths between September 1927 and March 1928.[36] German newspapers and periodicals increasingly criticized such attempts as foolhardy and dangerous. Walther Kleffel, writing in the aviation journal *Luftfahrt*, "excoriated the deadly *Reklamesucht* [desire for notoriety] of transoceanic pilots."[37] Reflecting the public mood, German government officials and Deutsche Lufthansa began to discourage any further attempts. After he refused to give up making the attempt, Lufthansa officials informed Captain Köhl that he would not be granted leave. Fred Hotson notes that aviation authorities sought to prevent any attempt from German soil: "Instructions, clearly aimed at the *Bremen*, also went out to airport managers across Germany to detain any aircraft attempting a heavily loaded takeoff from a German airfield."[38]

Köhl made the decision to leave Germany and begin the flight from Ireland, both to avoid official interference and to lessen the headwind resistance. After secretly touring possible airstrips during February 1928, Köhl and von Hünefeld decided to fly the *Bremen* to Ireland on

Monday, March 26. The next steps reflected the secrecy necessary to avoid official oversight. Early that morning, von Hünefeld boarded the aircraft, stationed at Berlin's Templehof Airfield, and hid in the fuel bay. Later, Köhl, accompanied by copilot Arthur Spindler, entered the airfield's flight control office and "registered a trial flight to Dessau."[39] The aircraft lifted off without incident and flew to Ireland, and just in time; over the weekend, an order arrived to seize the aircraft. Not surprisingly, the *Bremen* never arrived at Dessau, and upon learning of the deceit, Deutsche Lufthansa dismissed Captain Köhl. Taking off from Baldonnel Air Force Base on April 12, 1928, the *Bremen* successfully completed the Atlantic crossing from east to west, crash landing on Greenly Island off the Newfoundland coast thirty-six hours later. Enormous celebrations began when word reached Germany that the *Bremen* had completed the Atlantic flight successfully. Newspapers, so critical only days before, erupted with praise.[40]

For Junkers, the *Bremen*'s success lay in positive publicity, but it also represented an important step forward for the concern in its attempts to reassert its technical superiority in the face of challenges from other domestic rivals, particularly the Dornier Flugzeugbau, whose flying-boat designs dominated the market by 1927.[41] By the end of 1927, costs for the transatlantic ventures exceeded 250,000 marks. In February 1928, Junkers confessed in his diary that worrying about them prevented him from sleeping.[42] The following month, he outlined principal reasons why a successful flight mattered:

(1) [It will be] one step forward in transoceanic transport. As such, however, it must not be done immediately with contemporary means. We shall calmly examine whether circumstances are favorable. In the end, it is critical that it encourages commerce. Perhaps we will be better served if we wait on the completion of a suitable aircraft . . .

(2) For us however, the transoceanic flight has [an]other significance of perhaps more importance, namely as a prelude for the commencement of production and eventually involvement in air transport in the US[.] Here we must ask ourselves whether we need this flight for this purpose.[43]

Junkers correctly realized that civil aviation's real growth market lay in the United States. Earlier in the decade, his first venture into that market failed due to circumstances not entirely of his own making. Now he sought reentrance into the United States and again traveled to this country in the wake of the *Bremen*'s success. There he renewed his acquaintance with Henry and Edsel Ford, and engaged in negotiations with them over license fees for the production of Junkers aircraft. As in 1924, Ford refused to accept Junkers's asking price, and the negotiations led nowhere.[44] Junkers had hoped to build on the publicity and prestige generated by the *Bremen*'s flight to corner the apparently imminent transatlantic aviation market. Unfortunately, as with the G-38 and the A-50 programs, his vision outran the pace of contemporary reality.[45] Bitterly disappointed, he returned to Dessau in June 1928 and resolved to focus his attention on Europe, most of all in reestablishing a relationship with German state agencies.

This effort, the concern's second aim after 1927, now received priority. Despite past problems, the reputation of the Junkers Works as a research center remained undiminished. IFA remained Germany's largest aircraft producer. Junkers sensed the RVM might be persuaded into closer relations due to altered political circumstances. He offered the G-38 design as a seaplane to the RVM in a conscious effort to demonstrate his adherence to new state priorities. In response, the RVM agreed to fund the G-38's development, with several conditions: IFA was required to accept RVM supervision of construction, provide detailed cost analyses, and recognize the RVM's claim to exclusive use of the design upon successful completion.[46]

Additionally, the RVM demanded Gotthard Sachsenberg's removal from IFA's leadership. RVM officials such as Ernst Brandenburg considered Sachsenberg the principal obstacle to improved relations between Junkers and the government. During his career at Dessau, Sachsenberg's direct involvement first in the Fili negotiations and later as head of ILAG created many enemies for Junkers within both the Reichswehr and the RVM. Obliged to remove Sachsenberg from direct leadership, yet unwilling to release him completely, Junkers created an office for Sachsenberg in Berlin at the end of 1927, where he acted as the firm's unofficial representative, particularly in the Reichstag; in

May 1928, Sachsenberg entered the Reichstag as a representative of the *Wirtschaftspartei* (Business Party).[47]

The G-38 negotiations and Gotthard Sachsenberg's removal constituted significant victories for the RVM. They brought Junkers into line with the requirements placed by the state on other firms within the aircraft industry and, thereby, once more drew Junkers into the nexus of patron-client relations that characterized the state-industry relationship. Closer relations between all state organs responsible for aviation meant that Junkers's traditional strategy of exploiting interagency differences and rivalries lost its effectiveness. Covert rearmament's return to Germany removed one of Junkers's strongest official supporters, the Foreign Office, from any involvement in rearmament policy. Additionally, unification of RVM and Reichswehr policy aims decisively limited Junkers's freedom of movement; with the former Reichswehr officer Dr. Adolf Bäumker now directing and overseeing a centralized disbursement program for aviation research funding, and Deutsche Lufthansa receiving the bulk of Reich aviation subsidies, IFA and JUMO, like the rest of the German aviation industry, found themselves inexorably coordinated into the state's rearmament strategy.[48] Angered by these developments, yet increasingly powerless to alter them, Junkers found himself forced to adjust IFA's and JUMO's corporate strategies into line with the new reality.

This readjustment echoed the recommendations of several officials within IFA's leadership and the Hauptbüro, including Gotthard Sachsenberg and Hans Plauth, who insisted the concern abandon its myriad of development projects and focus on a small number of designs most likely to elicit state approval. More precisely, this meant tailoring the firm's design priorities explicitly toward military applications. Although up to this point Junkers designs incorporated a "dual" capability that allowed for military conversion, Sachsenberg and Plauth argued, although for different reasons, that IFA should focus on producing designs that could be immediately converted in emergencies without requiring extensive retrofitting.[49] New Reichswehr contingency plans that called for "emergency armament" of Deutsche Lufthansa aircraft bolstered this argument.[50] IFA executives accepted these new priorities, and by 1929, Junkers possessed four distinct military aircraft that appeared to satisfy the needs of any air force in the world.[51]

While Junkers hoped to sell these aircraft abroad, he focused attention primarily on events within Germany in 1928, specifically on the
Reichstag's allocation of aviation subsidies. Improved economic circumstances in 1927 and 1928 resulted in a record budget for the 1928
financial year. Reich aviation subsidies increased 25 percent from the
previous year, up from 43,803,500 marks to 55,534,395 marks.[52] Junkers
and Sachsenberg believed these increased funds—and more importantly the methods employed for their distribution—represented an opportunity to use the Reichstag in an attack on the existing aviation power
structure. Three broad goals motivated this attack: an end to Deutsche
Lufthansa's monopoly on German air transport; the dismantling of the
"aviation cartel" formed by the Reichswehr, the RVM, and the RDLI;
and a return of significant autonomy to private industry in aviation
planning and development.[53]

Junkers viewed the first aim as a personal obligation. Since the founding of Deutsche Lufthansa in 1926, Junkers had longed for an opportunity to end its state-supported monopoly and never missed a chance to
illuminate the problems inherent in state control of civil aviation.[54] On
November 29, 1927, at a meeting in Dessau, Junkers emphasized that
reestablishment of contact between the Junkers Works and Berlin politicians was a top priority. The woeful circumstances of 1927, in which
out of fifty-eight new aircraft ordered by Deutsche Lufthansa, Junkers
had received orders for only two, must be avoided. Junkers called for a
resumption of visits of prominent politicians to Dessau, a tactic used to
good effect earlier in the decade. He argued that such visits "are a suitable platform to create support for our goals."[55] At the same time, however, cordial relations with existing power structures had to be maintained and had to be cultivated in areas where no relationship existed.[56]
Aware of the resonant effects of 1926 and of his restricted freedom of
action, Junkers sought to avoid direct confrontation with state authorities until new political alliances crystallized.

Wary of press criticism, Junkers left direct action to Sachsenberg,
whose position in the Reichstag provided a suitable platform to criticize
the Reich's aviation policies.[57] Throughout 1928 and 1929, he wrote and
distributed several memoranda that called for a reevaluation of German
aviation policy and priorities in both military and civil spheres.[58] Concern-

ing military aviation, Sachsenberg adopted the argument of the Italian air theorist General Giulio Douhet, whose writings championed the superiority of the fast bomber fleet that could strike anywhere in Europe within hours.[59] Accepting the restrictions of the Treaty of Versailles, Sachsenberg proposed German defense needs would be better served through the creation of a fleet of fast transport aircraft that could be instantly converted into bombers should war begin. Sachsenberg's memoranda argued that such a fleet, with latent military capabilities recognized by Germany's enemies but which did not contravene Versailles obligations, would act as a strategic deterrent by guaranteeing a rapid and devastating response to any attack. With this force, Sachsenberg maintained, a "compulsory peace" could be maintained throughout Europe.[60]

Additionally, this fleet's development promised three further advantages. First, it significantly reduced costs associated with supporting covert rearmament; second, in contrast to existing rearmament strategy, it provided direct assistance and contracts to the German aircraft industry, and third, it presented a challenge to the rising prominence of the United States in the international aviation market.[61] Naturally, the design envisaged for such a fleet was the new Junkers J-52, and adoption of Sachsenberg's plan would reestablish Junkers as the central figure in German military and civilian aviation. Also Sachsenberg's vision, if realized, would mark a decisive turn in German aviation policy and end the dominance of the "aviation cartel": the RVM and the Reichswehr, as well as its subservient organs, Deutsche Lufthansa and the RDLI.[62]

Sachsenberg also called for an end to Lufthansa's monopoly on air transport routes within Germany, the transfer of authority over aviation subsidies from the RVM to the Reichstag, and the creation of an "Aviation Bank" supported by private credit institutions that would oversee distribution of aviation funding.[63] These proposals fell on fertile ground in both obvious and unlikely places.[64] Within the Reichstag, opposition parties, particularly the SPD, possessed a long history of opposition to the state's covert rearmament policies and saw Sachsenberg's proposals as an opportunity to weaken the power of their enemies, most notably within the Reichswehr.[65]

Most criticism centered on Deutsche Lufthansa. By the end of 1928, the airline carried debts of 19,800,000 marks, and SPD deputies echoed the critical appraisal of the airline and the RVM reached by the Reich Auditor-General's Office, which reported that the RVM's strict control of Deutsche Lufthansa's procurement policies had led to increased ministerial control of the airline and the aircraft industry without a corresponding increase in efficiency.[66] Income generated by the airline corresponded to only one quarter of expenditure, and only 100,000 passengers traveled on the airline throughout 1927. Compared with other transport systems, air travel's costs meant that ticket prices matched those of first-class rail fares, and high overheads meant that on a flight from Berlin to Dresden priced at 132 marks, 120 marks reflected costs.[67] SPD attacks on Deutsche Lufthansa increased throughout 1929, both in the Reichstag and in the party newspaper *Vorwärts*.[68] Other experts, even Junkers rivals such as Heinkel, also joined in and created a chorus of criticism.[69] This chorus reached a crescendo in March 1929, as the aviation budget arrived in the Reichstag for an initial reading.

Members of the "aviation cartel" wasted little time mobilizing their own resources in response. Accepting the terms and location of the struggle, Deutsche Lufthansa began paying Reichstag members to support its cause and defend it against these attacks.[70] Although members from both the SPD and Deutsche Volkspartei (DVP) received Lufthansa subsidies, most funds went to Hermann Göring, parliamentary leader of the National Socialists.[71] In a number of characteristically grandiose speeches, Göring admonished his peers for their criticism of the national airline and urged them to view support for Lufthansa as a "great patriotic task."[72] Lufthansa's opponents remained unmoved, and their attacks continued.

Junkers closely followed the debate over aviation in the Reichstag and the press. Unlike Sachsenberg, who relished his new role as "public advocate," Junkers recognized the great risks inherent in the firm's new strategy. On January 20, he noted, "I fear that the objections to the existing system may be perceived as merely expressions of a personal standpoint and (as such) will generate spiteful repercussions. One exposes oneself to the danger of being cast as a troublemaker. The recent public discussions have encouraged a certain weariness and a justified aversion toward aimless mudslinging. . . . One runs the risk of not only preaching to deaf ears, but of also running into considerably united opposition."[73]

Declining economic circumstances warranted Junkers's concerns. The onerous burden of reparations combined with rising social welfare expenditure to severely compromise the Reich budget. By the end of 1928, the German economy carried short- and long-term debts totaling over 13 billion marks, and the Reich budget deficit had ballooned to over 600 million marks.[74] Calls to balance the budget provided ammunition to the enemies of the RVM, and in 1929, the ministry's budget allocation fell by 48 million marks. Cuts fell heavily on the Aviation Department, where subsidies for air transport decreased by one third. State funding reductions halved the Lufthansa subsidies for 1929, a move that encouraged the new director of the airline, former Junkers employee Erhard Milch, to begin restructuring and streamlining the airline's activities.[75] Support for the aviation industry received even sharper reductions, declining from 15 million marks to 5 million, and the budget for covert rearmament fell from over 9 million marks to less than 2 million.[76]

New financial realities resulted in two immediate consequences: first, the RVM's interest in transatlantic aviation ended, and in May 1929, it informed the industry that no new projects were under consideration. Second, it superseded Sachsenberg's calls for reform, although the Reichstag attempted to alleviate some of the cuts by providing loans to Deutsche Lufthansa and private firms totaling 9 million marks. Significantly, these loans were supervised not by the RVM, but by a "Key Commission" appointed by the Reichstag. IFA and JUMO received 2,350,000 marks through these loans.[77] Thus, Sachsenberg's efforts were not entirely fruitless.[78] Additionally, the awareness generated by the debate over aviation also led to a recognition of private industry's common interests versus the state's and a rapprochement between Junkers and the RDLI. In May 1929, the industry group reorganized, removing Deutsche Lufthansa from its membership and enrolling Junkers.[79] The aircraft industry attempted to join forces against the prevailing power interest, but found its arms tied by a lack of private capital and weak private markets. Sachsenberg's proposed "Aviation Bank" never materialized, and the state remained in control of the industry's future. Even before the global economic crisis began in October, the budget reductions began to claim victims, most notably the Rohrbach Flugzeugfabrik.

Rohrbach's path through the decade since the war's end paralleled that of Junkers in many ways. The firm was owned and directed by its namesake, Adolf Rohrbach, who, like Junkers, entered metal aircraft construction immediately in 1919. Also like Junkers, Rohrbach pioneered the use of light metal internal reinforcement in wings and fuselages and developed a series of large transport aircraft based on these design characteristics. The required high capital investment taxed the firm's resources to the limit, and the state stepped in to save the firm twice, first in 1924 with extensive loans, and then in 1927, unfortunately, in the immediate wake of the Junkers Affair. Rohrbach fell victim to the state's increased oversight of its investments. RVM and Reichswehr representatives intervened directly in the firm through STAMAG. In exchange for saving the firm from bankruptcy, STAMAG took over a controlling interest in the firm and reserved the right to liquidate Rohrbach in the event of subsequent difficulties. Gambling everything on winning a transatlantic contract, Rohrbach invested all his remaining resources into giant flying-boat research, a field he barely knew. By 1929, the firm again lacked sufficient capital for continued operations without state funds. In July 1929, STAMAG exercised its right, and liquidation began.[80] Many other small firms either followed Rohrbach's demise or attempted mergers. Realizing that the industry faced a crisis on par with that of 1920, the RVM's Aviation Department and the Reichswehr began a process of calculated rationalization, choosing to support certain companies as a nucleus for future rearmament programs. Foremost among those saved were the Heinkel and Dornier concerns.

Claudius Dornier's prowess in flying-boat design made him the crucial contributor to Weimar Republic marine aviation. Despite this position, his large investment in the transatlantic program, represented by the gigantic Dornier X, placed the firm in financial difficulties by 1929. Dornier found few customers for the huge craft, and in the wake of the Hoover Moratorium suspending Germany's reparations payments, Yugoslavia canceled the firm's only large order. RVM funds maintained the firm with a sharply reduced workforce throughout the economic crisis between 1931 and 1933. Ernst Heinkel's enthusiasm for covert rearmament paid off in 1929, as the RVM also protected him through the worst of the crisis by awarding the firm a Deutsche Lufthansa contract for a fast postal aircraft. Additionally, Heinkel's foreign contracts, particularly with the Soviet Union, provided crucial foreign currency and kept the firm alive until conditions improved in 1933.[81]

The Junkers Works found itself completely exposed in 1929. Sharp declines in Reich aviation subsidies rendered Sachsenberg's efforts moot and combined with the end of the transatlantic program to render substantial domestic orders unlikely for the foreseeable future. International and domestic circumstances now converged as the global economic crisis took hold after the collapse of the New York Stock Exchange in October; these circumstances magnified Junkers's contemporary financial difficulties and revealed several key deficiencies within the group's corporate structure.

Understanding the severity of this convergence requires a brief examination of Germany's financial course between 1900 and 1929. From the turn of the century, inflationary effects significantly compromised Germany's economic and financial health. Lack of a broad direct taxation base forced the state into reliance on income through indirect taxes, tariffs, and foreign loans. Increased defense spending compounded inflationary pressure; it began with naval appropriations between 1898 and 1912 and culminated in the expense of World War I, which left the Weimar Republic with debts of 156 billion marks by 1919. Faced with this huge deficit, now magnified by reparations obligations, demobilization costs, and unemployment insurance demands, successive Weimar cabinets resorted to increased production of treasury notes and reliance on foreign capital, a course that led to the hyperinflation of 1923. The stabilization of the currency with the creation of the *rentenmark* alleviated the worst effects of hyperinflation but failed to stem Germany's need for external capital, both in the private sector where profitability relied on exports, and in the public sector where government expenditure came to rely on foreign loans, above all from private US banks.

These loans were the first victims of the Wall Street Crash, as US firms attempted to shield themselves from collapsing stock prices. The fragile platform supporting the German economy vanished, and the subsequent collapse of the international economy precluded any possibility of foreign rescue. Lack of funds rendered Weimar's welfare state provisions—always a point of contention between employers and workers in

Germany, despite the acceptance of the *Zentralarbeitsgemeinschaft* in November 1918—insufficient and unsatisfactory, and the drastic austerity measures introduced by Chancellor Heinrich Brüning in 1930 and 1931 worsened the situation by removing capital from the economy.[82] Dissatisfaction with the Republic reached a critical level, and German voters across all social levels abandoned centrist parties in favor of more radical political solutions.[83] As unemployment worsened throughout 1930 and 1931, the state's social welfare responsibilities rapidly exceeded budgetary estimates, and drastic cuts occurred in other budgetary sectors, particularly in transportation. Initial hopes for a rapid end to the crisis soon faded, and mass unemployment gripped Germany until 1934.

Confronted by these circumstances, many aircraft firms simply collapsed.[84] For Junkers's two aviation firms, IFA and JUMO, the global economic crisis not only removed the possibility of international orders by severely contracting the international aviation market and encouraging foreign nations to protect their domestic industries, but also exposed several critical problems within the Junkers Works corporate structure. Lack of capital support ranked foremost among these problems. Always a perennial concern for IFA and JUMO, capital shortages became acute by 1929 as the funds garnered by Junkers Works after the 1926 bailout ran out. Between 1926 and 1929, these funds, totaling 13.5 million marks appeared in Junkers's account records as profits, offsetting actual losses and masking the firm's increasing financial difficulties. Significantly, aircraft production never reached self-supporting levels throughout this period, and after the surplus disappeared, funding for IFA and JUMO increasingly flowed from Junkers's core firm, Junkers & Company (ICO).

The 1926 settlement also concealed the problematic relationships that permeated the group's financial structure. Throughout the 1920s, the Junkers Works corporate structure resembled a loose confederation, with overall control of policy formally directed from the Hauptbüro and then passed to the individual firms themselves. Additionally, the Hauptbüro oversaw research and development for all Junkers companies and set research priorities in aviation and aero-engine development for the Forschungsanstalt (Research Institute). Funding for the Hauptbüro came from two sources: first, from license fees for use of Junkers patents and foreign licensed production of Junkers products;

second, from monthly contributions from the four production firms: ICO, the Kaloriferwerk Hugo Junkers, IFA, and JUMO.[85] Funding for the Forschungsanstalt nominally derived from "proceeds from research work," which meant from license fees also earmarked as Hauptbüro funds. These financial arrangements required both imaginative bookkeeping and favorable economic conditions.[86] Under difficult economic conditions, the symbiotic relationship between the productive firms, the Hauptbüro and the Forschungsanstalt, became a liability, as the large overhead costs of the aircraft and engine divisions combined with research costs to place an unbearable strain on the group's viability. By September 30, 1929, IFA possessed only 375,000 marks of liquid capital, while monthly obligations for the Hauptbüro and the Forschungsanstalt exceeded 400,000 marks.[87]

Junkers, continuing to direct the firm's policies, also became a liability. As the economic crisis worsened, Junkers refused to modify IFA's or JUMO's research programs or construction schedules, despite the fact that many current projects, such as the Ju-49 high altitude research aircraft, enjoyed no prospects of future production.[88] These research priorities required the maintenance of a large scientific workforce within the Forschungsanstalt, whose numbers remained constant regardless of economic circumstances and whose salary obligations, when combined with the Hauptbüro's executive salaries, totaled half of the Junkers Works employee costs.[89] Motor research consumed an increasing amount of research time and funding, as Forschungsanstalt researchers and JUMO designers sought to produce and refine a diesel aero-engine and improve existing benzine engine designs.[90] As Budrass correctly notes, Junkers continued faith in the viability of self-funding aviation research dovetailed with the realization that further progress within the field, particularly in Germany, lay in development of improved aero-engine designs. Through successful production of JUMO's new diesel and benzine designs, Junkers hoped to regain market dominance through technical superiority in German and world aviation.[91] Unfortunately for Junkers, although lack of quality engines proved a lasting problem for German aviation, the Junkers Works internal funding mechanisms proved unable to support the high costs of engine research for an indefinite period, and the slow technical progress combined with poor economic conditions to transform Junkers's aero-engine operations from a promising venture to a critical financial burden.

Junkers's continued influence also proved detrimental within IFA, as his insistence on limited series production and development of several designs concurrently meant that in 1930, out of no less than ten different aircraft types then under construction at Dessau, only one, the W-33, sold in significant numbers.[92] As the international Depression deepened, unsold aircraft began to accrue at the IFA plant; between 1929 and 1930, only fifty-two aircraft were sold, less than half of those produced. By the end of 1930, IFA possessed an inventory of two hundred aircraft with a value of 12,500,000 marks.[93] Turnover fell steadily from a high of over 10 million marks in 1927–28 to less than 5 million marks two years later.[94] Seventy years old in 1929, Junkers proved resistant to change, and he continued to oppose rationalization or reductions of the group's research initiatives.[95] As financial woes increased, opposition to Junkers within the Junkers Works executive branches mounted.

Rising production and raw material costs compounded the group's financial problems. In an increasingly competitive marketplace, Junkers agreed to modify aircraft to suit customers' individual needs; the result was higher costs due to longer production times and use of more expensive materials.[96] Wages also rose substantially in the aircraft industry throughout the 1920s due to successive state arbitration awards and inflation. All of these factors meant that the sales prices of Junkers aircraft typically exceeded those of their competitors by 1929.[97] More problematically, these competitors in many instances outperformed their Junkers counterparts, most of which still incorporated Junkers's now obsolescent design principles.[98] Junkers's attempt to offset the loss of Junkers Luftverkehr through creation of a global sales and marketing organization added a further drain on the firm's resources without yielding tangible returns. Between 1926 and 1929, advertising costs for the United States alone exceeded 1.5 million marks.[99] By 1930, only ICO and the Kaloriferwerk remained profitable, and their turnovers had declined significantly since 1928.[100]

Junkers, by now used to recurrent financial crises, met the difficulties head on. Correctly surmising that his sole ownership of IFA limited the firm's credit opportunities, Junkers transformed the firm into a joint-stock company in 1928.[101] On July 5, 1929, before the onset of the global economic downturn, he met with colleagues in the Hauptbüro and formulated plans to increase income through "a fundamental examination of all ways and means that appear suitable to encourage and guarantee the fructification of Junkers research products."[102] Junkers recommended three courses of action: first, tighter management of patent policy, including increased monitoring of patent infringements by foreign firms, more consultation with foreign patent experts, and cultivation of closer relations between the Junkers Works and the Reich Patent Office; second, a renewed focus on the development of effective sales networks and advertising; and third, the development of relationships with influential personalities both within Germany and internationally.[103] Junkers hoped these relationships would ultimately lead to the creation of an advisory body charged with encouraging licensed production of Junkers aircraft by foreign firms.[104]

For his part, Junkers began this process by writing to both Hjalmar Schacht, president of the Reichsbank, and Reich President Paul von Hindenburg during 1929 and 1930.[105] Schacht, by this time embroiled in the Young Plan negotiations and aware of Germany's burgeoning capital crisis, balked at providing direct financial assistance and instead advocated the pursuit of partnerships with other firms, particularly in aero-engine development.[106] On August 2, JUMO executives met to discuss Schacht's suggestions, and while they declared themselves prepared to enter into partnerships, they reiterated Junkers's perception of the firm as "principally a facility involved in the creation of new technology and products. . . . Therefore naturally we are not suited to mass-production."[107] On November 26, Junkers traveled to Berlin to consult with Schacht and other Reichsbank directors. At this meeting, Junkers explained that the distinctive character of the Junkers Works as a research concern resulted in "perpetual financial strain" and that research required "long-term pre-financing. Often large sums must be expended over a period of years before tangible economic and financial success is achieved."[108] In this meeting with Schacht, Junkers exposed the fundamental problem of the Junkers Works; the concern's focus on long-term, uncertain research projects requiring large capital investment without guaranteed returns was incompatible with financial institutions' lending practices, which sought to ensure safe, guaranteed returns over short periods of time. Germany's particular circumstances exacerbated this incompatibility, and by 1929, even those banks that had supported Junkers for over a decade found themselves unable to continue support.[109]

During the discussion with Schacht, Junkers also employed his most consistent claim concerning the Junkers Works—that the group's principal worth lay not in its material assets, but in its latent assets, in the primary research and new product development that produced both patents and new technological innovations. As Schacht's refusal to provide direct financial support demonstrated, this argument proved hard to sell to financial institutions. However, as subsequent events demonstrated, other parties within Germany, most notably the Reichswehr and the RVM, recognized this latent worth and sought to use the financial difficulties of the Junkers Works to gain control over it.[110] As the firm's financial problems worsened, this opportunity drew closer.

Junkers's letter to President Hindenburg revealed the professor's other central theme—that the Junkers Works occupied a position within Germany's aviation industry of "primary national importance" and therefore required state assistance in difficult economic times. Cleverly anticipating the martial perspective of the letter's recipient, Junkers outlined the contemporary state of German aviation in relation to its military utility and preparedness for anticipated threats:

> Germany's political situation is characterized by the vicinity of power-politics oriented states. These neighbors have military forces at their disposal that can in emergencies deliver a destructive strike against the centers of power and population of Germany within a few days or even hours.
>
> Therefore it appears necessary to sufficiently strengthen German military forces in a way that on one hand proves capable of successfully repulsing such an attack, and on the other hand is not subject to the limitations of the Versailles Treaty.
>
> No service arm corresponds to the requirements more than the Air Force. Instant combat readiness, a greater radius for action and rapid effectiveness enable this force to protect against and forestall enemy actions through the threat of severe attacks against their own nations.

. . . However, aviation in Germany has in fact developed in ways that
prevent these aims being achieved. Over and above the limitations of
the Versailles Treaty, Germany has self-imposed severe limitations on
the remaining freedom for development of its aviation. . . . The mo-
nopolization of air transport has . . . forced aviation within an official framework and cut off private initiative as the driving force of all
economic development. . . . The productive power of already limited
funds is thereby used in unsuitable ways and in unsuitable areas. . . .
German security requires . . . the release of German aviation from official shackles.[111]

Ultimately, however, Junkers's efforts yielded few returns. Appeals
to higher authorities fell on deaf ears throughout 1930, while much-
hoped-for orders for either the G-38 or Junkers engines failed to materialize.[112] Morale declined throughout the concern, particularly within
executive ranks.

While Hugo Junkers continued these machinations, other Junkers
executives began implementing reforms and austerity measures in an
attempt to stave off the approaching financial disaster. Within IFA these
measures included a reduction in the number of aircraft types and an
end to custom retrofitting.[113] As these measures took effect, they encountered increasing opposition from Junkers himself, who perceived these
measures as potentially harmful to the essential nature of the Junkers
Works as a research-oriented organization. Junkers's approach toward
mergers or granting of "world licenses" to other firms to manufacture
Junkers aircraft and products exemplified this resistance. In a memorandum that outlined his thoughts on these matters, Junkers raised a long
list of objections on grounds that the unique corporate structure of the
Junkers Works, with its intricate connections between research bureaus
and production facilities, and its reliance on patent protection for self-
financing precluded successful partnerships. The necessary knowledge
and technology transfer required for mergers or licenses would critically
undermine this structure by removing its most valuable resources.[114]

Junkers's viewpoint correctly summed up the status quo within the
Junkers Works by 1930 and confirmed what many within and outside
the firm already knew—that no other firm operated according to the

professor's principles and that these principles precluded friendly mergers or collaboration with outside investors.[115] Release of IFA's balance
for 1929–30 confirmed the company's financial woes; the aircraft firm
recorded a loss of 1,455,152 marks, despite state loans and payments of
more than 1,600,000 marks during this period.[116] By the end of the year,
the financial difficulties of the Junkers Works mirrored those of 1925.

Junkers's continued confidence in the soundness of his corporate
vision combined with contemporary economic circumstances to con-
firm that the group's recovery required his removal. Recognizing that
Junkers would not deviate from his long-held corporate designs, other
executives within the Junkers Works increasingly criticized the professor's sole direction of the concern and cited the need for a revamped
corporate strategy to avert imminent financial collapse. This criticism
emerged in 1931 and led to a shake-up of the firm's executive leadership.
On January 15, 1931, IFA's financial management produced a statement
that outlined further rationalization measures:

> The last two financial years have seen marked drops in turnover due
> to the depression of world market prices. . . . This raises the question
> of which new income sources can be developed that will bridge the
> timespan until the recovery of Germany, which for the firm as far as
> can be judged will provide sufficient opportunities. . . . The first prior-
> ity is the commitment of management to produce sales. . . . For the
> time being, new areas of work (housing construction) are not decisive-
> ly productive. The last reserves of the aircraft factory are exhausted,
> having been transferred to JUMO. Existing orders are pre-financed.
> Delaying payment of pending debts has already led to their increase
> to unbearable levels. . . . Given that funds are not available within the
> concern, outside funds are necessary if the time until considerable
> state demands arise is to be bridged over without heavy damage. . . .
> The supply of outside funds does not release us from the necessity of
> vigorously continuing the rationalization measures currently underway.
> These measures include: adjustment of luxuriously operated offices to
> material realities (Büro Berlin, Limhamm [Sweden], . . . Turkey), con-
> tinuation of voluntary salary reductions by executives in the course
> of current general salary and wage reductions, and conformity of the

entire IFA-apparatus to a monthly budget of 650,000 marks. All of these measures are totally unobtrusive and can be introduced and carried out without damaging the strength of the firm. . . . In no way can we choose whether or not we wish to reduce costs; we simply have to decide whether we will survive and develop further or go under. The bloated organism of the Hauptbüro requires a particularly sustained inspection of its viability. In its existing form it is unacceptable for the concern. . . . Over the last few years, no visible reductions have taken place in the Hauptbüro, while the rest of the firms have experienced far-reaching reductions.[117]

This criticism echoed statements of JCO Director Paul Spaleck, who in a series of statements throughout the year urged Junkers to accept financial reality and scale back the extensive research programs of the Junkers Works: "I believe that the previously proposed measures aimed at rapid utilization of existing research products, as important and necessary as they are, still will not be suitable for overcoming the acute financial difficulties of the coming weeks and months. These measures will not take effect as quickly as the financial crisis we find ourselves in."[118] Junkers refused to accept these arguments and responded by reemphasizing the group's raison d'être: "When Spaleck infers that in current circumstances our research's lack of viability led to our financial difficulties, he labors under a misapprehension. . . . Absurd conclusions result if only current revenues from mass-production and license utilization form the revenue sources for research. . . . It is self-evident that mass-production is the ultimate goal of any innovation. . . . At the same time however, one cannot disregard the fact that the concern's entire character still firstly is and shall remain that of a research institute. . . . All Junkers [Works] efforts move toward a fundamental improvement in the viability of the entire concern and, as its leading component, the research."[119]

None of the participants in these debates disagreed on the need for outside funds. Unfortunately, Germany's worsening economic crisis now took on financial dimensions, creating a credit crisis that made obtaining credit from private sources impossible. Germany's financial position worsened throughout 1930 and 1931 due to two factors: first, foreign investors' loss of confidence in the political system due to the elections of September 1930, which saw radical political parties make huge gains at the expense of their moderate rivals. This loss of confidence led to a further flight of foreign capital from Germany, resulting in the cancellation of many short-term foreign loans and a rapid constriction of the Reichsbank's reserves.[120] Second, Reich Chancellor Heinrich Brüning's decision to use Germany's financial crisis as a lever to end reparations obligations. This strategy backfired badly in June and July 1931 in the wake of two parallel developments: first, in pursuit of his policy designed to circumvent reparations through demonstrations of Germany's inability to pay, Chancellor Brüning announced two measures, the Third Emergency Decree for the Reform of the Economy and Finances on June 5 and the Tribute Appeal on June 6. The Emergency Decree called for widespread cuts in salaries, social services, and national subsidies to states and municipalities, while the Tribute Appeal, directed at the Allied Powers, inferred that Germany no longer possessed the means to meet reparations obligations.[121]

Foreign creditors perceived these announcements as de facto declarations of insolvency, and the flight of foreign capital from Germany accelerated.[122] At the same time, Austria's largest private bank, the Österreichische Creditanstalt (Austrian Credit Institute), collapsed. Within days, the banking crisis spread to Germany, and on July 13, after the collapse of several large firms compromised their solvency, the Darmstädter und Nationalbank (Danat) and the Dresdener Bank, the second and fourth largest banks in Germany, stopped payment.[123] Over the next two days, all German banks were closed, and even after they reopened, banks only allowed customers to withdraw a fraction of their assets.[124]

Now the flight of foreign capital became a flood, triggering a wave of withdrawals not only from private banks but also from the Reichsbank. In response, the Reichsbank found itself forced to constrict general credit activity throughout Germany in order to slow the flight of capital and avoid complete financial collapse. Refinancing of loans for private banks became much more difficult, and the overall volume of loans was significantly curtailed. The seriousness of the situation required immediate action, and on July 16, the government issued the Emergency Decree for the Protection of Credit. This decree created a government-controlled acceptance and guarantee bank, a shared liability consortium of major banking institutions from both public and private sectors. Most significantly, the new institution "provided for tighter government oversight of the credit system by giving the national government far-reaching control over private credit transactions and making it the majority shareholder in the Deutsche and Dresdener banks. The re-privatization of the banking system did not occur until 1933."[125]

Germany's banking crisis spelt disaster for the Junkers Works through the effective removal of private credit sources. Since 1925, Danat Bank had been one of the concern's most consistent sources of private credit, and Jakob Goldschmidt, Danat's director, was one of Junkers's most ardent supporters.[126] Two other consequences resulted from the state takeover of the banking system. First, in an effort to protect rapidly declining capital reserves and avoid a repeat of 1923, the Reichsbank restricted loan refinancing and curtailed loan volume throughout Germany.[127] Credit restrictions combined with state oversight of the financial system to end any hope Junkers had of private financial support. Second, municipal governments ranked among the hardest-hit by the new credit environment. Local governments relied on access to short-term loans for fiscal solvency. Already strained to the limit by budget cuts and increased social welfare responsibilities, municipalities now faced bankruptcy as their credit sources evaporated.[128] For Junkers, this meant the Anhalt state government, long a supporter of the Dessau factory complex and his last possible option for financial assistance, could not help him. As summer progressed, the financial situation of the Junkers Works became increasingly precarious. In August, Junkers was forced to curtail donations and membership dues.[129] IFA's monthly report for the same month made gloomy reading—forty-five aircraft in inventory valued at 1,953,500 marks and short-term debts totaling 1,210,643 marks.[130]

Acrimony within the concern's management peaked in November 1931, as IFA executives continued to press Junkers to abandon his focus on research until the concern's fortunes improved.[131] Sachsenberg led this attack, supported by his former men within IFA's management.[132] Junkers interpreted these attacks as a prelude to hostile takeover. He used the opportunity to end his decade-long relationship with Sachsenberg and remove his influence from Dessau. On November 20, 1931, all executives connected with Sachsenberg were removed from IFA, and Junkers replaced them with men he considered more loyal, including his former secretary, Adolf Dethmann, and his twenty-five-year-old son, Klaus Junkers.[133] These replacements reflected Junkers's awareness that only one source of funding remained to keep the concern's aviation activities alive—the "aviation cartel" of the Reichswehr and the RVM. Both agencies refused to deal with Sachsenberg, and thus his departure was seen by Junkers and IFA's new executive as an avenue toward better relations.[134] The priority Junkers placed on improving this relationship reflected his recognition of contemporary political developments. On May 21, 1931, he summarized the political consequences of the economic crisis:

> In my opinion throughout the coming months domestic politics will move strongly to the right due to the magnitude of the national crisis, whereby the position of the Defense Ministry and above all the position of the Reichswehr within the state will considerably strengthen. The outcome of this will be that the Reichswehr exerts a stronger influence on both foreign policy and domestic matters than hitherto, particularly in areas other Ministries consider their spheres. Primarily this development affects aviation. It appears possible that this development will affect our foreign sales. It is therefore all the more necessary that we secure domestic orders, in which once again the Defense Ministry will play the main role. . . . Whether these developments are desirable remains an open question. In any case, however, we must reckon with them. Therefore, we must place the highest value on creating an extremely favorable relationship with the Reichswehr.[135]

Junkers also correctly divined the Reichswehr's future intentions, noting contemporary military aviation planning reflected the army's attempt to move simultaneously in two different directions: first, toward creation of a small but powerful secret air force designed for an isolated war against Poland, and second, in preparation for a future free and independent air force "through the arrangement and mobilization of industry, especially through the placement and funding of development priorities."[136] Given these realities, Dethmann argued, the Junkers concern either resolved its differences with the military or faced collapse.

Philosophical objections to military involvement in the firm's research programs meant little if they compromised the concern's financial health: "Above all . . . it appears necessary to express the view that we desire a close collaboration with and are willing to accommodate the views and demands of the Defense Ministry. This appears all the more urgent as the Defense Ministry has not awarded us any development contracts for one and a half years. . . . In certain ways the criticisms of the Rw.M. [the Defense Ministry] (too expensive, not simple enough, too little consideration of the requirements of the Rw.M. in technical respects) appear not totally unjustified, particularly currently as suitable new designs are either unavailable or under review and the existing design program is already backdated about two years. The causes within the firm are predominantly perceived as internal."[137]

In response to these criticisms, Dethmann and Klaus Junkers instituted a series of reforms designed to increase efficiency and decrease costs. Their efforts, which included strict observation of working hours and reductions in work days for office staff managed to reduce IFA's salary costs from 97,000 marks to 84,000 by the end of the year.[138] Unfortunately, these initiatives proved unable to offset the firm's growing debts, and IFA, together with the rest of the Junkers Works, lurched toward insolvency. On December 10, 1931, Junkers wrote in his diary that he intended to withdraw from the concern's day-to-day affairs to focus exclusively on research.[139] Three weeks later, due to the drain placed on them by their sister firm, JUMO, IFA executives began considering insolvency proceedings in an effort to stave off bankruptcy.[140]

Financial difficulties within JUMO provided the catalyst for the entire concern's insolvency. Junkers's founding of the firm in 1923 reflected his desire to control all aspects of aircraft development and free IFA from dependence on outside engine manufacturers. JUMO's importance within the concern steadily rose after 1927. At this time, Junkers became convinced that better engine designs held the key to aviation's future and that Germany's lack of satisfactory aero-engines offered an opportunity for JUMO to dominate the market in the same way as the F-13 after its appearance in 1920. Engine development followed two paths: further refinement of high-performance benzine engines for use at higher altitudes and the systematic development of a diesel aero-engine known as the JUMO 4.[141] A prototype of the JUMO 4 appeared in early 1928, and expectations quickly rose that JUMO soon would form another foundation of the concern's self-financing structure. Between 1927 and 1933, the JUMO 4 served as the power-plant base for aircraft design, and IFA's J-52, destined to be the last great aircraft created and produced under Junkers, incorporated plans to use the engine as its primary power plant.[142]

Yet the firm never realized these expectations, partly due to the global depression after 1929, but more directly because of the nature of engine research, with its long and expensive development phases and prolonged timelines. Engine development and production required heavy investments in time, personnel, and materials, all of which increased in price between 1927 and 1930. The JUMO 4 required two years of workshop and flight testing before it could be considered for production, and endurance testing continued until September 1930.[143] Thus for over two years, despite advances in technical areas, no return materialized. Meanwhile, global depression and competition from superior foreign designs removed any chance for significant export of the firm's benzine engines. Additionally, JUMO's structure as an engine research facility meant it lacked means to mass produce its own designs and thus likely would not have avoided its increasing debt even had a large order appeared. When the iconic Junkers Ju-52 appeared in October 1930, Deutsche Lufthansa expressed interest and declared they would purchase the design, but with three engines rather than one, and with engines designed in the United States produced under license by JUMO's rival, BMW.[144] The Ju-52, or "Tante Ju" (Aunty Ju) would go on to be not only the culmination of a design arc that began with the J-1 in 1915 but would also be the Junkers design produced in the largest numbers, in continuous production around the world until the late 1950s. It would also become the most famous and recognizable Junkers aircraft, serving as the transport backbone of the Nazi Luftwaffe during the 1930s and 1940s. Thousands were built, and several flying examples survive today. Ju-52s ferried Francisco Franco's armies across the Straits of Gibraltar and also transported thousands of wounded German soldiers out of the siege of Stalingrad. Rugged, durable, and dependable, they served in dozens of roles across the world into the 1970s. Ironically, they would also serve to unwittingly tie the firm, and its founder, to the Third Reich after 1945.

Subcontractors' payment demands proved the final straw. JUMO's largest subcontractor, August Borsig GmbH, agreed in 1928 to offset JUMO's payments through a combination of long-term bills of exchange and production licenses for future JUMO products.[145] This system allowed JUMO to defer debt owed to Borsig until the JUMO 4 and other new designs matured, but left JUMO exposed should Borsig encounter difficulties. In December 1929, JUMO's sales collapsed, and by March 1930, with JUMO's debt to Borsig totaling over 1 million marks, the two firms signed a moratorium delaying JUMO's obligations by eighteen months, with the first payment due on October 1, 1931. Within this period, JUMO's debt increased to 3.5 million marks.[146] The moratorium stipulated an initial payment of 15 percent of the total debt, followed by a payment of half the original balance at the end of the year.

On August 22, 1931, Spaleck wrote to Junkers at his retreat in Bayrisch-zell, Bavaria. Spaleck outlined JUMO's imminent financial crisis; JUMO lacked the means to make even the first payment, let alone the second. Already the Junkers Works lacked the funds to support its own budget, and, Spaleck added, even without moratorium payments, a shortfall of 600,000 marks loomed. To make matters worse, Borsig's own financial difficulties ensured the involvement of its major creditors, specifically the Deutsche Bank and Commerz-Bank, in any moratorium negotiations. Both these banks had made extensive loans to the Junkers concern, specifically to JUMO, IFA, and ICO, whose value exceeded 1 million marks. The involvement of the Reichsbank, particularly since the banking crisis of July 1931, could therefore be expected and, with it, other state organs. Borsig's financial difficulties deepened, and during insolvency negotiations in August 1931, the firm noted the direct connection between its own capital shortages and the debts owed it by JUMO.[147]

Borsig's reorganization, overseen by the RVM, resulted in two consequences for Junkers: first, a controlling interest in Borsig passed into the hands of the state through the Reichsbank, and second, negotiations over further extensions of JUMO's moratorium collapsed. JUMO found itself confronted with a charge of 700,000 marks, due immediately. Faced with a debt that he could not pay, and with the concern's resources already stretched to the limit, Junkers began negotiations with the RVM for an extension of credit in an effort to avoid complete collapse.[148] For its part, the RVM recognized the importance of the Junkers Works both for the local economy and also as an integral part of any future rearmament plans, yet the ministry remained wary of its experience in 1925 and realized that it no longer possessed access to unlimited funds. In September 1931, the RVM declared itself ready to negotiate but called for a thorough examination of the firm's financial status before further credit could be extended. At the same time, an agreement between Junkers and the RVM granted a further moratorium of one year on JUMO's Borsig debts in exchange for the mortgaging of 7.5 million marks worth of IFA shares.[149] This agreement effectively made the RVM the majority shareholder of IFA. Seven years after the last state takeover of the Junkers Works, RVM financial and accounting experts again appeared in Dessau and began an examination of the entire concern's financial status.

These examinations and their accompanying negotiations proceeded slowly, hampered by arguments between Junkers and the concern's creditors and trustees over the actual worth of the "latent value" contained within Junkers's research programs and patents. In March 1932, Junkers stressed that no agreement would be finalized without acceptance by both sides of common goals and leadership principles, and that eventual recovery of the firm by either himself or his family must remain an option.[150] By this point, however, with capital resources exhausted, Junkers was in no position to dictate terms. Faced with bankruptcy, he declared the Junkers Works illiquid on March 22, 1932, suspended all wage and salary payments, and requested the commencement of insolvency proceedings.[151] Two days later, the Anhalt state court approved this request; later that week, all Junkers contractual employees saw their terms of employment reduced from three months to day-to-day.[152]

Realizing that recent internal reforms gave the concern hope of regaining viability, and that his continued involvement in IFA and JUMO might compromise any agreement with the RVM, on April 11, Junkers declared himself ready to retire from the concern's directorships and boards "if the decision was made that he was no longer suitable."[153] Junkers's declaration reflected the concern's corporate structure; as sole owner of ICO, the Kaloriferwerk Hugo Junkers, the Hauptbüro, and the Forschungsanstalt, as well as owning majority interests in IFA and JUMO, he held personal liability for the concern's debts. On April 20, the RVM wrote to Klaus Junkers and recommended the creation of a new holding company overseen by the firm's trustees and creditors. This company would be freed from the concern's existing debts and obligations and would allow the concern to continue operations, and the RVM intimated that this reorganization would encourage the granting of orders from the Reich.

On April 29, the RVM formally presented its demands to Junkers. In addition to support for the creation of a new holding company, the RVM demanded that Junkers support any measures "deemed necessary" by the firm's trustees in the concern's reorganization and grant the new holding company a free license to use all patents owned by Junkers related to aircraft design for five years.[154] In return, the RVM would cover all wage and employee costs for the firm until insolvency proceedings concluded. Later that day, the RVM's trustees arrived at Dessau to begin their investigation into the concern's finances.[155] The following day, Junkers agreed to the RVM's terms, which included formal settlement of claims registered against Junkers by IFA's previous management in 1930. These claims centered on Junkers's personal responsibility for debt incurred through IFA's financing of the Hauptbüro and the Forschungsanstalt.[156] At this point, however, negotiations began to flounder.

Differences persisted between Junkers and the RVM trustees over valuations of Junkers's patents and research programs. Junkers argued the trustees' disregard of the "latent worth" of these factors—which he regarded as central to arriving at a reasonable estimate of the concern's value—resulted in not only an underestimation of this worth but also an overestimation of his personal financial responsibility. Specifically he questioned the creditors' assignment of 2 million marks of debt against him personally and countered this assessment with figures that showed Hauptbüro expenses charged to IFA totaled only 1,272,615 marks throughout 1930.[157] He also criticized the terms of the license agreement regarding patent use, noting that many patents applied to multiple applications rather than just aviation and that by granting their free use he would be deprived of his rights as owner.[158] Junkers noted that the cost of patent application and maintenance needed to be included in overall calculations of the concern's assets.[159] As May began, more layoffs occurred within the concern.[160] Against this background, discussions began between Junkers and the Anhalt state government; as Dessau's largest employer, the Junkers Works held an important position within the local economy. If the concern collapsed, many of Dessau's citizens would lose their jobs and become wards of the state.[161] Unfortunately for Junkers, these negotiations led nowhere, as Anhalt's financial situation resembled that of the Junkers Works. Only federal agencies possessed the means to rescue the firm, and these agencies indicated that if a rescue occurred, it would be on their terms.

RVM actions appeared to illustrate this underlying agenda throughout early 1932. Since March, in the wake of the start of insolvency proceedings, the RVM had suspended all payments and subsidies to IFA. By May, with all financial reserves exhausted, and with the concern's workforce no longer receiving wage payments, Junkers ordered work at IFA to cease and attributed the firm's closure to the RVM's lack of support. On May 5, 1932, IFA Director Dethmann wrote to Reich Transport Minister Gottfried Treviranus and expressed his displeasure over the lack of progress. Dethmann also accused the RVM of pursuing an agenda contrary to the best interests not only of the concern but also the general public: "After four months of fruitless negotiations with the RVM as well as the desire within the Ministry to use the pressure of the current situation to ensure the subjugation of Professor Junkers and the leadership of IFA and JUMO, it is clear that your Ministry desires the immediate shutdown of IFA. . . . This decisive exertion of influence occurred through the RVM without—according to my information—any recognition of the legal responsibility of the RVM for the fate of IFA through its capacity as trustee of the public interest."[162] The RVM's inaction between March and May 1932 reflected the state's desire to influence the concern's reorganization with the goal of removing Junkers from control of the Junkers Works aviation divisions. This strategy succeeded, and on May 13, the Creditor Committee released its findings and recommendations. Per the RVM's recommendation, the Creditor Committee ordered the creation of a new company, Junkers Flugzeugwerk Betriebs GmbH, with new management independent of the Junkers Works. Faced with bankruptcy and the dismissal of his entire workforce, Junkers had little choice but to accept the committee's decrees.

Terms of the agreement between Junkers and the committee meant the effective end of Junkers's involvement in aircraft production. IFA was required to suspend operations, and the new firm would take over all IFA production facilities at Dessau and lease them for 150,000 marks a year. All current IFA orders passed to the new company, which agreed to immediately hire four hundred IFA workers. In exchange, all profits generated by Junkers Flugzeugwerk Betriebs GmbH flowed to IFA, the trustees agreed to approve a loan to the rest of the concern, Junkers retained majority ownership of ICO and the Kaloriferwerk, and the RVM agreed to finalize all outstanding debts and place orders with the new firm.[163] With the signing of this agreement, work recommenced immediately within the aircraft factory, which benefited from its new financial independence, the reforms of the previous year, and reduced sales prices for its products.[164] By the end of 1932, these reforms resulted in the aircraft factory realizing a small profit, a dramatic improvement from the previous year's loss of 2,205,838 marks.[165]

Although the May agreements resolved IFA's and JUMO's immediate problems, the fate of the Hauptbüro and the Forschungsanstalt remained unclear. Junkers and the Creditor Committee continued to argue not only over the assessed patent worth but also over the means used to determine this value. These arguments continued throughout summer 1932 as the creditors insisted that the terms of the agreement of May 13 required Junkers to hand over all patents connected with aviation and aero-engine development, while Junkers steadfastly maintained that no transfer could occur without satisfactory compensation.[166] Meanwhile, the separation of the Hauptbüro and the Forschungsanstalt from the rest of the concern disconnected these agencies' funding sources, resulting in further layoffs and wage delays throughout May, June, and July.[167] Financial need drove Junkers into negotiations with locomotive firm Oskar Henschel & Son over IFA's possible sale, but the two sides failed to reach an agreement, again due to Junkers's insistence on what he perceived as a fair price for the company.[168]

Some uncertainty ended as investigations into IFA's and JUMO's finances concluded. Germany's official arbitration body, Deutsche Revisions und Treuhand AG, announced its decision on JUMO on July 22, and on IFA on September 9. Terms of the arbitration included a moratorium on all creditor claims for a further year, with the mortgaging of all IFA and JUMO shares under the supervision of a trustee.[169] Despite these resolutions, no agreement emerged concerning the properties and assets formally recognized as wholly owned by Junkers himself. As sole owner of all 178 patents registered by the concern, he sought to use them as a lever to retain control. These patents were his only remaining assets, as ICO and the Kaloriferwerk had been reorganized as limited liability companies under the terms of the May agreement. Junkers hoped to use the patents' value to offset any further personal debts and stubbornly refused to accept any agreement that lacked this proviso; meanwhile, the RVM, as principal IFA and JUMO creditor, sought to force Junkers into surrendering his patents to the state.

Close connections between the Reichswehr and the RVM explain this aim. Gaining control of Junkers's patents became an important aspect of the Reichswehr strategy after 1929 as part of the military's larger rearmament initiatives. Partly in response to the enforced austerity brought by the global depression, and also due to planning programs that called for production numbers only achievable through licensed mass production, Reichswehr aviation planners advocated the creation of a state-controlled "patent pool" that contained all militarily useful aviation patents. Such a pool would greatly facilitate production during open rearmament and had been used successfully during World War I. The need for such a pool increased once Reich authorities decided to begin stockpiling aircraft after November 1930.[170]

By 1932, after examining Germany's aircraft factories, Reichswehr officers realized that the aircraft industry's maximum production capacity totaled one hundred aircraft per month and that existing reserves combined with industry capacity to give German air forces an expected combat life span of only six weeks.[171] Despite this depressing forecast, in February 1932 Hellmut Felmy, chief of staff of the Reichswehr's Air Inspectorate, called for a massive rearmament program that envisioned an air force numbering one thousand aircraft by 1938. In November that year, Hans Jeschonnek, another member of the Air Inspectorate, published a study that called for the integration of all Reich aviation offices within the Defense Ministry to centralize and coordinate all aspects of state aviation planning. Jeschonnek's proposal also called for the creation of the new air force as a separate defense arm, independent of army control. These proposals received authorization from Chancellor Kurt von Schleicher later in the month, and future plans called for the appropriation of Reichstag aviation subsidies in their entirety for military purposes and the establishment of a new air force on April 1, 1934.[172] On January 24, 1933, a new Defense Ministry department appeared under Hellmut Felmy, Inspectorate of the Air Force. Six days later, the Weimar Republic fell, and the situation changed again.

Faced with the knowledge that the only forces who possessed the power to assist him instead wished to see him removed from Dessau, Junkers became increasingly frustrated. Late in September 1932, he reflected on his circumstances and the RVM's proposals:

So we are getting nowhere: This proposal is nothing more than a ruthless rape with the aim of removing Junkers and placing everything that he has produced in 40 years of work in the hands of a prospective buyer for a song.

On one hand they demand that I a) maintain good will and protect the interests of the Creditors b) guarantee unconditionally that they will be protected.

On the other hand they a) hold me by the throat in order to bankrupt me and b) put me in a straitjacket and take from me any possibility of protecting creditors' interests.

This theater, *playing with the mouse*, must now stop: Either they give me the freedom I need to protect them and the interests of the Junkers Works, . . . or bankruptcy occurs. . . . In this tough fight over the existence of the Junkers Works[,] serious, fundamental mistakes have been made. . . . Public opinion has been completely misled; it has no idea how things really are and operates on the belief that the public interests . . . are best served by opposing Junkers. All of this is the result of the view that Junkers is neither businessman nor manager and has brought the Junkers Works to the edge of ruin through unreasonable research programs. The worst of the matter is the view that Junkers wishes neither to learn nor suffer, so outside managers and financial experts must be brought in to lead the firm. . . . The indisputably worst mistake from Junkers's side was allowing the enemy to dictate the terms and place of battle. . . . We have done nothing for a year, except to run and beg to the RVM . . . where our real enemies reside and greet us with kicks, and where we are completely powerless while they are invulnerable. Fighting shoulder to shoulder with the RVM are our so-called "trustees," . . . who want the Junkers Works sold to Henschel. The Creditor Committee has also recently opposed us and all these powers have now raised their arms in one last attack against Junkers in order to

a)   completely remove him from his concern
b)   prevent and curtail his research activities
c)   impose on him obligations that will make him a perpetual debtor, like a bear who through the ring in his nose is compelled for all time to dance to their pipes.

The means of this violation is the newest settlement proposal—a strangulation proposal—in which Junkers, under threats, is presented with the request to kindly place a rope around his own neck, so that he also endures the odium of the executioner.[173]

Even Junkers knew his circumstances precluded resistance beyond these internal exhortations. On October 6, he accepted settlement terms that included the establishment of a board of trustees, phased satisfaction of creditor claims over the following year, and mortgaged ICO shares valued at 1 million marks as security. Settlement terms also decreed the creation of "special agreements" between Hugo Junkers, IFA, and JUMO that allowed the firms to use applicable patents and exercise limited patent rights.[174] On November 6, 1932, both sides formally signed the agreement with two further caveats: first, 75 percent of incoming license fees for the year 1933 were added to the security, and second, the "special agreement" with JUMO offset the outstanding balance of 1,900,000 marks claimed by JUMO against Junkers himself.[175] The signing of this agreement ended the insolvency proceedings at the Junkers Works. On November 14, Junkers sent a memo to his employees thanking them for their loyalty, "united cooperation and willing subordination of every individual to the common interest" during the insolvency proceedings. Two weeks later, he announced the cancellation of all planned layoffs.[176]

Although Junkers managed to emerge from near bankruptcy and retain control of his concern for the second time in seven years, this time liberation came at a heavy price. On November 4, in order to redeem IFA shares mortgaged under the terms of the aircraft firm's settlement, Junkers was forced to sell the concern's core company, ICO, to Robert Bosch AG for 3 million marks.[177] ICO, founded in 1897, had borne the financial burden of Junkers's research priorities for over three decades; its sale removed this financial source and destroyed the "organic unity" of the Junkers Works. ICO's sale also meant the end of Junkers's corporate vision, developed since 1920 and created within the Junkers Works— a vertically integrated aircraft complex that incorporated research, development, and production. ICO's contribution of thermodynamic knowledge and research capital were vital elements of this vision, and their removal rendered the entire system unworkable. Although Junkers continued to struggle with the state over control of his patents, never again would he possess the means to return to aircraft production.

Between 1927 and 1932, the state managed to regain and consolidate its hold on the Junkers Works. Impetus for this takeover stemmed from the decision of successive Weimar governments to begin actively supporting covert rearmament measures, particularly after 1928. As part of larger plans designed to coordinate and rationalize German rearmament, the Defense Ministry sought to use its increased influence within political circles and the global depression to bring IFA and JUMO, as well as all relevant patents, within the circle of government supervised firms. The Junkers Works possessed crucial technology and factory capacity vital to this rearmament effort. Distribution of Junkers's patented technical knowledge would allow rapid licensed production on a scale far larger than that reached during World War I.

Junkers's poor management decisions throughout this period simplified the state's task; overly optimistic strategic planning, insufficient capital resources, expensive research programs, and an absence of available credit rendered the concern insolvent by 1932. Insolvency led to the sale of ICO and the replacement of Junkers as the concern's director and proprietor by his former secretary, Adolf Dethmann. As 1932 ended, Junkers found himself in an increasingly confined position. Still sole owner of IFA and JUMO as well as his patents, yet no longer able to use them, he attempted to stall for time through the courts, but could not escape the terms of the 1932 agreements. These agreements called for resolution of outstanding debt by the end of 1933 and the unconditional transfer of all licenses and patents. By the time this legal battle began, Adolf Hitler was Chancellor of Germany, and a new world was emerging.

5

Twilight and Eclipse, 1932–1935

With the sale of ICO, Hugo Junkers faced the painful realization that his dream of creating a worldwide aviation network incorporating aircraft production and airlines was no longer achievable. His
transference of daily control to Adolf Dethmann reflected this realization, as well as the recognition that his departure would improve the
firm's chances of gaining state contracts. Yet even after this transfer of
power, Junkers remained defiant. From the state's perspective, his continued defiance reinforced perceptions of him as a liability. Also, his
continued ownership of majority shareholdings of IFA and JUMO, as
well as the concern's patents, encouraged further action against him.

Responsibility for these actions passed from the hands of RVM officials to their successors in the new *Reichsluftfahrtministerium* (State
Aviation Ministry, or RLM) established under the National Socialists
after they took power on January 30, 1933. At the same time, however,
Junkers also came under attack from other sources, in particular, elements of the Anhalt National Socialist party, who had focused their efforts on gaining local control of the Junkers Works since their takeover
of Anhalt's state legislature in early 1932.[1] Significantly, these attacks
were initiated without central direction and reflected the myriad of
agendas pursued by local, state, and national branches of the National
Socialist party after 1932. The party's relationship to the Junkers Works

reflected the disparate aims of these agendas, as the local party organization sought to gain control of the Dessau complex for itself, while the RLM desired the incorporation of IFA and JUMO into a national rearmament structure controlled from Berlin. Junkers faced increasing pressure from both of these groups as 1933 progressed.

Local National Socialists made the first move. As early as December 1930, representatives of the Dessau Party Branch sent an anonymous letter to Junkers that warned, "Germany is Awake! Now is the time for the big clean up! Now order will be maintained in our Fatherland and Germany will be liberated from the parasites of democracy, for which the Third Reich has no place. . . . The public shall know what's what and then heaven help you. You old Democrat!"[2] On May 22, 1932, the National Socialists triumphed in Anhalt state elections, and soon after, their attention turned to the Junkers Works as the largest employer in Dessau. Concerns immediately centered on the firm's leadership. Both Junkers's past activities in Russia and membership in the German Democratic Party made him a liability in the eyes of local National Socialists. Other members of the concern's executive workforce also possessed questionable pasts. This was particularly true of Adolf Dethmann, Junkers's anointed successor. Dethmann had participated in the sailor's mutiny at Kiel in 1918, and then joined the Independent Social Democratic Party (USPD). By the time he traveled to Moscow in 1921 as a German representative of the Third International of the Communist Party, Dethmann was a member of the German Communist Party (KPD). Although Dethmann's political career was long behind him by 1932, National Socialists sought to use these past associations as grounds for his removal in preparation for a takeover of the concern by local party representatives. These plans gained momentum after the National Socialists gained power in Berlin on January 30, 1933. Events in Berlin led to increased hostility toward Junkers from federal authorities. In December 1932, Junkers reaffirmed his obligation to transfer patent rights to IFA and JUMO, but word of imminent new orders from the RVM in January 1933 and the change in government later that month encouraged him to draw the process out, in the hope of reaching a new compromise.[3] During this time, Germany's aviation administration changed dramatically. On February 3, 1933, new Reich

Chancellor Adolf Hitler appointed Hermann Göring, former Junkers sales representative in Scandinavia, to head a new Reich Commission for Aviation. Aware that Göring wished to extend his control over all aspects of aviation policy, existing state agencies united in an attempt to maintain their autonomy. Edward Homze notes that the Defense Ministry hoped to keep control of aviation under their jurisdiction through the creation of a new Air Defense Office that combined the aviation departments of the Reichswehr, Reichsmarine, and the RVM. Defense Minister General Werner von Blomberg ordered the creation of the office on February 8, and it appeared on April 1, 1933. It lasted only one month. On April 27, Reich President Hindenburg upgraded the Reich Commission for Aviation to ministry status, and on May 15, the new RLM appeared and took over the newly born Air Defense Office.[4] The RLM also assumed responsibility for the continued negotiations with Junkers; this change brought Erhard Milch, former Junkers employee and new state secretary for aviation, to the table opposite his old superior.

Initially, Junkers viewed Hitler's appointment as chancellor of Germany positively. Budrass argues that Junkers's conception of life as a struggle combined with his traditional distrust of finance capital and conservative social views to encourage an initially favorable view of the National Socialist "*Machtergreifung*."[5] Junkers also knew the National Socialists supported aerial rearmament plans, a stance confirmed when he met with Göring in Berlin on February 13, 1933. During this meeting, Göring outlined plans for a massive expansion of German military aviation, at first secretly and then later openly. For his part, Junkers declared himself ready to serve the state's needs and again committed to handing over patent rights to IFA and JUMO.[6] The RVM, at this time still involved in the negotiations, realized that Junkers's commitment was really an attempted sleight of hand since Junkers's declarations since November 1932 possessed no legal validity and could be revoked at any time.[7] In response, they refused to commit any orders to either IFA or JUMO until the patent issue was resolved. Subsequent meetings between Junkers and RVM officials during March 1933 failed to break this impasse; for his part, Junkers argued the Reich Commission for Aviation had placed additional demands on patent transfers that far exceeded the terms of the 1932 agreements and continued to repeat his mantra that only free research could best serve Germany's national interests.[8] This impasse remained as Reich aviation agencies reorganized.

Two further developments occurred that provided Junkers's enemies with grounds for action against him. Since November 1932, Dessau National Socialist officials had been searching for ways to expel "politically unreliable elements" from the Junkers Works. Anhalt State President Freyberg met with Dessau Senior Public Prosecutor Lämmler and charged him with this task. Early investigations focused on the publication of IFA sales figures in both domestic and foreign press reports in 1932. These reports revealed the Junkers Works military activities.[9] Lämmler initially pursued Dethmann on the grounds that this release of militarily sensitive information constituted an act of treason. Yet little evidence linked Dethmann to these revelations, and it was only in the wake of the Reichstag fire on February 27, 1933, that more legal foundations appeared.

In response to the Reichstag fire, the Decree for the Protection of Reich and State appeared on February 21 and was enshrined in law. Although the decree contained only six paragraphs, its conditions effectively destroyed the Weimar Constitution and opened the door for the National Socialist dictatorship.[10] Within the decree, a provision legalized "confiscation of and restrictions upon property outside normal legal limits"; this provision emasculated Weimar Republic common law and provided Lämmler with the means to attack Dethmann and others at the Junkers Works. As the investigation proceeded, Lämmler's investigation widened to include Junkers himself, as well as his children, Klaus and Anneliese.

Federal authorities now entered the picture. Erhard Milch formally accepted a position as state secretary for aviation within Göring's Reich Commission for Aviation on February 2, 1933. Charged by Göring with preparing Germany's aircraft industry for rearmament, Milch focused his attention on the stalled negotiations between Junkers and the RVM. On March 10, Milch confronted his old employer and made two demands: first, a speedy resolution to the patent negotiations, and second, the removal of certain Junkers employees identified by the new regime as "security risks." When Junkers refused, Milch responded with force.

On March 23, Milch requested the Interior Ministry begin investigations into employees of the Junkers Works under provisions of the Decree for the Protection of Reich and State. The Interior Ministry, aware of Public Prosecutor Lämmler's preliminary investigations, charged him with control of this new wider investigation.[11]

On the night of March 23, 1933, Dessau police arrested Dethmann, Junkers's son-in-law Peter Drömmer, and IFA engineer Fiala von Bernbrugg. All three men were accused of "attempting to establish communist cells within the Junkers Works and contact with foreign communist elements."[12] Milch encouraged these arrests, hoping to force Junkers to resolve the patent negotiations. As police pressure increased on Junkers's own family, particularly his children, he took additional steps to remove himself from the concern. Following a conversation on April 6 between Milch and Junkers in which Milch reiterated the state's demand of unconditional patent transfer, on April 7, Junkers formally resigned from all management positions within the Junkers Works.[13] At the same time, he stated his intention to "bow to the pressure of circumstances" and formally transfer patent rights to IFA and JUMO.[14] These agreements required completion of these transactions "over the next week."[15]

However after weeks passed without a formal agreement, Milch increased pressure even further. On April 28 1933, Milch allowed Lämmler to increase the scope of his investigation to include possible charges of treason against other Junkers employees, including Klaus Junkers. That day, Dessau police informed Junkers that his position as an important witness in treason investigations required the imposition of travel restrictions on him.[16] Reich officials matched their threats with incentives. On May 6, the newly formed Reich Air Ministry informed Klaus Junkers that "with resolution of personnel matters and the patent question, nothing further stood in the way of the concern receiving orders."[17] The combined pressure of threats against his family and himself proved too much for Junkers, and on May 24, 1933, he agreed to hand over all relevant patent rights to IFA and JUMO. Formal agreements signed by both Junkers and representatives of IFA and JUMO followed on June 2.[18]

With the patent question apparently resolved, RLM officials proceeded to negotiate with IFA and JUMO leaders over the firms' role within

new rearmament programs. On June 12, the RLM confirmed its intention to place extensive orders with both enterprises.[19] While these negotiations took place, Dessau Public Prosecutor Lämmler continued to
explore allegations of treason arising from Junkers's activities in Russia.
These enquiries received a boost when Lämmler received information
from Gotthard Sachsenberg, now a sworn enemy of Junkers. Always an
opportunist, Sachsenberg sought revenge for Junkers's disregard of his
compensation demands that arose from the takeover of Junkers Luftverkehr by Deutsche Lufthansa in 1925.[20]

At the same time, RLM officials, many of whom had been absorbed
into the new ministry from the RVM and the Defense Ministry, questioned the ability of the Junkers Works to fulfill rearmament obligations
with current leadership. Many of these officials had participated in the
Fili project and the subsequent state takeover of the concern during 1925
and 1926, and thus held particular reservations about the Junkers Works
in general and Junkers in particular. The nature of the Third Reich's
rearmament plans, particularly the high level of responsibility accorded
to private industry within the wartime ABC (Albatros, Bayerische Flugzeugwerke [BFW], and AEG) program, encouraged a fear among Air
Ministry officials that a disaster reminiscent of Fili might recur.[21] Milch
decided that under the circumstances Junkers's complete removal from
the Junkers Works constituted the only remedy. Throughout summer
1933, this view gained ground within the RLM.[22] Milch saw an opportunity to carry out this onerous task through Lämmler and began plans
to formally charge Junkers with treason based on publication of state
secrets in 1926 and 1932.

The decision to formally charge Junkers came under scrutiny at an
RLM meeting on October 3, 1933. Although legal experts present at the
meeting noted the lack of precedent behind such action, Milch decided
to proceed, hoping that threats of further criminal action against the
now seventy-four-year-old Junkers might force him into submission.[23]
Use of the Decree of the Protection of Reich and State allowed for police surveillance and restrictions of movement, all designed to make life
uncomfortable for Junkers and encourage him to give up his remaining
shares of IFA and JUMO. To ensure the involvement of only a few actors

in this carefully orchestrated action, Lämmler also took up the post of Anhalt police director on October 9, 1933; this dual role allowed him to focus both legal and criminal sanctions against Junkers.

Throughout the summer of 1933, Junkers refused to enter negotiations with the RLM over the sale of his shares in IFA and JUMO, a situation Milch and the RLM could not tolerate indefinitely. At the October 3 meeting, Milch charged Lämmler with responsibility for "presenting Professor Junkers with a solution proposal." Milch outlined the following conditions: Junkers was required to sell his majority shares of IFA and JUMO. He would have twenty-four hours to accept the proposal before criminal proceedings against him commenced.[24] Lämmler began work immediately. On October 15, he sent a telegram to Junkers in Bayrischzell, Bavaria, that called for an immediate meeting between the two parties in Dessau. Junkers, in Bavaria for health reasons, replied by requesting three days to return to Dessau. Lämmler interpreted Junkers's request as recalcitrance and took two immediate actions on October 17. First, he dispatched Dessau police agents to Bavaria and charged them with arresting Junkers and returning him to Dessau by force. Second, in preparation for criminal proceedings against Junkers, Anhalt police agents arrived at the Junkers Works and confiscated all Junkers's files. Additionally, Junkers employees were subsequently forbidden to provide any documents to Junkers himself.

Dessau agents arrested Junkers in Bavaria and, on October 17, transported him back to Dessau via Munich. Junkers arrived in Dessau that evening tired and angry, yet still defiant. Lämmler's men conveyed Junkers directly to the Anhalt Chamber of Commerce in Dessau, where the meeting formally began at 8:00 p.m. Junkers, who had not been permitted to change or greet his family, squared off against his opponents, Lämmler and Johannes Müller, president of the Anhalt Chamber of Commerce.[25] Notes from the meeting convey Lämmler's threatening stance:

> **Senior Public Prosecutor.** Attorney Dr. Leutgebrune (Junkers's attorney) has declared that Junkers is ready—as the Reich desires—to separate himself from IFA and JUMO: Is this correct?

Junkers. Misunderstandings exist between Junkers and the Reich. There is no divergence between the goals of Junkers and those of the state. . . .

Senior Public Prosecutor. (States question precisely) Is Junkers prepared to hand over the majority of IFA and JUMO?

Junkers. When assessing the concern's worth one must consider that this is no normal factory, rather a research enterprise and it would be a pity if it lost this character. If however state interests require it, Junkers will step down. However, Junkers considers himself obliged to point out this threatened loss. . . . In any event Junkers will accept the negotiated decision.

Senior Public Prosecutor. The decision has been made. In the interests of clarity, an immediate transfer of the majority ownership of IFA and Jumo to a trustee is desired. . . .

Chamber of Commerce President. Junkers must immediately cede 51 percent; the final worth will be ascertained by an expert, however if arguments arise the Air Ministry has the final say.

Junkers. Asks whether negotiations over individual points have any purpose, since this is really a diktat.

Chamber of Commerce President. Sharply disagrees; the Reich does not think of it as a diktat.

Junkers. There is also no point in discussing economic questions. I wish to know the criminal charges against me.

Senior Public Prosecutor. In order to spare you from agitation I will not go into detail now, however since you desire it I will say this. You (have) maintained unacceptable leadership over the last few years. I refer to Dr. Dethmann, Drömmer, and Ehmsen, who was arrested today. To completely clarify the situation I must refer to your activities in the following areas during 1925: Legal quarrels with the state, the Quaatz Affair, and the publication of related materials. . . .

Junkers. (Avoids subsequent discussion of criminal matters) I hereby declare myself ready to cede my majority.

Chamber of Commerce President. If an agreement is not reached this evening, criminal proceedings will commence tomorrow morning.

Junkers. I am prepared to adopt your proposals. There are things that must be considered from an economic viewpoint. In my opinion negotiations cannot be rushed.

Chamber of Commerce President. The discussion must be concluded this evening. Leutgebrune and Junkers have led us up the garden path over the last few days.[26]

At 2:00 a.m., the meeting ended. After more than six hours, and with the threat of immediate criminal action against him, Junkers relented and gave in to the state's demands. With Lämmler and Müller looking on, Junkers agreed to sell 51 percent of IFA's shares; until a buyer could be found, Müller took control of the majority as trustee. On November 24, 1933, Junkers formally resigned as chairman of IFA and JUMO. Seven days later, Lämmler received 3 million marks worth of IFA shares from the RLM as payment for services rendered.[27]

Junkers's removal appeared to satisfy the aims of both the RLM and local National Socialist leaders, who sought to use the Dessau complex as a regional sinecure.[28] Yet questions remained, particularly in the mind of RLM Deputy Milch, over the firm's remaining leadership and its ability to execute the ABC rearmament program.[29] This plan envisaged a complete restructuring of IFA for its new role as a primary mass production facility; however, despite the departure of Dethmann and Junkers, the firm's traditional craft-based manufacturing techniques remained in place. Milch, aware that Public Prosecutor Lämmler's investigations continued, realized IFA needed a new leader who was both removed from possible further criminal proceedings and experienced in corporate reorganization. He selected Heinrich Koppenberg, who, despite a lack of experience in aviation, possessed a proven track record in technical management and corporate restructuring, particularly in the adoption of assembly-line production techniques at the Mitteldeutsche Stahlwerke during 1926.[30] Two days after Junkers agreed to hand over his majority, Koppenberg toured the Dessau complex and described the aircraft factory, with its complex, labor-intensive workshops as reminiscent of a "plumber's shop."[31] That same day, Milch met with representatives of the aircraft industry in Berlin and informed them of the ABC program.[32] Ten days later, the RLM deputy appointed Koppenberg as IFA's new chairman, with an annual salary of 150,000 marks. Koppenberg immediately began converting IFA's workshops into mass production facilities, and by early 1934, the Dessau complex bore little resemblance to its earlier form.

Koppenberg's ascendance effectively stymied the ambitions of Anhalt National Socialists to take sole control of the Junkers Works. National priorities superseded the creation of local empires, although local National Socialist representative Johannes Müller remained on IFA's board of directors under Koppenberg. In the meantime, however, State Prosecutor Lämmler's investigations into Junkers continued. Confiscated IFA files and Junkers employee interrogations appeared to yield sufficient evidence for prosecution of Junkers on treason charges over his actions during 1926. Conditions of the October 18 agreement included Junkers's permanent banishment from Dessau, and he was forbidden to associate with Junkers employees.

Junkers retired to his residence in Bayrischzell, Bavaria. On November 29, 1933, Lämmler again dispatched Dessau police agents to Bavaria to monitor Junkers's movements. Further restrictions followed; on December 13, Lämmler wrote to Junkers and informed him that henceforth he was confined to travel between Munich and Bayrischzell.[33] Junkers had left Dessau at the end of October 1933 and moved to an office in Munich on the Königinstrasse next to the Englischer Garten, where he began work in a new field, metal housing design and construction.[34] At the same time he took steps to counter Lämmler's ongoing investigation by hiring National Socialist legal counsel, including Walter Leutgebreune, a close associate of *Sturmabteilung* leader Ernst Röhm, in an effort to negate the treason allegations against him through political means.[35] Although these efforts proved unsuccessful, subsequent legal investigations revealed that the state possessed little hope of successfully proving its case based on the Decree of Protection of Reich and State, the threat of which had encouraged Junkers to accept the October 18 agreement.

Other circumstances now interceded into the process between Junkers, the RLM, and Prosecutor Lämmler. Göring's appointee as trustee of the Junkers Works, Wilhelm Keppler, reported that Junkers's continued minority shareholding in IFA and JUMO made it unlikely that private interests would purchase the majority of IFA and JUMO shares. Keppler recommended the complete takeover of the firm as a necessary precursor to attract potential buyers. For his part, Junkers, now aware of the fragility of the state's case, refused to sell his remaining stake in IFA and JUMO without a reevaluation of the firms' value. Additionally, Junkers demanded the severance of the Forschungsanstalt from the Junkers Works in exchange for any transfer of his remaining stake in IFA and JUMO. Execution of this arrangement would once again give rise to questions regarding ownership and use of patents, a circumstance the RLM sought to avoid. Throughout January and February, both sides exchanged legal briefs and memoranda outlining their respective cases.[36]

Aware of the legal problems behind his investigation, but committed to the task, Lämmler maintained pressure on Junkers throughout 1934. On February 2, 1934, Bavarian Political Police agents detained Junkers in the Englischer Garten. The next day, Junkers's seventy-fifth birthday, Munich police officials "on the orders of the Dessau State Police" arrived at the Junkers residence at 1:00 p.m. and announced further personal restrictions on Junkers's freedom. Junkers was now confined exclusively to Bayrischzell. All contact with former Junkers employees, even the professor's own son, Klaus, was forbidden. Police officers now maintained twenty-four-hour surveillance of the Junkers residence, and any time Junkers left the house, an officer accompanied him. All contact with Junkers's legal representatives was also forbidden, and both telephone and telegraph connections were cut.[37] These actions demonstrated the Air Ministry's growing impatience with Junkers, and also state officials' determination to use extra-legal means to pressure Junkers into a complete sale of IFA and JUMO.

Despite these new restrictions, Junkers continued the struggle. He arranged for details of his detention to be conveyed to his Berlin lawyers. He also managed to transfer ownership of seventeen patents to his wife, Therese. Junkers's lawyers continued to argue that the state trusteeship of IFA and JUMO lacked any legal validity while, in response, Lämmler reiterated accusations of treason and unlawful dissemination of state secrets. Lämmler also attempted to cast doubt on the validity of Junkers's patent rights by arguing, somewhat absurdly, that Junkers's 1909 "thick wing" patent lacked originality.[38] As the months progressed, Junkers grew increasingly confident that legal means would allow him to reclaim control of IFA and JUMO. On March 21, Junkers's legal representatives met with RLM officials in Berlin and announced their intention to pursue redress through the courts.[39] Lämmler responded by declaring his intention to begin treason proceedings on April 17. These efforts ran aground in the summer of 1934 as the Reich Supreme Court refused to hear the case due to lack of evidence. The court's decision, read by Reich Court President Walter Simons, appeared to open the way for Junkers's return to Dessau by invalidating the October 18 agreement. As Junkers lawyer Georg Eschtruth wrote to RLM trustee Keppler: "The question is not about Professor Junkers or several million [marks], but whether Germany is a state subject to the rule of law."[40]

The RLM responded to the court's decision in two ways: first, State Secretary Erhard Milch and Reichsminister Göring continued to threaten Junkers personally, and second, when these threats failed to elicit a response, the Air Ministry forced a change in German aviation law.[41] Under pressure from the RLM, the 1922 Laws of the German Aviation Industry, initially amended in 1933, were changed again. The new laws mandated that production of aircraft and aero-engines required the permission of the Air Ministry; additionally, the new laws gave the state the option to take over private firms for "reasonable compensation."[42] These legal changes rendered Junkers's legal successes moot, and only an arbitrated agreement on the value of Junkers's remaining assets now stood in the way of the state's complete takeover of the Junkers Works.

Before both sides reached an agreement, Junkers's health failed.

Throughout 1934 his health problems increased, possibly due to stress incurred by his circumstances. On February 3, 1935, his seventy-sixth birthday, Junkers passed away due to a heart attack at his home in Gauting, a suburb of Munich. News of his death appeared hidden on the inside of major German newspapers, although Therese Junkers and former Junkers employees published several full-page obituary notices in selected dailies, and international tributes to Junkers appeared throughout the world.[43] Milch attempted to send a party to the funeral with a wreath on February 9, but the Junkers family, incensed, threatened to hold it elsewhere. RLM officials were ordered off the train halfway to Munich and returned to Berlin.[44] Rudolf Hess appeared as the party's representative at the funeral ceremony held at Munich's Waldfriedhof Cemetery. Snow covered Munich like a blanket, and as Beethoven's *Eroica* played, Junkers's four sons carried a silver urn containing his ashes to his grave. Overhead, three Junkers aircraft appeared and passed over the cemetery in a final salute to their creator.[45]

With Junkers's death, all pressure from the RLM ceased, and negotiations between RLM trustee Keppler and Junkers's widow, Therese, concluded on April 30, 1935. Frau Junkers sold the family's remaining stake in IFA and JUMO for 9 million marks, and all patents and licenses for a further 3.5 million marks.[46] Now completely under state control, the Junkers Flugzeug- und Motorenwerke rapidly expanded and by 1938 controlled five manufacturing plants with a workforce of over forty-three thousand, by far the largest in Germany.[47] Junkers's production and training techniques also served as models for the rest of the German aircraft industry. Junkers designs would play key roles in World War II, and this close association with the National Socialist state ensured the company's destruction in 1945. After the war, the Dessau complex and many Junkers employees passed into the service of the Soviet Union, where old connections between Junkers researchers and Soviet aircraft designers were reestablished.

It is particularly ironic, and historically unjust, that Junkers aircraft emblazoned with swastikas became iconic symbols of Nazi attacks on Europe and the world after World War II. As this study shows, the reality of the two-decade relationship between Junkers and the German state was anything but harmonious.

Accelerated technological progress characterizes the last one hundred years more than any other phenomenon. Technology advanced rapidly throughout the twentieth century, propelling humanity at greater speeds and to ever greater heights. Aviation's evolution is one of the most recognizable examples of this acceleration. Peter Fritzsche compares the development of the aircraft to other great products of the industrial age: "Flying machines, like steam railroads, giant dynamos, and electric lighting, vastly increased humankind's power to control and manipulate the environment. Thanks to aviation, the globe became accessible in an unprecedented way. . . . For better or worse, airplanes offered modern men and women a heady dominion over the earth."[48] Fritzsche also notes that this process demonstrates the close connection between technical change and national ambition: "The histories of modern nationalism and modern technology are inexorably intertwined. . . . Aviation, perhaps better than any other field of technology, clarifies the links between national dreams and modernist visions. And Germany, the least satisfied among the great powers . . . is the most suitable ground on which to explore this troubled intersection."[49] Junkers is a central figure in aviation's development, and his story reveals more than just a career as a great researcher and inventor. His experiences also demonstrate themes such as the price of unfettered ambition, the perils of prophecy, and the risks of innovative entrepreneurship.

Aircraft matured during World War I. Nation states quickly recognized aviation's potential as a weapons delivery system and an instrument well suited to project power far over battlefields, visible horizons, and earthly boundaries. Within this new "air-minded" context, inventors, designers, and manufacturers within the aircraft industry assumed new, national importance and became recognizable actors creating products whose potential marked them as latent state property. Junkers's entry into aviation began just as Germany's war preparations peaked in 1913. Over the next four years, the German Empire attempted to harness all potential military resources. This effort required unprecedented intervention by the state into the private economy as it became obvious that the private sector lacked the means and the organization to produce armaments on the massive scale total war demanded. For Junkers, this meant closer contact with state officials at all levels as the army sought to accelerate technological development for military uses. Junkers's reluctance to deviate from his technical goals simply to satisfy state interests led to friction with state agencies such as Idflieg, whose attitude toward Junkers became increasingly critical as the war progressed. By 1916, war demands encouraged direct action against Junkers, and he was forced to merge with Anthony Fokker in a well-intentioned but ultimately unproductive union. The year 1918 brought an end to this union and the war, but Junkers's war experience left him with a lasting suspicion of state intentions and motives while, for their part, state agencies viewed the Junkers concern's poor production record as indicative of Junkers's lack of reliability.

Junkers's commitment to all-metal construction gave him a market advantage until 1925; unfortunately, contemporary economic conditions combined with external restrictions to prevent him from exploiting this advantage as he expanded his plant facilities and airline networks across Germany, Europe, Asia, and the Americas. During this period, with Allied restrictions on German military activity at their height, German Army Commander Hans von Seeckt pursued close ties with the Soviet Union in an effort to maintain German military capabilities by using Russian territory as a testing ground. With no other real options, Junkers gambled and invested heavily in Russia, convincing himself that the rugged characteristics of his aircraft designs would provide both civilian and military orders that would see the firm through difficult economic times. Ironically, he was right; the clandestine activities of the Reichswehr provided Junkers with capital that sustained the firm for several years. However, these funds came with a price—the loss of independent action through adherence to state procurement demands. Ultimately, the Soviet Union gained most from the Fili project when it inherited the complex for a fraction of the sums invested by both Junkers and the Reichswehr in 1926. The fallout from the Fili Affair permanently damaged Junkers's relationship with state aviation agencies, particularly the Reichswehr, and the financial difficulties stemming from the venture required state intervention in 1926. Continuity within the agendas and personnel of the state aviation agencies meant that negative attitudes toward Junkers shaped before and during the firm's state supervision remained throughout the rest of Junkers's aviation career.

From Junkers's perspective, the Fili venture drained valuable personnel and resources from the Dessau factory complex for several years, and
even creative accounting methods proved unable to save the concern
from insolvency at the end of 1925. Fearful of involvement with either
the state or Germany's banks, Junkers stuck doggedly to his unique business model, based on *Eigenwirtschaftliche Forschung*, or "self-funded research," in which practical innovations provided capital funding through
patent payments and license fees as well as market sales. Unfortunately,
the aviation market throughout the decade lacked both the participants
and the financial strength to sustain Junkers's model, and attempts to
create a customer base through spectacular technical achievements and
airline partnerships proved uneconomical and further drained the concern's capital reserves. Capital scarcity reached a critical point at the end
of 1925, and the RVM used Junkers's financial woes as a lever to establish
state control over Germany's airline network.

For the state, this development served two important purposes: first,
it established direct government oversight of state aviation subsidies, and
second, it strengthened the relationship between civilian and military
aviation within Germany's borders. Von Seeckt's departure encouraged
an end to foreign-based military aircraft production and a tightening
of links between civilian and military aviation agencies. State aviation
officials, such as the RVM's Ernst Brandenburg, now forged closer links
with their Reichswehr counterparts in an effort to oversee aircraft design,
procurement planning, and personnel training. These efforts envisaged
nothing less than the erection of a state-directed structure encompassing
all stages of aviation development, from planning and production strategies developed within the Reichswehr and RVM, through research and
development through the DVL and Deutsche Lufthansa, to production
financed by state institutions like Fertigungs GmbH within firms such as
Heinkel that were either controlled by the state or closely allied with its
objectives.

These developments mirrored those that occurred in other states
during this era, such as in the United States, the United Kingdom, and
the USSR. Actions of German aviation officials throughout the 1920s
reflected a larger consensus concerning aviation and military readiness;
twentieth-century war required massive industrial production of mili-

tary matériel. Past experience showed high production levels could not be achieved without significant state intervention into the private economy. Faced with both a fluid political elite and foreign restrictions on military development, Weimar Republic civil servants and army officials assumed responsibility for rearmament policy. By 1929, with political currents shifting in favor of restoring Germany's military presence in Europe, support for open rearmament increased. The sorry state of Germany's aviation industry prompted increased intervention from state agencies as they sought the establishment of a solid industrial foundation for mass production. As Germany's largest and best-recognized producer, Junkers's concern became a target of this process.

Despite the obvious role of the state in his demise, Junkers's personal responsibility cannot be overlooked. An obstinate, pugnacious man, Junkers viewed life as a struggle, and this neo-Darwinian outlook shaped his interactions with both state officials and private rivals. Junkers refused to alter his plans to accommodate state interests on several occasions, particularly when these interests focused on mass production of aircraft for military purposes. Junkers's experience during World War I served as the foundation for his subsequent attitude toward state involvement in aviation. In his view, state interests undercut aviation development and retarded research by restricting design parameters. Junkers's refusal to accept official instruction to alter construction and design characteristics during the war years created the perception of him in official circles as an obstructionist, a designer who sacrificed state needs to pursue his own technological objectives. His subsequent actions during the Fili Affair further emphasized his aloofness and self-interest–centered agenda, as he sought to use state-supplied capital to dominate Russian aviation and support his Dessau complex. When these efforts failed, Junkers denied responsibility for his part in his difficulties and pressed the Reichswehr for more funds. During the state takeover of the concern in 1926, an action that avoided certain bankruptcy, Junkers defied authorities by releasing details of the German-Russian military relationship. All these actions led to permanently damaged relations between Junkers and state authorities, who concluded that Junkers could not be bargained with and therefore had to be removed.

Within the concerns he owned and controlled, Junkers's actions and direction also contributed to his downfall. Convinced of the soundness of his corporate vision, he refused to alter or scale back research, even after it was clear aviation development had rendered Junkers design characteristics obsolete, and economic realities required immediate reductions in research expenditure. Junkers ignored advice from his oldest associates and interpreted reform measures as attacks on his leadership. As criticism mounted, he dogmatically retreated behind long-held mantras extolling research as the key to the concern's vitality and refused to consider compromise. Junkers's actions alienated supporters and reinforced enemy portrayals at a critical time, when no credit lifelines existed, and the firm faced bankruptcy. Unlike state officials, who learned from their mistakes between 1915 and 1933 and altered their plans accordingly, Junkers, certainly due to his advancing age, remained set in his ways until the end. His intransigence proved fatal as Germany's political geography shifted to the right between 1930 and 1933. National Socialist ideology demanded total subservience by industry to state requirements, and Third Reich leaders viewed aerial rearmament as an essential component of the new state's security; no place existed for mavericks like Junkers within this vision.

Viewed from a purely economic standpoint, Junkers's aviation career appears flawed, a series of ambitious but ultimately unsuccessful attempts to create a dominant market position in both aircraft production and airline development. Yet this view ignores Junkers's remarkable technical successes in aviation and aero-engine design and also the impact of his visions on aviation's subsequent history. Few saw aviation's potential earlier or clearer than Hugo Junkers. His dream of a large fleet of modern airliners transporting millions of people each year across borders and oceans became a reality twenty-five years after his death. His vision of an aviation "system" that included international airline alliances, aircraft sharing, and common marketing arrangements closely resembles today's airline industry, particularly firms such as Richard Branson's Virgin network. Due primarily to erroneous connections between Junkers and aircraft bearing his name that served in Germany's Luftwaffe in World War II, his role in world aviation development has been generally underestimated by non-German historians. Junkers's role in the creation of the Soviet Union's aviation industry has also, for political reasons, been considerably underestimated.

Perhaps Junkers's most lasting achievement lies in his conception of the airplane as one part of an aviation system whose sum total of many related innovations become something greater than their parts. Junkers would have been proud of, but not surprised by, events like the Berlin Airlift of 1947–48, where aviation directly affected the course of human lives in an overwhelmingly positive way. If aircraft are explicitly political instruments, as both Junkers's contemporaries and subsequent commentators maintain, then his conception of that potential far exceeded that of his peers and still has resonance today. Professor Junkers's greatest legacy is his belief that through the conquering of borders, geography, distance, and time, aircraft not only bring individuals but also cultures closer together.

NOTES

Introduction

1. The mythology surrounding Hugo Junkers, woven during the Nazi era and still influential today, has been the subject of recent research by German scholars. For an example in a literary context, see Bielke, *Der Mythos*.

2. Aviation history scholarship has broadened and deepened considerably over the last twenty years. For English, see examples such as Higham, *100 Years*; Kinney, *Airplanes*; Winter and van der Linden, *100 Years of Flight*; and Crouch, *Wings*.

3. The Third Reich's cynical but calculated decision to continue to use the Junkers name and brand after the firm was nationalized in 1934 contributed enormously to this misunderstanding. Nazi aviation officials—such as former Junkers employee and later Luftwaffe Field Marshal Erhard Milch—recognized the advantages the Junkers brand delivered in terms of quality and excellence, and sought to maximize its use politically and ideologically over the life of the regime. Consequently, aircraft such as the iconic Junkers Ju-87 Stuka, long synonymous with the *Blitzkrieg* attacks of 1939–41, remain fixed in popular memories of the war *and* of the firm, even though these designs appeared long after nationalization and the termination of any family involvement. Examples of East German scholarship on Junkers include Schmitt, *Hugo Junkers*; and Groehler, *Hugo Junkers*.

4. For more on this, see Byers, "Unhappy Marriage," 1–30, and the discussion in chapter 1 of this work.

Chapter 1

1. For Junkers's early life, see Schmitt, *Hugo Junkers*; Blunck, *Hugo Junkers*; and Wagner, *Hugo Junkers*.

2. Wagner, *Hugo Junkers*, 11.

3. Schmitt, *Hugo Junkers and His Aircraft*, 8.

4. Schmitt, *Hugo Junkers*, 8. See also Blunck, *Hugo Junkers*, 16–18.

5. Schmitt, *Hugo Junkers and His Aircraft*, 9.

6. Wagner, *Hugo Junkers*, 14.

7. Schmitt, *Hugo Junkers and His Aircraft*, 10–11.

8. Blunck, *Hugo Junkers*, 26–28. Blunck notes that despite their professional separation, the two remained friends, and Junkers always had a portrait of Oechelhauser in his personal office.

9. Blunck, *Hugo Junkers*, 32–36.

10. Schmitt, *Hugo Junkers and His Aircraft*, 11.

11. Ibid., 13.

12. For Mader's biographical information, see Wagner, *Hugo Junkers*, 29, note 11.

13. See Wohl, *Passion for Wings*.

14. For more on Germany's love affair with airships, see de Syon's excellent cultural history *Zeppelin!*.

15. Fritzsche, *Nation of Flyers*, 7 and *passim*.

16. Schmitt notes that during a lecture he gave in 1920, Junkers gave Reissner all credit for the Ente design, claiming that "other obligations, which could not be ignored, left me with little time on this occasion. . . . Hence the aircraft emerging from our work was, in essence, a result of his efforts." (Speech by Junkers to the Scientific Society for Aviation, 1920, reprinted in Schmitt, *Hugo Junkers and His Aircraft*, 18.)

17. Morrow, *Building German Airpower*, 14.

18. Ibid, 15–25, 8. The Europe-wide armaments race was also in full swing during this period, leading to a rise in overall defense budget requests that seriously strained the imperial political system in the years prior to the outbreak of war.

19. Ibid., 27. De le Roi would go on to become an employee of Luftverkehrgesellschaft, the sales agency for Albatros, Germany's largest aircraft manufacturer during World War I. This relationship between private industry and members of the military would be emulated by Junkers, whose general agent in Berlin after 1917, Major Wilhelm Seitz, formerly worked for the War Ministry.

20. Hugo Junkers, "Eigene Arbeiten auf dem Gebiete des Metall-Flugzeuges," within *Berichte und Abhandlungen der Wissenschaftlichen Gesellschaft für Luftfahrt*, Book 11, Munich, 1924, 1, cited in Schmitt, *Hugo Junkers and His Aircraft*, 21.

21. Junkers, "Grundsätze technisch-wirtschaftlicher Forschung," cited in Schmitt, *Hugo Junkers*, 121.

22. Internal memorandum on the development of the first Junkers metal aircraft, December 7, 1918, DMM JA propaganda 898. Photographs of these tests, housed today in the visual archive of the Deutsches Museum in Munich, show more than fifty men standing on each wing as a crude measure of the design's load bearing capacity.

23. Junkers invested 20,000 marks a month into the J-1 program from profits accrued by the boiler and gas heater departments of Junkers & Co. Such "cross-pollination" funding practices would continue for the rest of Junkers's career.

24. Budrass, *Flugzeugindustrie*, 42. See also Wagner, *Hugo Junkers*, 50. Junkers's research concentrated on production of an aero-engine powered by either diesel or a diesel derivative—the military, who initially supported these experiments financially, informed Junkers that as its energy infrastructure centered on benzine, a diesel engine would be of little use in wartime.

25. The motor engine facility at Magdeburg, founded in 1913, focused on marine engines. Junkers felt that the high expenses and limited commercial potential of such an operation during wartime precluded its economic viability. After the war, in 1919, the engine business reappeared with a focus on aero-engines. This operation will be discussed in a later chapter.

26. Schmitt, *Hugo Junkers*, 126.

27. Wagner, *Hugo Junkers*, 79. Wagner also notes that this decision came with some misgivings, as the military experts doubted that the machine would ever fly. They also ordered Junkers to develop a biplane aircraft, as they believed contemporary aero-engines lacked the power to lift an all-metal monoplane off the ground. Junkers vehemently resisted this demand, and the appearance of more powerful engines at the end of 1915 settled the issue.

28. Morrow, *German Airpower*.

29. Ibid., 17–19.

30. Ibid., 17–20. Morrow argues that the industry missed an opportunity to increase its leverage in the relationship, since the army would have been forced to agree to the industry's requests over time.

31. Internal memorandum on the development of the first Junkers metal aircraft, December 7, 1918, DMM JA propaganda 898.

32. Wagner, *Hugo Junkers*, 81.

33. Overview of the development of the construction methods of metal aircraft by Junkers—Aachen and the firm Junkers & Co. (1.5.14.–1.10.1917), March 14, 1918, DMM JA propaganda 474–896.

34. Wagner, *Hugo Junkers*, 81.

35. Letter from Junkers to Wagenführ, January 11, 1916, DMM JA Flugzeugbau 0201/4/4.

36. Notice to Junkers & Co. from the Inspectorate of Flying Forces, February 15, 1916, DMM JA Flugzeugbau 0201/4/12.

37. Junkers refers to this in a letter to the War Ministry on August 30, 1916, DMM JA Flugzeugbau 0201/4/31.

38. Letter from Junkers to Idflieg, September 1, 1916, DMM JA Flugzeugbau 0201/4/32.

39. Notice to Junkers & Co. from the Inspectorate of Flying Forces, March 30, 1916, DMM JA Flugzeugbau 0201/4/20.

40. Letter from Junkers to War Ministry, August 30, 1916, DMM JA Flug-zeugbau 0201/4/31.

41. Letter from Junkers to War Ministry, October 6, 1916, DMM JA Flug-zeugbau 0201/4/31.

42. Letter from Oschmann to Junkers & Co., October 24, 1916, DMM JA Flugzeugbau 0201/4/31.

43. Ibid.

44. Wagner, *Hugo Junkers*, 93.

45. Protocol of negotiations with Director Fokker on December 16 and 18, 1916, DMM JA Flugzeugbau 0201/11/1. Parts of this section were previously published as a journal article, Byers, "Unhappy Marriage," located at http://www.ufv.ca/jhb/volume_3/volume_3_byers.pdf.

46. Dierickx, *Fokker*, 38.

47. Protocol of negotiations with Director Fokker on December 16 and 18, 1916, DMM JA Flugzeugbau 0201/11/1, 2.

48. Ibid., 5. Interestingly, Dierickx writes that Fokker remarked that he was unable to begin production of the Junkers design in his factories, a circumstance not recorded in the protocol. Despite this small error, Dierickx's work provides the best portrait of the eccentric Dutchman yet produced.

49. Letter from Junkers to Wagenführ, January 2, 1917, DMM JA Flugzeugbau 0201/11/4.

50. Internal memorandum: Position toward the proposal of Fokker regarding the granting of a license for the aircraft patent, February 1, 1917, DMM JA Flugzeugbau 0201/11/8. By this point, it had become clear to Junkers that Fokker felt he did not need to enter into a corporate union and sought only to use the advances made by Junkers within the J-4 design for his own ends. Regarding Fokker's business history, Junkers was surely aware of the controversy surrounding Fokker's control of synchronized machine gun manufacture, a circumstance made possible by the army's decision to lessen patent protection during the war. See Dierickx, *Fokker*, 33–35; and Morrow, *German Airpower*, 20–22. Patent conflicts are a much understudied aspect of modern aviation history in particular, and modern history in general.

51. Protocol of conversation between Horter and Lottmann, February 2, 1917, DMM JA Flugzeugbau 0201/11/10.

52. Ibid.

53. Letter from Fokker to Junkers, April 16, 1917, DMM JA 0201/11/12.

54. Inventory of research costs within internal memorandum, July 28, 1918, DMM JA 0201/8/10.

55. Founding agreement of the Junkers-Fokker-Werke AG (IFA), October 20, 1917, DMM JA 0201/11/31.

56. Report of a confidential conversation with Horter by Director Eggers, June 13, 1917, DMM JA 0201/11/14; and letter from Fokker to Junkers, July 27, 1917, DMM JA Conzelmann, NL 123, box 30.

57. Letter from Fokker to Junkers, July 27, 1917, DMM JA Conzelmann, NL 123, box 30; and founding agreement of IFA, October 20, 1917, DMM JA 0201/11/31.

58. Table of Junkers metal aircraft delivered to the military authorities until March 31, 1919; April 7, 1919, DMM JA Conzelmann, NL 123, box 39.

59. See the reports of Company Representative Schmidt, April 1, 1918, and Reserve Lieutenant Wagner, May 23, 1918, DMM JA Conzelmann NL 123, box 39. Wagner noted that his machine had over 128 bullet holes in it and that he was convinced that it had saved his life.

60. See Dierickx, *Fokker*, 41–43.

61. Budrass, *Flugzeugindustrie*, 48.

62. Loose stenogram, March 6, 1918, DMM JA NL 21/2. Junkers goes on to characterize Wilhelm Horter, Fokker's business manager, as a "shady character and a paid spy."

63. See Schmitt, *Hugo Junkers*, 137–38. The subsequent awarding of the army contract to Fokker, for four hundred planes at 25,000 marks apiece, supports the remarks of IFA Director Schliessing, who noted that "all evidence points to the fact that [Fokker] committed the act with consideration."

64. Loose stenogram, March 24, 1918, DMM JA Conzelmann NL 123, box 22.

65. Ibid.

66. Loose stenogram, April 17, 1918, DMM JA Conzelmann NL 123, box 22.

67. Report of long distance call with the Inspectorate of Flying Troops, April 17, 1918, DMM JA Conzelmann NL 123, box 39.

68. Ibid.

69. Ibid.

70. Morrow, *German Airpower*, 119.

71. Letter from Junkers & Co. to Inspectorate of Flying Troops, May 8, 1918, DMM JA Conzelmann NL 123, box 39.

72. Report of conversation between Director Spaleck and Düren Directors Beck and Gunkel, Continental Hotel, Berlin, April 18, 1918, DMM JA NL 21/2.

73. Loose stenogram, May 23, 1918, DMM JA Conzelmann NL 123, box 22. Emphasis in original.

74. Letter from Spaleck to Company Representative Seitz, July 26, 1918, DMM JA Conzelmann NL 123, box 39.

75. Table of Junkers metal aircraft delivered to the military authorities until March 31, 1919; April 7, 1919, DMM JA Conzelmann, NL 123, box 39.

76. Personal memorandum, July 28, 1918, DMM JA Flugzeugbau 0201/8/10.

77. Draft of a letter from Junkers to Seitz, September 26, 1918, DMM JA Conzelmann NL 123, box 39.

78. Morrow, *German Airpower*, 128. Morrow argues, "The fragmentation of the inspectorate may . . . be interpreted as an attempt to decrease even more the inspectorate's power in favor of the frontline airforce [*sic*] in the all-important area of fighter development."

79. Letter from Seitz to Junkers, August 17, 1918, DMM JA Flugzeugbau 0201/8/50.

80. Letter from Seitz to Junkers, August 18, 1918, DMM JA Flugzeugbau 0201/8/50.

81. Ibid. General Ernst Wilhelm von Höppner, formerly a Cavalry officer, commanded the German air forces from 1916 to 1918.

82. Letter from Seitz to Junkers, September 26, 1918, DMM JA Flugzeugbau 0201/8/51.

83. Morrow, *German Airpower*, 139.

84. Mommsen, *Rise and Fall*, 1–50.

85. Dierickx, *Fokker*, 52–55.

86. Letter from Fokker to Seitz, November 13, 1918, DMM JA Flugzeugbau 0201/12/43.

87. Letter from Seitz to Fokker, November 13, 1918, DMM JA Flugzeugbau 0201/12/43.

88. Letter from Fokker to Seitz, November 14, 1918, DMM JA Flugzeugbau 0201/12/43.

89. Letter from Seitz to Fokker, November 14, 1918, DMM JA Flugzeugbau 0201/12/43.

90. Letter from Seitz to Fokker, November 18, 1918, DMM JA Flugzeugbau 0201/12/43.

91. Letter from Seitz to Junkers, November 27, 1918, DMM JA Flugzeugbau 0201/8/54.

92. Letter from Wagenführ to Seitz, December 9, 1918, DMM JA Flugzeugbau 0201/8/39.

93. Letter from Seitz to Frank, December 9, 1918, DMM JA Flugzeugbau 0201/8/39.

94. Zürl, *Deutsche Flugzeugkonstrukteure*, 58.

95. Dierickx, *Fokker*, 42.

96. Table of Junkers metal aircraft delivered to the military authorities until March 31, 1919; April 7, 1919, DMM JA Conzelmann, NL 123, box 39. The total for all aircraft is that cited with reservations by Morrow, *German Airpower*, Appendix 1, 202.

97. Protocol of proposed restructuring and organization of the Junkers firms under consideration of the current political situation, October 15, 1918, DMM JA Flugzeugbau 0201/8/24.

98. See Schmitt, *Hugo Junkers and His Aircraft*, 40.

99. On the granting of peacetime orders by the current military authorities, November 18, 1918, DMM JA Flugzeugbau 0201/8/35.

100. Loose note, November 16, 1918, DMM JA Conzelmann NL 123, box 39. Emphasis in original.

101. See Wagner, *Hugo Junkers*, 140; and Schmitt, *Hugo Junkers and His Aircraft*, 39.

102. Loose stenogram, October 24, 1918, DMM JA Conzelmann NL 123, box 22. Groehler and Erfurth, *Hugo Junkers*, 23: "Junkers saw his creations and his firms as concentrated expressions of invention and quality. . . . Subordination and command economies—like those of the World War—were horrifying to him. From this perspective he often spoke of how lucky Germany had been to lose the war. Junkers viewed the war's end as the end of an epoch of Armaments, the overcoming of class, hierarchy and ossification, of militarized economies and compulsory state intervention, of stupidity and intellectual narrow-mindedness, of bureaucracy and uniformity."

103. Morrow, *German Airpower*, 105.

104. In an interview in 1939, Major Wagenführ repeated this assertion, arguing that he did all he could to further Junkers's research and that after the war Junkers wrote to him recognizing his achievements. He also noted he only brought Fokker and Junkers together to help Junkers. See interview with Lieutenant Colonel (retired) Felix Wagenführ, March 17, 1939, DMM JA Conzelmann NL 123, box 45/2.

Chapter 2

1. See Schmitt, *Hugo Junkers*, 218; Morrow, *German Airpower*, 152.

2. Blunck, *Hugo Junkers*, 113.

3. Transcript of conversation between Major Wagenführ, Captain Zahn, Lieutenant Goering, Major Seitz, and Dr. Mader, Berlin, February 10, 1919, DMM JA Conzelmann NL 123, box 39.

4. Ibid.

5. Morrow, *German Airpower*, 147.

6. Ibid., 149–52.

7. For details of Fokker's daring escape, see Dierickx, *Fokker*, 52–63.

8. Morrow, *German Airpower*, 152.

9. See Schmitt, *Hugo Junkers*, 153; Wagner, *Hugo Junkers*, 185; and Blunck, *Hugo Junkers*, 115.

10. Opinion regarding claims of Junkers for injury, January 6, 1920, DMM JA 0071, also cited within Budrass, *Flugzeugindustrie*, 70.

11. Budrass, *Flugzeugindustrie*, 70.

12. Morrow notes that German Army officials, after claiming that only seventeen hundred frontline aircraft existed in November 1918, later confided to civilian agencies that over nine thousand aircraft remained in army hands after the handover. See *German Airpower*, 146–58.

13. See Budrass, *Flugzeugindustrie*, 56–57; and Morrow, *German Airpower*, 159.

14. Morrow, *German Airpower*, 165.

15. See Wagner, *Hugo Junkers*, 144–46; and Schmitt, *Hugo Junkers*, 153–63, for details of the increasingly acrimonious relationship between Junkers and Larsen throughout 1919 and 1920.

16. Schmitt, *Hugo Junkers*, 154.

17. Ibid.

18. See table in Wagner, *Hugo Junkers*, 146–47.

19. See Schmitt, *Hugo Junkers*, 162–63. Schmitt notes a contemporary headline from the *Cleveland Press*, September 16, 1920, "Death Planes Made in Germany." The original source for the fuel problems of the F-13 in the United States is Leary, *Aerial Pioneers*.

20. Decision of Inter-Allied Control Commission, May 4, 1920, DMM JA Flugzeugbau 0301/3/18.

21. Morrow, *German Airpower*, 163.

22. Budrass, *Flugzeugindustrie*, 58.

23. "Regular Information Bulletin No. 19: A Confidential Document of the French Sub-Secretary of State for Aeronautics, 18 Jan 1921," within *Germany: A Compilation of Information for the Period August 1914 to May 1920*, Smithsonian Institution, US Air and Space Museum, 6, cited by Morrow, *German Airpower*, 164–65, and Budrass, *Flugzeugindustrie*, 60.

24. Letter from Seitz to Junkers, September 24, 1920, DMM JA 0301/4/14.

25. Opinion regarding confiscation of eleven Junkers aircraft and its consequences, Dessau, July 9, 1921, DMM JA Hauptbüro 0301/5/41, cited also within Schmitt, *Hugo Junkers*, 165.

26. Diary entry, May 28, 1920, DMM JA NL 21, diary no. 68, 3407–10.

27. Renamed in order to adhere to the Treaty of Versailles, the Truppenamt in fact was a smaller version of the abolished General Staff.

28. Carsten, *Reichwehr and Politics*, 70. The precise order of events surrounding who established contact first may never be known. For a more recent interpretation, see Zeidler, *Reichswehr und Rote Armee*.

29. See Budrass, *Flugzeugindustrie*, 104; and Wagner, *Hugo Junkers*, 186.

30. Carsten, *Reichswehr and Politics*, 135; and Budrass, *Flugzeugindustrie*, 104.

31. Budrass, *Flugzeugindustrie*, 105.

32. Draft of letter to Emanuel Nobel, February 25, 1921, DMM JA NL 21, diary no. 78, 4607, also cited by Wagner, *Hugo Junkers*, 186.

33. Letter from Seitz to Junkers regarding conversation between Wagenführ, Seitz, and Director Schliessing, January 7, 1920, DMM JA Hauptbüro 0301/3/5. The following discussion of Junkers's early Russian contacts derives from Budrass, *Flugzeugindustrie*, 106–7.

34. The Sachsenberg brothers, Hans (1889–1937) and Gotthard (1891–1961), played important roles in the destiny of the Junkers firm. Related to Paul Sachsenberg, director of a shipyard and factory on the Elbe near Dessau and an old friend of Junkers, the brothers enjoyed a level of trust with him that propelled them into positions of responsibility after the war's end. Hans, initially an engineer in the aircraft factory, later ran an ill-fated joint venture with the

Turkish government (see chapter 4). Gotthard, nicknamed "the Napoleon of Dessau," represented the firm at the Fili negotiations and also ran the firm's airline department. For the role of Gotthard Sachsenberg in the firm's subsequent financial difficulties, see chapter 3.

35. Exposé concerning the erection of an airline company on the route Berlin-Königsberg on the one side and Königsberg-Kovno-Riga-Revna on the other side, not dated, within the files of the Dessau public prosecutor, State Archive Oranienbaum, no. 155, folder 126, cited also by Budrass, *Flugzeugindustrie*, 106.

36. Letter from Seitz to Junkers, January 6, 1921, DMM JA Hauptbüro 0618/1/10.

37. Draft of letter from Junkers to Hesse, June 1, 1921, DMM JA NL 21, diary no. 77, 4557–58.

38. Opinion regarding confiscation of eleven Junkers aircraft and its consequences, Dessau, July 9, 1921, DMM JA Hauptbüro 0301/5/41.

39. Carsten, *Reichswehr and Politics*, 137.

40. Oskar von Niedermayer (1885–1948), educated in Russia, was known as "the German Lawrence" for his exploits in Persia and Afghanistan during World War I. During World War II, he commanded troops on the Eastern and Italian fronts. Captured by Soviet forces in 1948, he died of illness in captivity. A fascinating and enigmatic figure, he awaits a modern English-language biography.

41. Schleicher would later become the final chancellor of the Weimar Republic and would subsequently be murdered by the Schutzstaffel SS during the infamous "Night of the Long Knives" in 1934.

42. Undated note, DMM JA NL 21, diary no. 77, 4555. Budrass is probably correct when he estimates the date around the end of May 1921. See *Flugzeugindustrie*, 112.

43. Among those who entered Junkers's service with Sachsenberg was Erhard Milch, later the director of Lufthansa and a field marshal in the Luftwaffe. See chapter 3 and also Irving, *Rise and Fall*, 13–15.

44. With the retirement of Major Seitz in 1922, Sachsenberg became the senior Junkers employee in charge of relations between the firm, the Bolshevik Russian government, and the German Army authorities.

45. Notes of Seitz concerning report of Offerman on October 25, 1921, DMM JA Hauptbüro 0618/1/15.

46. Niedermayer's promises far exceeded the bounds of reality and included the creation of an "armaments city" adjacent to St. Petersburg for the production of all types of munitions, with the German government and private firms supplying all raw materials, skilled workers, and expertise. A skilled speaker, Niedermayer convinced many Russian officials, including People's Commissar for Foreign Affairs Georgi Chicherin, that this plan was feasible. Not surprisingly,

Russian representatives expressed anger when the plan fell through. See Budrass, *Flugzeugindustrie*, 115–17.

47. Gotthard Sachsenberg, transcript of the conversation concerning the Rumanian matter on November 25, 1921, DMM JA Hauptbüro 0618/1/17. To maintain absolute secrecy, Junkers correspondence referred to all Russian references as "Rumania."

48. In the interests of secrecy, no company legal officials attended the meeting, a circumstance that returned to hurt Junkers in subsequent legal battles with the Reichswehr. See Wagner, *Hugo Junkers*, 190. Wagner also notes that Junkers's Major Seitz, surely with the professor's assent, gave Oskar Niedermayer legal authority to conduct negotiations with the Russians throughout 1921 on the firm's behalf, a decision that also returned to haunt the firm in later years.

49. See Wagner, *Hugo Junkers*, 190.

50. Davies, *Lufthansa*, 30.

51. See Budrass, *Flugzeugindustrie*, 115; and Wagner, *Hugo Junkers*, 191.

52. Letter from Junkers to Spaleck, January 20, 1922, DMM JA Conzelmann NL 123, box 16.

53. Original translation of agreement between the Russian government and the Junkers firm, February 6, 1922, written for People's Commissar Trotsky, cited by Wagner, *Hugo Junkers*, 192.

54. Copy of secret Reichswehr document entitled "Development of the Junkers Concern in Fili (Russia) and Its Relationship with the Ministry of the Army up to Spring 1925," January 13, 1926, DMM JA Flugzeugbau 0301/14/4.

55. See previous document citation. The currency conversions within this document show the debilitating effects of the German currency crisis. While the March 27 payment of 40 million paper marks converted to US$118,168, the 35 million marks transferred on July 10 converted to only US$66,313. The consequences for Junkers require no further elaboration.

56. Diary entry, January 17, 1922, DMM JA NL 21, diary no. 77, 5552.

57. In the Reichswehr document from January 13, 1926, the authors cite a note written by Junkers from March 15, 1922, the day of the March Agreement. Perhaps hoping to encourage a timely conclusion to the negotiations and thus a prompt transfer of Reichswehr funds, Junkers declared himself "convinced that a contractual obligation of the Russians to permanently purchase half of the total production was unnecessary" due to the clear superiority of his aircraft. He continued, "The removal of this compulsory requirement will not endanger the existence of the concern." This unwise assertion undoubtedly bolstered the Reichswehr's determination to limit its commitment to the project.

58. Budrass, *Flugzeugindustrie*, 117. For discussion of Aero-Lloyd, see chapter 3.

59. Telegram from Sachsenberg to Junkers, March 24, 1922, DMM JA Hauptbüro 0618/1/25.

60. President Ebert's opposition to Seeckt's Russian plans was well known. In a meeting with Count Ulrich von Brockdorff-Rantzau on September 13, 1922, soon to be the German ambassador in Russia, Ebert remarked on Brockdorff-Rantzau's position against any military involvement with the Russians: "I can only say that I fully agree with the ideas expressed in your memorandum; a different opinion would be madness. About six months ago, when Radek was in Berlin, I saw signs that there were certain currents in the direction you indicate; I immediately opposed those tendencies in the strongest terms and strictly forbade any such attempt, even before Genoa. According to the constitution I am entitled to do so. I appoint the minister of defence and I am chief of the army. Since then I have not heard anything about it." (Source: Notes of Brockdorff-Rantzau on his conversation with Ebert, September 13, 1922, within Carsten, *Reichswehr and Politics*, 142.) Ebert's remarks demonstrate both the level of secrecy surrounding the Reichswehr-Russian negotiations and also the Reichswehr's attitude toward its commander-in-chief and the Weimar Constitution.

61. Carsten, *Reichswehr and Politics*, 142.

62. Diary entry, April 9, 1922, DMM JA NL 21, diary no. 88, 5805–6.

63. Diary entry, June 24, 1922, DMM JA NL 21, diary no. 90, 6124.

64. "Development of the Relationship between Junkers and the State Concerning the Collaboration in Russia," n.d., DMM JA NL 123 Conzelmann, box 16.

65. Diary entry, October 23, 1922, DMM JA NL 21, diary no. 94, 6585.

66. Copy of secret Reichswehr document entitled "Development of the Junkers Concern in Fili (Russia) and Its Relationship with the Ministry of the Army up to Spring 1925," January 13, 1926, DMM JA Flugzeugbau 0301/14/4. For a view of the mark's dramatic devaluation throughout 1922 and 1923, see Feldman, *Great Disorder*, particularly the table on page 5.

67. See "Factual Account of the Army Ministry in the Mediation Proceedings of Junkers against the German State, Transcript, 13 January 1926," cited by Schmitt, *Hugo Junkers*, 203; and Wagner, *Hugo Junkers*, 197. See also Wissmann, "Zur Geschichte," chapter 2.

68. Budrass, *Flugzeugindustrie*, 120.

69. Ibid., 121.

70. Junkers could only blame himself for this requirement. In December 1921, after learning of the Russians' interest in creating an indigenous aluminum industry, he purchased a license to manufacture aluminum and duralumin in Russia from the Düren Metal Works. Clearly, he hoped to establish an aluminum monopoly in Russia that would provide both additional capital funds for the Fili project as well as its vital raw materials. See Budrass, *Flugzeugindustrie*, 118–19.

71. Diary entry, May 13, 1923, DMM JA NL 21, diary no. 100, 7356.

72. Diary entry, November 1, 1923, DMM JA NL 21, diary no. 106, 7991.

73. See Feldman, *Great Disorder*, 653.

74. These funds found their way to the GEFU and totaled 70 million gold-marks.

75. "Development of the Junkers Concern in Fili (Russia) and Its Relationship with the Ministry of the Army up to Spring 1925," January 13, 1926, DMM JA Flugzeugbau 0301/14/4. Schubert later argued that he thought Hasse asked him whether the factory could produce one hundred aircraft over the course of 1923.

76. Budrass, *Flugzeugindustrie*, 126. The order was later halved to fifty aircraft and engines.

77. Copy of contract between the Special Section and Junkers Aircraft Works AG, November 5, 1923, DMM JA Flugzeugbau 0301/32, enclosure 8. The contract notes that Junkers bears responsibility for repayment of the sum if the order fails to materialize.

78. Budrass, *Flugzeugindustrie*, 125–26.

79. "Development of the Junkers Concern in Fili (Russia) and Its Relationship with the Ministry of the Army up to Spring 1925," January 13, 1926, DMM JA Flugzeugbau 0301/14/4. The J-21 failed to reach the required top speed, rate of climb, maximum ceiling, and weight limits established in 1922, clearly demonstrating its obsolescence by 1924. The Reichswehr argued Junkers deliberately slowed production at Fili in the hope of receiving a second, larger contract from the Russians. This assertion is not supported by other evidence, which suggests factors beyond Junkers's immediate control, such as the Ruhr Occupation, exerted significant influence.

80. Budrass, *Flugzeugindustrie*, 127.

81. Junkers noted in his diary that other agendas lay behind BMW's interest in production at Fili, an interest Junkers regarded as deceptive. "BMW's intentions focus on their factory within Germany. They make a pretense of declaring themselves ready to work in Russia to gain orders for their German factory." See diary entry, February 12, 1924, DMM JA NL 21, diary no. 108, 8317, cited also by Budrass, *Flugzeugindustrie*, 127. For the connection between Junkers's refusal to include BMW and the cancellation of the November 5 order, see statement of the Reichwehr Ministry in response to the account of Junkers, March 15, 1926, DMM JA Flugzeugbau 0301/14/8.

82. Letter from Sachsenberg to Waffenamt, March 25, 1924, DMM JA Flugzeugbau 0301/32, enclosure 12.

83. Ibid.

84. Letter from Sachsenberg to Waffenamt, April 15, 1924, DMM JA Flugzeugbau 0301/32, enclosure 13.

85. Development of the relationship between Junkers and the state regarding the cooperation in Russia, n.d., DMM JA NL 123, box 16, 48–49. See also the identical view within the document "Opinion of the Foreign Office," Summer 1924, DMM JA Flugzeugbau 0301/32, enclosure 1.

86. "Opinion of the Foreign Office," Summer 1924, DMM JA Flugzeugbau 0301/32, enclosure 1. This solution matched a proposal made by Junkers to the Reichswehr on April 26, the day before Sachsenberg visited the Foreign Office. See Budrass, *Flugzeugindustrie*, 127–28.

87. Feldman, *Great Disorder*, 833–34.

88. Development of the relationship between Junkers and the state regarding the cooperation in Russia, n.d., DMM JA NL 123, box 16, 50.

89. For an image of the R-1 concept, see the central photo gallery within this volume.

90. Diary entry, June 18, 1924, DMM JA NL 21, diary no. 112, 8695–98. Junkers also noted the rising prominence of US aircraft producers, describing Boeing of Seattle as a "strong firm . . . inexpensive and competitive." Ford's own forays into aircraft production, most notably the 4-AT Trimotor, possessed design characteristics such as thick-wing construction so clearly derived from Junkers principles that Junkers successfully sued him twice for patent infringement. Several Trimotors are still flying today.

91. Copy of letter from Junkers to von Seeckt, July 22, 1924, DMM JA Flugzeugbau 0301/32, enclosure 16.

92. Ibid.

93. Letter from von Seeckt to Junkers, August 18, 1924, DMM JA Flugzeugbau 0301/32, enclosure 15.

94. Letter from Junkers to von Seeckt, October 22, 1924, DMM JA Flugzeugbau 0301/32, enclosure 18.

95. Letter from von Seeckt to Junkers, November 26, 1924, DMM JA Flugzeugbau 0301/32, enclosure 20.

96. Budrass, *Flugzeugindustrie*, 123, note 264.

97. Junkers created two sets of financial records, one showing sums nominally set aside for and used at Fili, and another set showing valuation adjustments for supposed expenditures at Fili that actually flowed back to Dessau. The existence of these two separate sets of records was revealed in 1934 by Otto Pupke, Junkers's chief accountant. See Budrass, *Flugzeugindustrie*, 181–82.

98. Diary entry, 26 April 1922, DMM JA NL 21, diary no. 88, 5857.

Chapter 3

1. Fritzsche, *Nation of Fliers*, 1–59. Fritzsche notes the contrast between the Prussian Army's tepid official response to the Zeppelin as a military platform and the popular perception of the craft as a wonder weapon. See also de Syon, *Zeppelin!*

2. Wagner, *Der Deutsche Luftverkehr*, 11.

3. Morrow, *German Airpower*, 144.

4. Radandt, "Hugo Junkers," 95.

5. Wagner, *Der Deutsche Luftverkehr*, 13.

6. Comments of Dr. Emil Georg von Stauss for the magazine *Motor and Sport*, January 1927, originally from a Deutsche Bank file notice, January 11, 1927, cited by Radandt, "Hugo Junkers," 95.

7. Radandt notes the courier service began in Germany on February 15, 1918.

8. Deutsche Luftreederei (DLR), founded with a capitalization of two and a half million marks, became the cornerstone of Deutscher Aero-Lloyd AG (DAL), Junkers's principal rival until 1925. DLR's insignia, the crane, survives today through its descendant, Lufthansa, the German national airline.

9. Wagner, *Der Deutsche Luftverkehr*, 13.

10. Morrow, *German Airpower*, 152–62.

11. Wagner, *Der Deutsche Luftverkehr*, 18–20.

12. Ibid., 20. Ironically Euler's proposal, which fell on deaf ears in 1920, closely resembled the ultimate framework for the establishment of Deutsche Lufthansa in 1925–26. Euler would not be in office for the creation of the national airline; his critical attitude toward collaboration with military authorities led to the preparation of a law that allowed for the removal of authority in aviation affairs from his office. Attacked by both the Reichswehr and its supporters in the aviation press, as well as war veterans critical of the state of German aviation after the war, Euler retired in December 1920. The Aviation Office became the Air and Motor Vehicle Office, attached to the newly created Reichsverkehrministerium (State Transport Ministry, RVM) in October 1920. Euler's successor, Major (ret.) Ernst Brandenburg, a former bomber pilot personally appointed to the RVM at the request of General von Seeckt, ensured the reestablishment of close ties between the Reichswehr and the industry. See Morrow, *German Airpower*, 166; and Wagner, *Der Deutsche Luftverkehr*, 20–21.

13. See Wagner, *Der Deutsche Luftverkehr*, 17, for a list of these restrictions, which came into effect on April 14, 1922, and remained in force until 1926. The most important included restrictions on top speed, engine size, maximum ceiling, and weight limits. In these cases, the performance limits were considerably below those of wartime aircraft and well below the next generation of civilian designs.

14. The subsequent Paris Agreement of May 21, 1926, removed all restrictions on German aircraft manufacture. The German Reichstag ratified the Paris Agreement on July 8, 1926.

15. With the founding of DAL, DLR's parent company, AEG, withdrew from its involvement in air transport.

16. See Davies, *Lufthansa*, 8–13, for a detailed breakdown of the numerous components of DAL.

17. See Blunck, *Hugo Junkers*, 128; and Wagner, *Der Deutsche Luftverkehr*, 57. Sachsenberg assumed full control over all airline matters and employed

many of his wartime comrades, including Erhard Milch, in the organization. See Schmitt, *Hugo Junkers*, 220–22.

18. For North America, see chapter 2 and accompanying references. In South America, an ambitious flight program commenced that led to the formation of SCADTA (Sociedad Colombo-Alemana de Transportes Aéreos) on November 5, 1919. Two F-13 floatplanes and Junkers pilot Fritz Hammer connected the Colombian capital, Bogotá, with the Caribbean coastline, a day's journey that previously took two weeks. The airline, supported by the Colombian government, played an important role in Colombian history and in 1925 completed the Trans-Caribbean Survey, an event of tremendous significance for the subsequent US aviation development. Tragically for Junkers, his oldest son, Werner, died in an accident outside Buenos Aires in 1923. Junkers aircraft pioneered and founded South American commercial aviation. For more on SCADTA and other developments in South America, see Davies, *Lufthansa*, 28–29; and Blunck, *Hugo Junkers*, 142–52.

19. For a complete list of the vast number of airlines associated with Junkers between 1919 and 1933, see and compare the lists of Radandt, "Hugo Junkers," 89–91; Wagner, *Der Deutsche Luftverkehr*, 57–58; and Schmitt, *Hugo Junkers*, 241.

20. Radandt, "Hugo Junkers," 97–98. See also the examples of the Luftverkehrsgesellschaft Ruhrgebiet AG, affiliated with Junkers, and the Luftverkehrs-AG Westfalen, affiliated with DAL, in Budrass, *Flugzeugindustrie*, 172.

21. Budrass, *Flugzeugindustrie*, 174.

22. Ibid.

23. In 1924, the "Ost Europa Union" changed its name to the "Nord Europa Union." For routes and members of both unions, see Davies, *Lufthansa*, 16–17. For details surrounding the proposed founding of the Europa Union see Prospekt für die Gründung der "Europa Union": Kommanditgesellschaft auf Aktien, DMM JA propaganda 533=920.

24. See Groehler and Erfurth, *Hugo Junkers*, 37, cited also by Budrass, *Flugzeugindustrie*, 177.

25. For figures, see Junkers company pamphlet, "Junkers im Weltluftverkehr," DMM JA propaganda 592. See also Blunck, *Hugo Junkers*, 154.

26. The Europa Union's prospectus envisaged the Junkers Luftverkehr's role within the new firm as "executive shareholder." See Prospekt für die Gründung der "Europa Union": Kommanditgesellschaft auf Aktien, DMM JA propaganda 533=920.

27. These firms included the four based around the greatly enlarged Dessau complex—Junkers & Co. Apparate Fabrik, Junkers Kaloriferwerk, Junkers Flugzeugwerk AG, and Junkers Motorenbau GmbH—as well as the Junkers-Werk Moskau, overseeing the Fili project; Junkers Corporation of America, based in New York; the Aachener Segelflugzeugbau GmbH, in Aachen; and the newly

founded AB Flygindustri, in Limhamm, Sweden. Negotiations also began in 1925 concerning the establishment of an aircraft factory in Turkey.

28. Diary entry, December 17, 1922, DMM JA NL 21, diary no. 96, 6874.

29. Milch's later defection to Deutsche Lufthansa undoubtedly rankled Sachsenberg as much as Junkers.

30. Schmitt, *Hugo Junkers*, 221.

31. Ibid., 229.

32. Diary entry, June 25, 1923, DMM JA NL 21, diary no. 101, 7435. See also Schmitt, *Hugo Junkers*, 227–29.

33. At this time, Junkers employed a young graduate student, Hans Bongers (later Dr. Bongers) to investigate the financial records of Abteilung Luftverkehr. Bongers later described what he found: "Until then nothing had been scrutinized or defined in a business management sense. Nothing existed to clarify what was regarded as an efficient standard; whether it should be a flight, or a flight hour, or a flown kilometer or perhaps a flight route. Transport charges point to this experience. Only much later were the costs distinguished between supplied seats and those actually used by passengers. Up to that point no-one had attempted to establish and develop price-fixing or cost-analysis principles for air transport. The undertaking, an attempt to produce standardization, was laughed at, the purpose hardly understood, the whole matter seen as utopian" (Bongers, *Es lag in der Luft*, 27–28, cited by Schmitt, *Hugo Junkers*, 230.)

34. Diary entry, 23 June 1923, DMM JA NL 21, diary no. 101, 7435.

35. Schmitt, *Hugo Junkers*, 229. Schmitt describes the source of this quotation as "Reminisces of A. Weise: Particulars of the life history of Professor Junkers and the history of the Junkers Works," which he locates within the archives of the Deutsches Museum in Munich. This author proved unable to locate this source, perhaps because Schmitt provides no archive reference number and the Junkers collection has been reorganized several times since the publication of his work in 1986.

36. See chapter 2. For a more detailed analysis of these developments, See Budrass, *Flugzeugindustrie*, chapter 3, passim; and Homze, *Arming the Luftwaffe*, 10–40.

37. See chapter 2.

38. For an overview of the development of this relationship, see Boog, *Conduct of the Air War*, 55–85.

39. These struggles expanded outside Germany's borders, reaching such a level that Denmark, tired of the incessant rivalry and its effect on services, revoked both Junkers Luftverkehr and DAL's operating licenses in favor of the French firm Farman Air Transport. See Radandt, "Hugo Junkers," 101.

40. See Siefert, *Der deutsche Luftverkehr*, 9–11.

41. Ibid., 10.

42. Fritzsche, *Nation of Flyers*, 175. Fritzsche cites Fischer von Poturzyn,

Junkers press director, who published several articles on German aviation politics in the 1920s, many of which can now be found in the Junkers Archive at DMM JA propaganda 718=919.

43. Diary entry, January 19, 1924, DMM JA NL 21, diary no. 108, 8288.

44. Diary entry, March 28, 1924, DMM JA NL 21, diary no. 110, 8444.

45. See chapter 2.

46. See the numerous declarations against capital in Junkers's diaries throughout his life, such as that from January 24, 1923, diary no. 96, on page 6895: "Relationship to Capitalism; If something characterizes Junkers's career, it is the fight against capital, his entire industrial life is a fight for the freeing of work from the hegemony of capital."

47. Diary entry, September 1924, DMM JA NL 21, diary no. 115, 9150.

48. Diary entry, December 19, 1924, DMM JA NL 21, diary no. 118, 9501.

49. See Budrass, *Flugzeugindustrie*, 178–79.

50. Due to Swedish laws prohibiting foreign ownership of firms, Junkers cleverly designated AB Flygindustri's majority owners as Adrian and Carl Florman, two brothers whose relationship with the firm began the previous year when Junkers supplied their air transport firm, AB Aerotransport, with two F-13s. It later emerged that the Florman brothers were merely front men for the concern, with Junkers owning 82 percent of the firm's shares. The Limhamm factory acted as a satellite of the Dessau concern, completing construction of the G-24 until 1926 and modifying Junkers designs for military use until 1931, when the financial difficulties of both Junkers and the Florman brothers initiated Junkers's withdrawal. Unfortunately for all concerned, the factory never realized a profit due to a lack of orders for either aircraft or modifications, creating an additional drain on the parent firm's financial resources. For a closer examination of the Limhamm venture, see Bohme and Olsson, "Swedish Aircraft Industry," 146–70.

51. The Turkish firm, abbreviated to "Tomtasch" in company records, demonstrated the divergent aims of German state ministries regarding aviation. The Auswärtige Amt (Foreign Office), a consistent enemy of the Reichswehr, provided Junkers with 2 million marks for the Turkish venture, in the hope that Junkers's presence in the region would lead to a growth of German influence, checking the aims of France, England, and the Soviet Union. The region's abundant oil supplies lay behind these moves, as Germany, unable to exert military power in the area, sought other means to press national claims. For its part, the Reichswehr, through General von Seeckt, strongly advised against the venture. The Auswärtige Amt replied sharply, noting that the Reichswehr "had frittered away 100 million" in Russia. Two circumstances prevented the success of the Turkish venture: first, following a change in bureaucratic leadership, the Turkish regime chose to adopt an autarkic course in air transport, removing foreign companies from routes in Turkey; and second, as in the Soviet Union, the performance of the military aircraft produced by Junkers for the Turkish

Air Force, the A-20, failed to match either the contractual obligations established at the firm's founding or the expectations of the Turkish military, who subsequently refused to pay the firm or purchase any of the aircraft. The firm, led ably but ultimately unsuccessfully by Hans Sachsenberg, suffered recurring losses before filing for bankruptcy in 1930. See Wagner, *Hugo Junkers*, 288; and for Junkers's views on the venture, see his diary entry of August 11, 1925, DMM JA NL 21, diary no. 124, 10153.

52. These cost increases occurred despite a marked improvement in worker productivity through September 1925. See memorandum on profitability overview, November 20, 1925, DMM JA Flugzeugbau 0301/10/38.

53. Most material in this section relies on Budrass, *Flugzeugindustrie*, 180–83. Budrass notes that tailoring aircraft to each customer's special needs increased production prices considerably, while the firm's pledge to provide aircraft at a significant discount to airline allies removed any significant profit from these transactions. One statistic from this period illustrates these problems clearly— out of forty-seven F-13s produced in 1923, only three reached the open market. See the customer list of November 1924, DMM JA Flugzeugbau 0303/1/1.

54. List of competitors' prices for Transport Aircraft, April 4, 1924, DMM JA Flugzeugbau 0301/9/9.

55. Stock of completed F-13 aircraft, DMM JA Flugzeugbau 0301/9/9, cited also by Budrass, *Flugzeugindustrie*, 183.

56. See statistical reports of the Junkers Works: personnel graphs, November 1925, tabulated within Schmitt, *Hugo Junkers*, 263.

57. Budrass, *Flugzeugindustrie*, 188.

58. Ibid, 187.

59. Ibid.

60. Ibid., 188–89.

61. Letter from Brandenburg to Junkers, October 7, 1925, DMM JA Flugzeugbau 0301/10/30.

62. Outline of letter from Junkers to Brandenburg, October 7, 1925, DMM JA Flugzeugbau 0301/10/30. Whether Junkers ever sent this letter to Brandenburg, or simply used it as an expressive outlet, could not be determined by this author. Interestingly, the document copy possesses Junkers's signature.

63. Letter from Dr. Rambach, financial administration of Junkers Luftverkehr, Berlin, to Junkers Flugzeugwerke, Dessau, October 14, 1925, DMM JA Flugzeugbau 0301/10/31.

64. Diary entry, October 9, 1925, DMM JA NL 21, diary no. 125, 10290–92.

65. See Budrass, *Flugzeugindustrie*, 189–97, for a meticulous examination of these and subsequent events. For a list of the officials named to the board of IFA after October 20, see the letter from Reichsverkehrminister von Krohne to Junkers, December 10, 1925, DMM JA Flugzeugbau 0301/10/30.

66. Budrass, *Flugzeugindustrie*, 188.

67. Diary entry, October 20, 1925, DMM JA NL 21, diary no. 126, 10397.

68. For an excellent narrative of the events leading up to Deutsche Lufthansa's founding, see Siefert, *Der Deutsche Luftverkehr*, 9–14. The name of the new airline derived from an essay written by Junkers Press Chief Fischer von Poturzyn published in 1925 as *Lufthansa Luftpolitische Möglichkeiten*. Ironically, Germany's national airline retains the same name today.

69. See Irving, *Rise and Fall*, 13–38, for Milch's version of his relationship with Junkers between 1920 and 1934. Milch had been chosen by Brandenburg over Gotthard Sachsenberg, who the Transport Ministry viewed as primarily responsible for Junkers's financial mismanagement of Junkers Luftverkehr. During World War II, Field Marshal Milch would become the second most powerful officer of the Luftwaffe.

70. Budrass, *Flugzeugindustrie*, 191–92.

71. See the company memorandum on damage to Junkers through the press regarding the events of fall 1925, DMM JA Flugzeugbau 0301/10/35.

72. These operations included the aircraft testing ground and flight school at Lipetsk and the army armored vehicles school at Kazan. See Homze, *Arming the Luftwaffe*, 9–10; and Carsten, *Reichswehr and Politics*, 272–84.

73. Transcript of conversation between Junkers, Veiel, Kottmeier, and Plauth at the Kaiserplatz, morning of January 12, 1926, DMM JA Flugzeugbau 0301/12/6.

74. Remarks of Junkers regarding further action in the "Arbitration SG" Affair, January 13, 1926, DMM JA Flugzeugbau 0301/12/6.

75. See chapter 2. For the Reichswehr's view, see their letter to Simons on January 13, 1926, DMM JA Flugzeugbau 0301/14/4.

76. See thoughts of the board of directors regarding the reduction of sales due to the unknown business policies of Deutsche Lufthansa, March 2, 1926, DMM JA Flugzeugbau 0301/12/45.

77. Budrass, *Flugzeugindustrie*, 192–93.

78. Letter from Junkers to von Schlieben, January 14, 1926, DMM JA Flugzeugbau 0301/12/10.

79. Letter from Finance Committee to von Schlieben, May 4, 1926, DMM JA Flugzeugbau 0301/12/53. All three plans proposed a dramatic reduction in the firm's workforce and production output for the rest of 1926.

80. See Budrass, *Flugzeugindustrie*, 193–94.

81. Transcript of conversation from February 1 and 2, 1926, at the Kaiserplatz, DMM JA Flugzeugbau 0301/12/20.

82. File note regarding arbitration, February 13, 1926, DMM JA Flugzeugbau 0301/12/20. See also Junkers's notes during February regarding the arbitration process, DMM JA Flugzeugbau 0301/14/6.

83. See Wagner, *Hugo Junkers*, 211.

84. See Budrass, *Flugzeugindustrie*, 194. Simons, whose son-in-law formerly

worked at the Junkers plant, noted in a letter to Foreign Minister Stresemann on April 23, 1926, that, regarding the Fili Affair, "both the Reichswehr and the Russian government had aroused expectations in Junkers that were unrealizable from the outset." See Groehler and Erfurth, *Hugo Junkers*, 41.

85. Groehler and Erfurth, *Hugo Junkers*, 41.

86. Budrass, *Flugzeugindustrie*, 195.

87. See Radandt, "Hugo Junkers," 108–19.

88. Ibid.

89. See, for example, the article by Widerhold, "Die Wahrheit über Junkers," 806–10. Widerhold concluded the article, essentially a critique of government actions toward Junkers over the previous ten years, by remarking that Junkers's possible move overseas constituted "new proof of the bankruptcy of German military and military-economic policy." Such views would become anathema after 1933.

90. Letters from Kuhlenkampff to Stresemann, April 24, 1926, and to Luther, May 1, 1926, cited by Budrass, *Flugzeugindustrie*, 194. See also Junkers's diary entry of April 17, 1926, DMM JA NL 21, diary no. 132, 11114.

91. Stresemann's stance was surely also influenced by other factors such as national prestige, given that Junkers's products ranked among the most recognizable of German exports. This assumption had encouraged his own ministry's investment of over 2 million marks in Junkers's Turkish factory.

92. Letter from Janssen to Junkers, April 20, 1926, DMM JA Flugzeugbau 0301/12/46.

93. See transcript of meeting at the Kaiserplatz, 9:00 a.m., April 27, 1926, DMM JA Flugzeugbau 0301/12/49.

94. See Junkers's diary entry on February 13, 1926, DMM JA NL 21, diary no. 130, 10949.

95. Groehler and Erfurth, *Hugo Junkers*, 41. For a copy of this first brief, see the undated document DMM JA Flugzeugbau 0301/14/1.

96. Ibid.

97. See letters from Junkers to Marx, May 20, 1926, and June 7, 1926, DMM JA Flugzeugbau 0301/12/63. Junkers sent copies of the June letter to every ministerial head.

98. See the copy of this brief, dated June 25, 1926 in DMM JA NL 123 Conzelmann, box 16.

99. Company report of the balance and loss/profit calculations of the Junkers Flugzeugwerk AG, Dessau to September 30, 1925; July 9, 1926, DMM JA Flugzeugbau 0301/10/29.

100. See the Army Weapons Office's secret statement on Junkers's brief from July 25, 1926; August 8, 1926, DMM JA Flugzeugbau 0301/14/13. Within the statement, the Reichswehr pointed to IFA's production activity in 1925 as the main cause of the firm's difficulties, with the factory producing more aircraft

than any previous year without receiving any advance orders. It also questioned, with some justification, Junkers's recounting of events, arguing that Junkers knew of the difficulties inherent in the Fili venture but chose to involve himself regardless, even after he knew he lacked the means to fulfil his contractual obligations.

101. See top secret record of the Transport Ministry Conference concerning the Junkers Works, August 18, 1926, DMM JA NL 123 Conzelmann, box 16. After the meeting, Junkers identified his opponents' diverse motivations: "a) The Reichswehr Ministry needs a plant to mass produce military aircraft in case of war b) the Transport Ministry desires a research institute funded by the state c) the Finance Ministry wants IFA run according to sound budgetary principles." See diary entry, August 15, 1926, DMM JA NL 21, diary no. 138, 11839.

102. Budrass, *Flugzeugindustrie*, 196.

103. Groehler and Erfurth also note that during August 1926 the Russian Concessions Bureau approached the Foreign Office about the possibility of concluding a new contract with Junkers over the Fili plant. The Russians additionally expressed their intention to drop all claims against Junkers for breach of the previous contract. The Foreign Office, hoping to both maintain good German-Russian relations and also to silence Junkers, therefore opposed liquidation of IFA. See Groehler and Erfurth, *Hugo Junkers*, 41–42.

104. File notice, meeting in Berlin concerning tactical analysis of current situation, September 9, 1926, DMM JA Flugzeugbau 0301/13/15. The October Contract refers to the RVM takeover conditions of 1925, which Junkers compares in his diary to the Treaty of Versailles later that year. (See diary entry of October 29, 1926, DMM JA NL 21, diary no. 142, 12305–6.) GEFU refers to the Gesellschaft zur Förderung gewerbliche Unternehmungen (Society for the Funding of Commercial Enterprises), the Moscow holding company established by the Reichswehr to finance its Russian projects; see chapter 2. Later that month Junkers repeated his strategy in his diary, "Tactics: General Campaign Plan (1) Play off opponents against each other. (2) Establish good relations with individuals whose power can be directed at our opponents. Allow to mature" (diary entry, September 28, 1926, DMM JA NL 21, diary no. 140, 12103).

105. Letter from von Krohne to Junkers, September 18, 1926, DMM JA Flugzeugbau 0301/13/18.

106. Carsten notes that von Seeckt's eclipse also indicated a recognition that the new president, Field Marshal von Hindenburg, desired to lead both army and nation. See Carsten, *Reichswehr and Politics*, 245–50.

107. See enclosure 24, excerpt from the protocol of the National Budgetary Committee on February 9, 1927, regarding the Junkers case and the budget of the RVM, DMM JA Flugzeugbau T0301–32.

108. See the discussions within documents contained in DMM JA Flugzeugbau 0301/13/2.

109. See conversations between Sachsenberg, Loewenfeld, and Quaatz in Berlin, November 12, 1926, DMM JA Flugzeugbau 0301/13/2.

110. Carsten, *Reichswehr and Politics*, 255–56.

111. See copy of *Manchester Guardian* article of December 6, 1926, as enclosure 46 within DMM JA Flugzeugbau T0301–32. The close resemblance between the *Guardian* report and Junkers's second memorandum of June 1925 did not escape the notice of those familiar with both documents, and the article later reappeared as evidence in allegations of treason leveled against Junkers by the National Socialist Regime during 1934. See chapter 4.

112. See Hauptbüro file of December 10, 1926, DMM JA Flugzeugbau 0301/13/53. Junkers additionally requested the right to purchase a stake in Deutsche Lufthansa, a request the RVM refused.

113. Letter from Loewenfeld to Quaatz, December 10, 1926, DMMJA Flugzeugbau 0301/13/54.

114. Budrass, *Flugzeugindustrie*, 195.

115. An excerpt of this speech appears in Mason, *Rise of the Luftwaffe*, 155–56.

116. Letter from Reichsverkehrminister Krohne to Quaatz, December 19, 1926, DMM JA Flugzeugbau 0301/13/61. The state also required Junkers to provide severance pay for all outside members of IFA's board of directors.

117. See protocol and copy of official agreement, December 23, 1926, DMM JA Flugzeugbau 0301/13/62.

118. Letter from Junkers to Simons, December 30, 1926, DMM JA NL 123 Conzelmann, box 24.

119. Memorandum from RVM to Junkers, December 31, 1926, DMM JA Flugzeugbau 0301/13/65.

120. See chapter 3.

121. The RVM ordered only thirteen aircraft from Junkers throughout the year 1927, down from twenty-two in 1926. See table in Wagner, *Hugo Junkers*, 286.

122. See abstract of petition of Reich President Ebert and the chancellor regarding air transport, July 10, 1925, DMM JA NL 123 Conzelmann, box 22, within which Junkers argues that "the peaceful side of the effects of air transport must be emphasized against the prevailing view that only military measures guarantee the security of the people."

123. Junkers was well aware of the state's agenda by 1926, which involved the systematic takeover of the industry through the coordination of research, procurement specifications, and production facilities. See the document entitled "The Situation on July 9," DMM JA Flugzeugbau 0301/12/78.

124. Unlike Junkers, whose share of the new national airline became part of the state's holding, DAL's shareholders were able to exchange their DAL shares for those of Deutscher Lufthansa.

Chapter 4

1. Junkers originally configured the G-38 as a seaplane, in response to a RVM request for an aircraft capable of flying long sea postal routes. Behind this request also lay possible military uses, as the Naval Transport Office within the ministry initially offered to provide orders for the craft through its civilian shell company, Severa GmbH. RVM officials vetoed this proposal by changing the order for a land-based machine only. See Wagner, *Hugo Junkers*, 295. For Severa, see Carsten, *Reichswehr and Politics*, 287; and Homze, *Arming the Luftwaffe*, 38–39.

2. Blunck, *Hugo Junkers*, 222–23.

3. The high costs of the G-38's development placed a severe burden on IFA's finances, soon exceeding the grants of 1,959,764 reichsmarks for the aircraft and 222,135 reichsmarks for the engines provided by the RVM and the German Aviation Research Institute (DVL). Once again Junkers had gambled that sufficient orders for the craft would offset these costs. When these orders failed to materialize in the wake of the global depression, Junkers found himself unable to pay for either the costly publicity flights of the craft during 1930 or its maintenance, deepening the firm's financial problems at a critical juncture. Risks associated with large aircraft design and profitability remain today. See Wagner, *Hugo Junkers*, 299–300. Although Junkers concluded a license agreement with Peugeot for construction of the G-38 in France, the global economic crisis together with the G-38's high costs discouraged the French firm from building the aircraft. See DMM JA Flugzeugbau 0301/26/9.

4. See Blunck, *Hugo Junkers*, 224–25.

5. IFA's yearly balance for 1928–29 showed cash reserves of only 375,075 marks, against debts of 1,389,609 marks. The firm's final losses for the year totaled 455,545 marks. See the table within Geschäfts-Bericht der Junkers-Flugzeugwerk Aktiengesellschaft zu Dessau für das XII Geschäftsjahr 1928–29 (Company Report of the Junkers Aircraft Works for 1928–29), DMM JA Flugzeugbau 0301/26/6.

6. Junkers's position in Turkey depended critically on its supporters in the Turkish government, in particular officers within the Turkish War Ministry, such as Kadri and Murad Bey. Throughout 1927, Junkers's reputation diminished, partly as a result of poor performance of Junkers aircraft in the field and also due to rumors circulating within the Turkish government concerning the Dessau firm's precarious financial situation. See the excerpt of a letter from Hans Sachsenberg to Gotthard Sachsenberg, November 7, 1927, DMM JA Flugzeugbau 0301/21/25.

7. Budrass, *Flugzeugindustrie*, 198.

8. JUMO's research and development costs increased from 600,000 marks in 1926 to 2,300,000 marks in 1929. Over the same period, IFA's research and

development expenditure expanded from 1,700,000 marks to 4,500,000 marks. See the summary of research and development costs derived from Hauptbüro figures between 1919 and 1929 throughout DMM JA Hauptbüro 0307, cited also by Budrass, *Flugzeugindustrie*, 242, table 7.

9. Wagner notes that the RVM only ordered thirteen aircraft from IFA throughout 1927, and the Reichswehr ordered none at all (*Hugo Junkers*, 286).

10. Budrass describes the outcome of the "Junkers Affair" as a "paradigmatic experience for the aviation policy of the Transport Ministry and the Reichswehr." See *Flugzeugindustrie*, 198–99.

11. With the signing of the Paris Air Agreement on May 21, 1926, all restrictions on German civilian aviation development were lifted, and the supervisory body, the Allied Aviation Guarantee Committee, ended its oversight beginning September 1. See Homze, *Arming the Luftwaffe*, 19.

12. Homze notes that prior to 1926, aviation policy "suffered from administrative decentralization . . . with personnel, tactics and training under the control of the Truppenamt, while aviation equipment was under the Waffenamt [Ordnance Office]" (*Arming the Luftwaffe*, 23).

13. Ibid., 24. The following analysis of Fertigungs GmbH and its activities is based on his research.

14. Ibid.

15. Ibid., 25. He also notes that these problems were not unique to Germany during this period; similar problems existed in the British and American aircraft industries. For the British experience, see Higham, *Armed Forces in Peacetime*, and Hayward, *British Aircraft Industry* (1989).

16. See chapter 2.

17. For the Rohrbach restructuring, which took place concurrently with the Junkers takeover, see Budrass, *Flugzeugindustrie*, 199–204.

18. Ibid., 204.

19. Personnel transfers exemplified these closer ties between the RVM and the Reichswehr; in May 1927, Adolf Baeumker, a senior officer within the Truppenamt's aviation department, assumed a new post within the RVM as a civilian aviation expert. See Budrass, *Flugzeugindustrie*, 204.

20. See ibid., 205–40.

21. Aktennotiz (file note), entitled "Zur Lage am 9. Juli (1926)," DMM JA Flugzeugbau 0301/12/78.

22. In a situation report on March 29, 1927, Junkers Press Chief Fischer von Poturzyn expressed this sentiment:

> An important moment in the relationship between Junkers and the state is the change of leadership of the RVM. The successor of Dr. Krohne is Dr. Koch, formerly national Trade Union Secretary. All signs indicate that he does not view aviation questions from the perspective of the Civil Service. Evidence for

this lies in his comments within a pronouncement of the Reichstag Budgetary Committee that took place on March 13. A discussion arose over the granting of subsidies and the "Junkers Affair" was mentioned. In his declaration the Minister gave the impression that in the solution of the Junkers question the opinion of himself and the Reich Cabinet on the one side and the opinion of the officials in the RVM on the other side was not unanimous: "The gentlemen of the RVM have only reluctantly gone along with the resolution. However there is no doubt that the agreement, now that is has been concluded, must be supported by the government and the officials of the RVM both internally and publicly."

See Junkers News Service situation report 293/771, March, 29, 1927, "Relationship between Junkers and the State Authorities," DMM JA Flugzeugbau 0301/19.

23. Diary entry, April 6, 1927, DMM JA NL 21, diary no. 148, 13017.

24. Ibid., 13033–36.

25. These attacks, which played out both privately and in the press, form the subject of a letter from Reich Privy Councilor Otto Köpcke to Deutsche Lufthansa Chairman Emil Georg von Stauss, in which Köpcke asks Stauss to censure Colsmann, who in addition to his position at Dornier was on Lufthansa's board of directors. Köpcke argued that since the Junkers Affair had been resolved, such attacks "were not in the state's interest." See enclosure from Werner Wagener to Junkers, March 29, 1927, DMM JA NL 123 Conzelmann, box 24. Other firms were also tired of paying Junkers patent royalties for design features in their own aircraft, such as for the "thick-wing" patented by Junkers in 1909. Throughout the 1920s, Junkers consistently instigated legal proceedings against his rivals over these patent infringements, with varying degrees of success.

26. See Schmitt, *Hugo Junkers*, 267–68. Recognizing that they lacked the power to challenge Junkers directly, Dornier and other firms, such as Rohrbach, Heinkel, and Arado, sought to use the RDLI as a leverage instrument to gain government support. This stance had some justification, due to publication of the enormous amounts required to maintain IFA and JUMO during 1926. Between 1924 and 1928, the RVM distributed 26 million marks in loans and advances to the aircraft industry. Junkers received 19,400,000 marks, over 16 million during 1925 alone. See the table within Budrass, *Flugzeugindustrie*, 213; for more on the RDLI, see also ibid., 229–32.

27. See Blunck, *Hugo Junkers*, 232–33. Blunck also notes that diesel fuel was one third cheaper than benzine in 1933.

28. Schmitt, *Hugo Junkers and His Aircraft*, 202. For an examination of JUMO, see Ittner, *Dieselmotoren*.

29. The development of the J-52 reflected this closer collaboration, as new IFA chief designer Ernst Zindel envisioned the J-52 as the test bed for a variety of

configurations incorporating the Junkers diesel engine, the JUMO 4. See notice from Zindel to Hauptbüro, June 7, 1929, DMM JA Flugzeugbau 0302/8/13, cited also by Budrass, *Flugzeugindustrie*, 244. Homze points to the lack of domestic aero-engine development as the principal handicap of the German aircraft industry between 1919 and 1939, and notes that "in 1933 only three engine types existed in the 1,000-horsepower range suitable for military aircraft. . . . Two of the three were of foreign design" (*Arming the Luftwaffe*, 26–28).

30. See table in Schmitt, *Hugo Junkers and His Aircraft*, 122–23.

31. Lindbergh's success, although a spectacular achievement, reflected the increased US investment, from both public and private sources, in aviation development throughout the 1920s. State interest and involvement in aviation culminated in the Air Commerce Act of 1926, which created an Aviation Office within the Department of Commerce.

32. For a discussion of these preparations, and the subsequent events that led to the successful crossing, see Hotson, *Bremen*. In German, see Schmitt, *Hugo Junkers*, 268–74.

33. "Europa" and "Bremen" were also the names of Norddeutsche Lloyd's two largest ocean liners.

34. Hotson, *Bremen*, 27.

35. Junkers, *Eine Chronik*, 131, quoted within Radandt, "Hugo Junkers," 112–13. Emphasis in original.

36. See Hotson, *Bremen*, 28–29.

37. Kleffel, "Zum Jahreswechsel," 2–3, cited within Fritzsche, *Nation of Fliers*, 146–47, and 246, note 44. Fritzsche's work also includes the cover of the German satirical periodical *Simplicissimus* from April 16, 1928, which, under the title "Die Ozeanflug-Saison beginnt!" (Ocean flying season begins!), depicted a huge skeleton with a lighted beacon reflecting out of its eye sockets crouched on an ocean buoy, luring planes into the ocean while holding aloft a bag of money and a victory wreath. See cover of *Simplicissimus* 33 (April 16, 1928), reproduced within Fritzsche, *Nation of Fliers*, 148.

38. Hotson, *Bremen*, 34–35. Hotson also notes that insurance coverage became extremely difficult to obtain by early 1928.

39. Ibid., 34.

40. For the response in Germany once the victorious flyers returned in June 1928, see Fritzsche, *Nation of Fliers*, 149–51. Fritzsche argues that "for Germans the . . . *Bremen* crossing [was a] powerful affirmation of German honor and German destiny."

41. Claudius Dornier's greatest success, the Dornier Gs II, or "Wal" (Whale) first appeared in 1922. Throughout the 1920s, the size and weight of the "Wal" rose, and in 1926, in response to the emerging transoceanic aviation market, Dornier began construction of a successor, the Do X, or "Superwal" (Super Whale), a massive twelve-engine flying boat designed specifically for transatlantic travel. Junkers

became aware of the Do X in early 1927, and its development significantly spurred his support for both the *Bremen* flight and the Azores expedition. Originally a designer with Zeppelin, Dornier had received instruction from Junkers aircraft designers and metalworkers at Dessau in the early 1920s, a connection he later acknowledged as critical in furthering his aviation career. Like many of his peers, Dornier awaits a modern English biography. For more on Dornier, see Morrow, "Connections between Military and Commercial Aviation in Germany," in Trimble, *From Airships to Airbus*, 153–67.

42. Diary entry, February 1928 (precise date unknown), DMM JA NL 21, diary no. 160, 14543.

43. Diary entry, March 13, 1928, DMM JA NL 21, diary no. 163, 14825.

44. See Schmitt, *Hugo Junkers*, 273–75. On June 2, Junkers noted in his diary that his price for license fees had been US$2 million. See diary entry, June 2, 1928, DMM JA NL 21, diary no. 165a, 12.

45. Ultimately, direct crossings of the Atlantic failed to materialize, and Deutsche Lufthansa settled on an interim solution, launching aircraft by catapult from ocean liners to mail delivery. After 1932, a modified version of the Junkers W-34 equipped with floatplanes and designated as the Ju-46, took over these duties, and five aircraft were delivered to Deutsche Lufthansa between 1932 and 1936. For the Ju-46, see Schmitt, *Hugo Junkers and His Aircraft*, 163–65.

46. See notes of Rudolf Müller on a conversation with the RVM, January 16, 1929; letter from IFA to RVM concerning the J-38 contract, February 13, 1929; and file notice concerning the development contract for the J-38, February 18, 1929, DMM JA Hauptbüro 0503/26, cited also by Budrass, *Flugzeugindustrie*, 241.

47. See Schmitt, *Hugo Junkers*, 265. Junkers's continued retention of Sachsenberg, which included him remaining on IFA's board of directors, reflected more than just Junkers's personal loyalty to his employees. Sachsenberg possessed sensitive information concerning the firm's activities during the events of 1925–26, in particular the indirect financing of the Dessau complex during the Fili crisis; see chapter 2.

48. Homze, *Arming the Luftwaffe*, 29–30.

49. Plauth's argument reflected two assumptions: first, that IFA's technical superiority had ended, and that in order to maintain financial solvency the firm must rationalize its diffuse research and development program and focus on fewer designs with clear market potential. Second, following on from the first assumption, he argued that IFA's design priorities should focus on the second rank of world nations, those with "primitively trained pilots," such as Thailand, and that, therefore, designs should be simple and easy to fly. Sachsenberg agreed with Plauth on the broader orientation for IFA's design strategy, but he differed both on the need for simplification and the target market. After Plauth's death in 1927, Sachsenberg succeeded in ending Plauth's simplification

initiatives within IFA's design bureau. See the survey of (aircraft) types conducted by Plauth, December 1, 1926, DMM JA Hauptbüro 0302/7/36; and the file notes of Gotthard Sachsenberg on October 4, 1927, DMM JA Flugzeugbau 0302/7/45, and October 18, 1927, DMM JA Flugzeugbau 0303/10/15.

50. Homze, *Arming the Luftwaffe*, 26. Homze notes that these contingency plans existed until 1935.

51. See IFA marketing program, September 14, 1929, DMM JA Flugzeugbau 0301/24/17. These models included a military version of the gigantic G-38 as a heavy bomber, a two-engine fighter known as the K-37, a single-engine fighter called the K-47, and the J-52 bomber conversion. The G-38, K-37, and K-47 were all manufactured under license in Japan by Mitsubishi Aircraft Corporation. See Budrass, *Flugzeugindustrie*, 245; and Schmitt, *Hugo Junkers and His Aircraft*, 159–60.

52. See Homze, *Arming the Luftwaffe*, 29, table 1.

53. The following section draws from Budrass, *Flugzeugindustrie*, 245–52.

54. See, for example, the Hauptbüro file notice of principal viewpoints for and against the connection between aircraft manufacture and air transport, November 5, 1927, DMM JA Flugzeugbau 0301/21/24, which notes, "Under the present situation in Germany a firm is completely dependent on state authorities and must obey their special wishes. Because of this production is uneconomical and dependent on subsidies, and sound development work is impossible."

55. Memorandum of meeting of November 29, 1927, Kaiserplatz, 10:30 a.m., DMM JA Flugzeugbau 0301/21/32. See in particular page 6, where sixteen Reichstag representatives from five parties—the Zentrumspartei (Catholic Center Party), Deutsche Demokratische Partei (Democrats), Deutsche Volkspartei (People's Party), Deutschnationale Volkspartei (National People's Party), and the SPD (Social Democrats)—are named as potential supporters of the firm.

56. Memorandum of meeting of November 29, 1927, Kaiserplatz, 10:30 a.m., DMM JA Flugzeugbau 0301/21/32. See also situation report no. 4 on relations between Junkers and state authorities, December 8, 1927, DMM JA Flugzeugbau 0301/19.

57. See Junkers's response to the article entitled "The Never-ending Junkers Scandal," which appeared in both the *Berliner Arbeiter-Zeitung* and the *Nazionalsozialist* newspapers on March 4, 1928, DMM JA Flugzeugbau 0301/22/18. After meeting with Hugo Junkers's son, Klaus, in Berlin on April 4, Hermann Göring declared that henceforth Junkers would receive all articles relating to aviation within National Socialist newspapers prior to publication. Göring also declared himself "completely convinced of the legitimacy of Junkers's standpoint regarding its relationship with the Reich." Regarding Sachsenberg, he wasted little time beginning his work; on March 31, 1928, he met with Admiral Rudolf "Papi" Lahs, chief of the Naval Aviation Department within the

RVM and later chairman of the RDLI. During the meeting both men agreed that the dominance of the existing "aviation cartel" hindered both Junkers and naval aviation, and that increased autonomy within the aviation industry was urgently required. See transcript of the conversation within DMM JA NL 123 Conzelmann, box 2. See also personal note, March 4, 1929, DMM JA NL 123 Conzelmann, box 23, folder 2.

58. These memoranda are discussed in detail within Budrass, *Flugzeugindustrie*, 245–51.

59. Douhet's theories concerning the new status of air power as an independent and devastating strategic weapon were widely accepted throughout Europe by the late 1920s and served as the primary foundation for the establishment of civil defense programs. Germany's geopolitical position appeared to heighten the importance of digesting Douhet's "lessons," and most German experts accepted his dire predictions concerning the use of fast bombers in the next war. On Douhet's thought and influence, not only in Germany but throughout the world, see Corum, *Luftwaffe*, 89–107. One of Douhet's earliest converts was Göring, who would use Douhetian theory as a template for the creation of the Luftwaffe as a separate military arm. Douhet's most famous work, *Il Dominio dell'aria. Probabili aspetti della guerra futura*, first appeared in German in 1927. See Homze, *Arming the Luftwaffe*, 52–55. Douhet's predictions concerning aviation's decisive role in the next major war were proven incorrect between 1939 and 1945.

60. The title of this memorandum, "Air War Equals Compulsory Peace," incorporated this theme. See Budrass, *Flugzeugindustrie*, 247.

61. Sachsenberg distributed memoranda outlining these principles both to Reichstag deputies and also to military officials. See memorandum from Sachsenberg to Defense Minister Groener, April 4, 1929, DMM JA Flugzeugbau 0301/23/14. The arrival of the United States as a major player in world aviation was noted by German aviation experts in November 1928 at a round table discussion, where Gotthard Sachsenberg reminded his colleagues that US aircraft manufacturers sold over eighteen hundred aircraft worldwide during 1927. See transcript of a discussion entitled "Aviation and Politics," November 23, 1928, DMM JA propaganda 863=344.

62. Junkers's hand in these proposals can be seen from documentary evidence, in particular the notes within DMM JA Conzelmann NL 123, box 23, folder 2. On November 27, 1928, he expressed his thoughts on the content of the memorandum sent to state officials such as President Hindenburg and Defense Minister Groener, noting, "It is questionable, whether the [current] system is actually the most suitable for purposes of national defence. . . . The Versailles Treaty has placed us in a situation which makes a successful struggle against other great powers impossible unless we counteract the superior numbers of

our opponents with superior quality, quality in all areas, most of all in leadership of the population." See loose file note, November 27, 1928, DMM JA Conzelmann NL 123, box 30, 71463.

63. As he did with most of Sachsenberg's ideas, Junkers agreed with their aims in principle but worried about both their feasibility and their possible consequences. These issues occupied his mind throughout the first half of 1929, resulting in a large number of notes collected within DMM JA Conzelmann NL 123, box 23, folder 2, under the heading *Luftreiseverkehr und Luftpolitik*. Concerning the "Aviation Bank" proposal, see the note of February 19. See also transcript of conversation in Hauptbüro, June 3, 1929, DMM JA Hauptbüro 0502/6/18.

64. Fischer von Poturzyn noted in an enclosure to Dessau from Berlin that press coverage of Sachsenberg's proposals in newspapers such as the *Vossische Zeitung* and the periodical *Germania* reflected general support for reform of German aviation, particularly Deutsche Lufthansa. See Poturzyn's introduction to the transcript of "Aviation and Politics," November 23, 1928, DMM JA propaganda 863=344.

65. See chapter 3.

66. See Irving, *Rise and Fall*, 21–22; and Budrass, *Flugzeugindustrie*, 246.

67. Transcript of a discussion entitled "Aviation and Politics," November 23, 1928, DMM JA propaganda 863=344.

68. In a file note on September 28, 1929, Junkers Press Director Fischer von Poturzyn noted that the SPD planned to increase its public criticism of state aviation policy prior to the Reichstag vote on aviation subsidies. Poturzyn also mentioned that the SPD, through the writings of its aviation expert Walter Binder in *Vorwärts* displayed a "strong opposing attitude to the current air transport system . . . and agreed in principle with the speeches made by Sago [Sachsenberg] in the Reichstag." See file notice from Fischer von Poturzyn to Hauptbüro, September 28, 1928, DMM JA Flugzeugbau 0301/22/61. Poturzyn also observed the SPD planned to bring its own motion for reform of civil aviation, particularly the granting of airline routes to other firms beside Lufthansa, in an effort to weaken opposition criticism that Sachsenberg's plans were merely a transparent attempt to accrue business for IFA and JUMO.

69. By 1929, even firms within the RDLI began to protest against their lack of freedom to pursue designs other than those mandated by the RVM and Reichswehr. Spurred on by Sachsenberg's example, an unnamed group of RDLI members published their own memorandum that called for increased parliamentary control of aviation policy. See Budrass, *Flugzeugindustrie*, 250.

70. Under Weimar civil law, payment of Reichstag members by third parties was legal.

71. Irving, *Rise and Fall*, 21. In June 1929, Göring alone received at least 10,000 marks from Lufthansa through the Deutsche Bank. Irving identifies

Reichstag Deputies Keil (SPD) and Cremer (DVP) as other recipients of Lufthansa money.

72. Ibid., 22.

73. Personal note, February 20, 1929, DMM JA NL 123 Conzelmann, box 23, folder 2. Junkers's character resonates more clearly in the note's conclusion: "Junkers is a researcher and industrialist; his role is not to behave publicly as a politician. . . . However, if I see my interests fundamentally disputed, I must ask myself; isn't anyone who has the opportunity to view the situation objectively obliged to raise his voice and contribute, so that everyone appointed to decisively intervene in aviation affairs is fully informed?" See also the transcript of a phone conversation between Junkers and Fischer von Poturzyn on April 13, 1929, in which von Poturzyn points to the articles surrounding calls for aviation reform in that day's *Berliner Tageblatt* and *Deutscher Arbeiter Zeitung*. Junkers replies by declaring, "We must strike while the iron is still hot. It is pleasing to have a way out of such a dreadful situation as this one, and I am willing to indiscriminately adopt *any* proposal. Now is the time to attack, before the inevitable criticism becomes too great." See transcript of telephone conversation, April 13, 1929, within DMM JA NL 123 Conzelmann box 2, file Nr. 71731. Emphasis in original.

74. Mommsen, *Rise and Fall*, 271.

75. For the details of this process see Irving, *Rise and Fall*, 23–24. Milch acted just in time, and the airline managed to retire or restructure all of its debt by 1930 before the world economic crisis intensified.

76. Budrass, *Flugzeugindustrie*, 252.

77. Ibid. See table 8, 254. Junkers presented two formal proposals for funding, one each for IFA and JUMO. See drafts of both dated July 21, 1929, DMM JA Conzelmann NL 123, box 2.

78. Although Sachsenberg could argue his tactics achieved results, Junkers grew increasingly concerned over the possible consequences of identifying the Junkers firms' cause with Sachsenberg's public pronouncements. In October 1930, Junkers directed all senior management and employees to refrain from commenting publicly on aviation matters. See Hauptbüro file notice, October 17, 1930, DMM JA Flugzeugbau 0301/26/14.

79. For preparations for this action, see Hauptbüro situation report No. 7, April 29, 1929, DMM JA Flugzeugbau 0301/19. Despite this move, the new president of the RDLI, Admiral Rudolf Lahs, noted in his opening address on May 6 that further action against the state was futile and that "we cannot go against the state, only always with it." See opening speech of the president of the RDLI, May 5, 1929, DMM JA Hauptbüro 0502/6/19.

80. Adolf Rohrbach fought STAMAG's actions in the courts until 1931. Budrass notes that the Reichswehr and the RVM's Aviation Department considered creating an aviation conglomerate as an alternative to the Junkers Works

out of the remains of Rohrbach and several other firms affected by funding cuts—Albatros, Focke-Wulf, and BMW (*Flugzeugindustrie*, 256).

81. See Homze, *Arming the Luftwaffe*, 44.

82. For discussion of the Zentralarbeitsgemeinschaft (Central Working Association), see Kolb, *Weimar Republic*, 159–61. For Brüning's austerity measures, see ibid., 112–15, and Mommsen, *Rise and Fall*, 362–36. German historians now largely agree that Brüning sought to use the country's economic woes to remove the burden of reparations payments once and for all. Ironically, Brüning ultimately succeeded in ridding Germany of reparations obligations, but by then had himself fallen from power on May 29, 1932, two weeks before the Lausanne Conference ended between the financial triangle of Germany, Britain, and France, and the United States. Both Kolb and Mommsen also point toward the Ruhr ironworks dispute of November and December 1928 as a key event in the downfall of the Republic, as employers' rejection of state arbitration awards signaled the beginning of open hostility toward the state from employers and employees alike. Both groups blamed the state for the failure of negotiations, and both also viewed the failure as confirmation that the compromise of the Zentralgemeinschaft no longer applied. Increasingly, industrialists and workers took the view that the Republic had run its course.

83. Peukert noted the close connections between economic hardship and political extremism during the latter stages of the Weimar Republic, particularly among the young for whom political violence assumed a sense of purpose in an otherwise aimless existence:

> Street fighting became an essential part of the power struggle, and hence of the battle for a new political order in which the individual dreamed of being able to make a new start. In an age of personal, social and political dislocation . . . [radical parties] took on the role of collective sources of meaning that gave shape to their members' everyday lives. Men without hope attached themselves to a dynamic political movement that rekindled hope by promising revolutionary change. . . . The world economic crisis thus hastened the final crisis of the Republic on two levels of society simultaneously. The masses whose hope for the future had been blighted by the crisis became radicalized; the old élites and the politicians of the right, for their part, believed that the moment had come when they could dismantle, once and for all, the structures established in 1918 (*Weimar Republic*, 254–55).

84. Two examples are Rohrbach and the Bayerische Flugzeugwerke, whose chief designer, Willy Messerschmitt, would see his career resurrected under the auspices of Nazi rearmament.

85. See the internal memorandum entitled brief outline of the financial and economic standpoint of the Junkers Works, November 24, 1929, DMM JA Flugzeugbau 0301/24/35.

86. In hindsight, it is difficult to see how the Junkers Works could have survived in this configuration without the bailout of 1926; this realization encouraged the perception among both the Reichswehr and Junkers's competitors such as Ernst Heinkel that another bankruptcy was imminent even as early as 1928. See Budrass, *Flugzeugindustrie*, 260–61.

87. See Geschäfts Bericht 1928–29, DMM JA Flugzeugbau 0301/26/6; and internal memorandum, November 24, 1929, DMM JA Flugzeugbau 0301/24/35. This memorandum contains a snapshot of IFA's financial state on November 23, 1929, that shows liquid capital reduced to 317,900 marks, while IFA contributions to the Hauptbüro since October 1928 totaled 3,571,400 marks.

88. For the Ju-49, see Schmitt, *Hugo Junkers and His Aircraft*, 166–68. Junkers's continued belief in the viability of his research emphasis emanates from IFA's 1929 company report. See Geschäfts-Bericht der Junkers-Flugzeugwerk Aktiengesellschaft zu Dessau für das XII. Geschäftsjahr 1928–29, DMM JA Flugzeugbau 0301/26/6.

89. See the figures quoted by Schmitt in *Hugo Junkers*, 305–6.

90. For the course of these parallel processes, see Ittner, *Dieselmotoren*, passim. The retirement of Junkers's longtime collaborator and chief engine researcher, Otto Mader, encouraged Hugo Junkers during 1928 to take a closer interest in this research. Clearly, this renewed involvement encouraged Junkers to continue to invest large sums in engine research despite a lack of orders throughout 1929 and 1930. Costs for engine research rose steeply from 600,000 marks in 1926 to 2,300,000 marks in 1929. See the table in Budrass, *Flugzeugindustrie*, 243.

91. See ibid., 242.

92. Out of twenty-six W-33s produced, twenty were sold. In comparison, of the fifty-five A-50 "Junkers Junior" aircraft manufactured in 1929 and 1930, only thirteen sold. See Blunck, *Hugo Junkers*, 224.

93. Budrass, *Flugzeugindustrie*, 261.

94. DMM JA Flugzeugbau 0301/24/35 and 0301/27/4. The disastrous A-50 program contributed significantly to this downturn. In 1932, Sachsenberg noted that Junkers had personally advocated the A-50 program "in a dictatorial manner" despite almost united opposition from IFA and Hauptbüro executives. See Schmitt, *Hugo Junkers and His Aircraft*, 162.

95. Just as the financial crisis reached a crescendo in July 1931, the Hauptbüro released a notice outlining future research programs. The programs envisaged thirteen aircraft projects, including work on tail-less designs, flying wings, and helicopters. See Hauptbüro notice of July 7, 1931, DMM JA Flugzeugbau 0301/27/30.

96. In 1920, production time for an F-13 was five thousand hours; by 1930, this had increased to seven thousand hours. Wage costs for an F-13 built in July 1927 totaled 4,756 reichsmarks. Three years later, it had increased nearly

50 percent to 6,977 marks. Hidden costs also mounted during this period. Customer modifications increased the weight of the aircraft, requiring increased strengthening of the airframe and therefore higher material costs. See reply of Herr Scholl to Junkers, February 18, 1929, DMM JA Flugzeugbau 0301/23/7.

97. See the comparison in Budrass, *Flugzeugindustrie*, 257, between the BFW M-20, which is a one-engine transport design, and the three-engine Junkers G-24. In 1929, the M-20, a contemporary Messerschmitt design, outperformed the G-24, yet cost 87,000 marks less.

98. The Heinkel He-70 and the BFW M-20 exemplified the new technical direction of aviation by moving away from Junkers's principles of large, heavy transport designs to smaller, faster, more economical transport aircraft. Morrow notes that when the He-70 first appeared in 1932, it possessed a top speed exceeding that of most foreign military aircraft. See Morrow, "Connections between Military and Commercial Aviation in Germany," in Trimble, *From Airships to Airbus*, 162–63.

99. By April 1929, Junkers operated sales offices in Bolivia, Persia, Turkey, Portugal, Sweden, Spain, Japan, and Argentina, as well as the United States. Monthly operating expenses for the US office, staffed by Junkers's eldest daughter, Herta, reached 25,000 marks per month by August 1929. See situation report No. 7, April 29, 1929, DMM JA Flugzeugbau 0301/19; and internal memorandum, November 24, 1929, DMM JA Flugzeugbau 0301/24/35.

100. See the figures in DMM JA Flugzeugbau 0301/24/35.

101. See transcript of conversation of February 24, 1928, regarding credit negotiations, DMM JA Flugzeugbau 0301/22/51. Public sale of shares equal to 49 percent of the new firm, Junkers Flugzeugwerk Aktiengesellschaft (IFA AG), resulted in new capitalization totaling 10.5 million marks. Junkers retained control of the majority shares.

102. See the Hauptbüro file notice of July 5, 1929, DMM JA Flugzeugbau 0301/24/1.

103. Junkers sought to create circles of influential supporters at both the regional, national, and international level. See the file notices of March 28, 1930; May 17, 1930; May 19, 1930; and May 22, 1930, all located within DMM JA propaganda 703. The file notice of May 19 includes two pages listing possible candidates ranging from Gustav Krupp to Konrad Adenauer.

104. Hauptbüro file notice of July 5, 1929, DMM JA Flugzeugbau 0301/24/1. Neither this document nor subsequent evidence explain how this advisory body would have worked in practice.

105. See letter from Junkers to Schacht, June 26, 1929, and reply from Schacht to Junkers, July 19, 1929, DMM JA Flugzeugbau 0301/23/36. See also copy of letter from Junkers to Hindenburg entitled "Wehrmacht, Luftfahrt, Nation" (Army, Aviation, Nation), October 21, 1930, DMM JA Flugzeugbau 0301/26/16.

106. For the role of Schacht in the Young Plan negotiations and the sub-

sequent political turmoil, see Mommsen, *Rise and Fall*, 269–79. Mommsen notes that in 1929 Germany used 54 percent of all foreign loans to cover public expenditures. He argues Schacht hoped to use this dependency as a lever to demonstrate Germany's inability to make reparations payments as outlined under the Dawes Plan of 1924. Junkers also argued for pursuit of partnerships with French engine manufacturers, citing the sole license agreement with Peugeot as unsatisfactory. See DMM JA Flugzeugbau 0301/24/33. For details of the Peugeot license agreement, see document entitled "Concluded License Agreements," August 29, 1930, DMM JA Flugzeugbau 0301/26/9.

107. File notice, August 2, 1929, DMM JA Flugzeugbau 0301/24/7.

108. Protocol of conversation with Reichsbank President Schacht filed by Junkers Director Paul Spaleck, November 28, 1929, DMM JA Flugzeugbau 0301/24/36.

109. These banks included the Anhaltische Landesbank and the Diskontobank. The Reichsbank's position gave it the ability to regulate capital supplies within Germany, and recognition of this encouraged Junkers to approach Schacht directly.

110. Foreign firms also recognized this potential, and during the meeting with Schacht, Junkers divulged plans to merge JUMO with Peugeot's motor operations to form a joint German-French engine manufacturing concern, with Junkers providing the technology and Peugeot the capital. Unfortunately, these plans came to nothing, probably due to the effects of the global depression and Peugeot's reluctance to assume responsibility for JUMO's mounting debts.

111. See copy of "Wehrmacht, Luftfahrt, Nation," October 21, 1930, DMM JA Flugzeugbau 0301/26/16.

112. See file notice concerning financial mobilization of research, August 17, 1931, DMM JA Flugzeugbau 0301/27/44.

113. File notice, January 15, 1931, DMM JA Flugzeugbau 0301/27/4.

114. See Hauptbüro file, "Outline of World License," January 28, 1931, DMM JA Flugzeugbau 0301/27/7.

115. This was certainly the view of German and foreign banks, which concluded by 1930 that the Junkers Works was not economically viable in its current configuration. As Junkers noted in his diary, this conclusion made the task of securing further financing extremely difficult, if not impossible. See diary entry, July 17, 1930, DMM JA NL 21, diary no. 188, 17917–19.

116. Balance calculations included with letter from IFA management to Junkers and the IFA board of directors, June 13, 1931, DMM JA Flugzeugbau 0301/27/39. These losses forced IFA's management into action, and in late 1930, they attempted to charge Junkers personally for IFA's Hauptbüro contributions, a sum of 3,300,000 marks. Attempts by IFA management to reconcile this debt met with resistance from Junkers and contributed to the growth of criticism concerning his continued direction of IFA's affairs. See letter from

Junkers to IFA, December 30, 1930, DMM JA Flugzeugbau 0301/26/38; and letter from IFA management to Junkers and the IFA board of directors, June 13, 1931, DMM JA Flugzeugbau 0301/27/39.

117. IFA file notice, January 15, 1931, DMM JA Flugzeugbau 0301/27/4. IFA's extensive financial commitments to other divisions of the Junkers Works placed critical strain on the firm's viability by 1931. Monthly commitments over and above internal overhead costs included 60,000 marks to the Research Institute; 45,000 marks to the Hauptbüro; 8,000 marks to Sachsenberg's Berlin Office; 3,200 marks to the firm's official Berlin office; 27,000 marks to Junkers's Persian airline ventures; and 37,000 marks to the Swedish factory at Limhamm. None of these agencies produced tangible returns by this time. See Budrass, *Flugzeugindustrie*, 263–65. For Junkers's interest in housing construction, see Blunck, *Hugo Junkers*, chapter 16, and also the Junkers-designed microhousing structures installed today at the Technikmuseum Hugo Junkers in Dessau. Current interest and design trends in modular, prefabricated microhousing within architectural and engineering circles today would please Hugo Junkers.

118. Letter from Spaleck to Junkers, August 22, 1931, DMM JA Flugzeugbau 0301/27/46.

119. Remarks of Junkers concerning Spaleck, September 7, 1931, DMM JA Flugzeugbau 0301/27/46. Junkers's consistent resistance to any deviation from what he perceived as the Junkers Works principal function soured relations between himself and Spaleck, whose criticisms began toward the end of 1930. In November 1930, responding to Spaleck's concerns that the total burden placed on the Junkers Works by research priorities now exceeded 5 million marks per year, Junkers noted, "What Spaleck has in mind means in practical terms the budgetization [*Etatisierung*] and dependence of research on the production plants and with that the destruction of the freedom that the essence of research demands." See "Principles of Leadership of the Entire Enterprise: Remarks by Professor Junkers between 6 September 1930 and 2 January 1931," cited by Schmitt, *Hugo Junkers*, 307 and 369–70, note 507.

120. Mommsen, *Rise and Fall*, 379–80. Mommsen notes, "Reichsbank President Hans Luther . . . responded to this situation by raising the discount rate, thereby making credit even more scarce. By 1931 the cabinet had decided that drastic new cuts in public spending represented the only way that the budgetary expenditures could be covered."

121. Mommsen, *Rise and Fall*, 384–91. Mommsen notes, "The *Berliner Tageblatt* described the public's reaction to the decree as 'general horror.'"

122. Mommsen argues that "the withdrawal of loans compounded certain structural weaknesses in the German banking system. In comparison with the prewar period, credit institutions operated with very little capital of their own and with much smaller liquid reserves. The high proportion of short-term credits was not a particular problem as long as it was possible to compensate

for their withdrawal by contracting new short-term loans. The outcome of the elections of September 1930, however, had brought about a major change in this practice, for it seriously inhibited the influx of new loans, whether short- or long-term" (Ibid., 388).

123. Kolb, *Weimar Republic*, 115. Noted victims of this collapse included the Karstadt department store chain, the largest in Germany.

124. Ibid.

125. Ibid., 391.

126. Goldschmidt had been involved in discussions concerning Sachsenberg's "aviation bank." See Budrass, *Flugzeugindustrie*, 240.

127. Mommsen, *Rise and Fall*, 389.

128. Ibid., 388.

129. See letter from Junkers to Reichsbund Deutscher Technik, August 10, 1931, DMM JA propaganda 703. Junkers noted apologetically in this letter, "Extraordinarily difficult economic circumstances compel me to employ all of my strength in the coming times toward my concern's struggle for survival."

130. IFA monthly report, August 1931, DMM JA Flugzeugbau 0301/27/50. Total monthly expenditure for August reached 708,600 marks. July expenditures exceeded 1 million marks. IFA's total losses for the year 1930/31 totaled 1,839,610 marks. See balance of the Junkers Flugzeugwerke AG, September 30, 1931, DMM JA Flugzeugbau 0301/28/82.

131. See letter from Spaleck to Junkers, August 22, 1931, and Junkers to Spaleck, August 26, 1931, DMM JA Flugzeugbau 0301/27/46. See also Junkers to Sachsenberg, October 9, 1931, DMM JA Flugzeugbau 0301/27/64; and the ultimatum to Junkers drafted by IFA Directors Emil Becker, Rudolf Müller, and Dr. Gottfried Kaumann on November 19, 1931, and Junkers's reply on November 20, 1931, DMM JA Flugzeugbau 0301/24/70.

132. Sachsenberg's men, all former members of his Baltic fighter squadron, had established themselves within IFA and Junkers Luftverkehr after 1921. When Deutsche Lufthansa took over Junkers Luftverkehr, Sachsenberg's protégés, including Emil Becker and Gottfried Kaumann, moved into IFA. See chapters 2 and 3.

133. Sachsenberg's dismissal led to bitter relations between the two men, as Sachsenberg now sought to attack Junkers's interests through the Reichstag and in the press. Further acrimony surfaced over Sachsenberg's efforts to secure reimbursement for his share of the original foundation of Junkers Luftverkehr; Junkers ignored these claims, arguing that the hyperinflation of 1923 effectively wiped out the net worth of Sachsenberg's contribution. See Schmitt, *Hugo Junkers*, 265. For more on Dethmann and Klaus Junkers, see chapter 5.

134. See Hauptbüro file notices written by Dethmann, June 3, 1931, DMM JA Flugzeugbau 0301/27/17; and June 30, 1931, DMM JA Flugzeugbau 0301/27/20. See also Junkers's diary entry of March 27, which notes that poor

relations between Sachsenberg and Ernst Brandenburg had contributed to the firm's troubled relationship with state authorities; entry of March 27, 1931, DMM JA NL 21, diary no. 197, 18927. Junkers's corporate reshuffle led to an official reassessment of the firm's suitability for defense orders, particularly within the Reichsmarine, whose representatives wished to gain access to the JUMO 4 diesel engine. See transcript of conversation between Kottmeier and Lahs, December 2, 1931, DMM JA Flugzeugbau 0301/27/72; and file notice, June 3, 1931, DMM JA Flugzeugbau 0301/27/17.

135. Remarks of Junkers regarding meeting with defense minister, May 21, 1931, DMM JA Flugzeugbau 0301/27/17. Junkers's propensity for selective amnesia reveals itself as the document continues, as he professes that the reasons behind the current poor relationship between the concern and the Reichswehr "are not completely clear to me." Within his diary, Junkers discussed his reservations concerning once again allowing military involvement in the firm's research programs. On April 28, he noted that "collaboration is only conceivable when trust and a favorable atmosphere reigns over both sides. However, it appears to me that this is still too much to wish for, as the atmosphere created by the Russian Affair still remains." See diary entry, April 28, 1931, DMM JA NL 21, diary no. 198, 19067–69.

136. Remarks of Junkers regarding meeting with defense minister, May 21, 1931, DMM JA Flugzeugbau 0301/27/17. Junkers's accurate summary of the Reichwehr's intentions between 1931 and 1933 is confirmed by Budrass, *Flugzeugindustrie*, 266–73.

137. DMM JA Flugzeugbau 0301/27/17.

138. Schmitt, *Hugo Junkers*, 314.

139. Diary entry, December 10, 1931, DMM JA NL 21, diary no. 204, 19793.

140. Hauptbüro file notice, January 5, 1932, DMM JA Flugzeugbau 0301/28/2.

141. For discussion of these developments, see Ittner, *Dieselmotoren*, passim. Due to patent restrictions, Junkers referred to diesel engines as "schweröl [heavy oil] engines" within company documents.

142. Budrass, *Flugzeugindustrie*, 244.

143. Schmitt, *Hugo Junkers and His Aircraft*, 209–10.

144. Irving, *Rise and Fall*, 25–26. This variant, the J-52/3m, would go on to be the most successful aircraft ever designed by Junkers. Yet production would not begin until May 1932, too late to save Junkers's firms from state takeover.

145. Schmitt, *Hugo Junkers and His Aircraft*, 213; and Budrass, *Flugzeugindustrie*, 265.

146. Letter from Spaleck to Junkers, August 22, 1931, DMM JA Flugzeugbau 0301/27/46. The following description draws from this document.

147. Budrass, *Flugzeugindustrie*, 265.

148. Budrass notes that already in September 1931 wage payments through-

out the concern were being delayed by two weeks, and employee contributions to medical insurance were being deferred to cover overhead costs. See Budrass, *Flugzeugindustrie*, 265.

149. Blunck, *Hugo Junkers*, 249–50.

150. Hauptbüro file notice, March 14, 1932, DMM JA Flugzeugbau 0301/28/4. ICO Director Spaleck also noted, however, that "in his view the Reich would not participate in any solution other than one that awarded them a central influence in the concern."

151. Internal memorandum, March 22, 1932, DMM JA Flugzeugbau 0301/28/11.

152. Decision of Anhaltische Amtsgericht, March 24, 1932, DMM JA Flugzeugbau 0301/28/13; and notice from Junkers to IFA workforce, March 29, 1932, DMM JA Flugzeugbau 0301/28/16.

153. Letter from Junkers to Anhaltische Staatsministerium, April 11, 1932, DMM JA Flugzeugbau 0301/28/26. For internal reforms undertaken within IFA and the Hauptbüro in 1932, which included halving the Hauptbüro's workforce, reduction of IFA's product lines from eight to three, cuts in both numbers of white collar employees and worker wages, and massive cuts in the retail prices of Junkers aircraft, see Budrass, *Flugzeugindustrie*, 282–85.

154. Transcript of telephone conversation between Junkers and Spaleck, April 29, 1932, DMM JA Flugzeugbau 0301/28/36.

155. See Junkers/Reich, list of important dates, March 9, 1934, DMM JA propaganda box C1, 1234.

156. Copy of declaration of Hugo Junkers and the leaders of IFA and JUMO, April 30, 1932, DMM JA Flugzeugbau 0301/28/38. The declaration formally reduced Junkers's personal debt to IFA from 3,300,000 marks to 2 million marks.

157. See note 154. Junkers made these counterclaims in a letter to RVM official von Buttlar, the RVM's representative on the creditor committee overseeing the concern's valuation assessment, on May 25. See letter from Junkers to von Buttlar, May 25, 1932, DMM JA Flugzeugbau 0301/28/43.

158. See memorandum concerning valuation of the technical worth that Junkers entrusts to IFA and JUMO, May 23, 1932, DMM JA 0301/28/51.

159. Costs for the granting of patents in Germany averaged 1,200 marks and required regular maintenance payments thereafter. See Schmitt, *Hugo Junkers and His Aircraft*, 213. Schmitt estimates the Junkers concern held over 350 patents in Germany and more than 2,150 worldwide in 1932.

160. Notice of Junkers, May 1932, DMM JA Flugzeugbau 0301/28/39.

161. Hauptbüro file notice detailing meeting with Staatsminister Dr. Müller, May 3, 1932, DMM JA Flugzeugbau 0301/28/44.

162. Letter from Dethmann to Treviranus, May 5, 1932, DMM JA Flugzeugbau 0301/28/46. Treviranus's response is not recorded.

163. Situation report no. 2, May 21, 1932, DMM JA Flugzeugbau 0301/28/50. The creditors ordered ICO and the Kaloriferwerk merged and reorganized as a limited liability company.

164. Budrass notes that the price for an F-13 fell from 60,000 marks in 1930 to 16,000 marks by 1932; see the figures quoted in *Flugzeugindustrie*, 284.

165. Balances of the Junkers Flugzeugwerk AG, September 30, 1932, and September 30, 1933, DMM JA Flugzeugbau 0301/31/25. Profit achieved in the year 1932/33 totaled 171,157 marks.

166. The complex nature of the insolvency proceedings precluded a rapid resolution of the crisis. Although the concern was perceived by Junkers as an organic whole, legally the Junkers Works divided into three separate entities: Junkers Flugzeugwerke AG, a joint stock company; Junkers Motorenbau GmbH, a limited liability company; and all other firms within the complex defined as personal assets of Junkers as "Einzelkaufmann" (small business man). This definition meant that the Hauptbüro and the Forschungsanstalt were considered separate from IFA and JUMO, although as Junkers repeatedly emphasized, such divisions never existed in practice. See speech of Junkers at House of Technology, Essen, November 11, 1932, cited within Blunck, *Hugo Junkers*, 251–54.

167. See notices from Junkers to Hauptbüro and Forschungsanstalt workforce, June 25, 1932, DMM JA Flugzeugbau 0301/28/74; and July 29, 1932, DMM JA Flugzeugbau 0301/29/6.

168. Henschel would later found his own aviation company, which would become a beneficiary of the Third Reich's rearmament programs of the 1930s. Junkers also investigated other means of outside financing during this period, including the creation of independent "cells" that combined external capital with Junkers research to accelerate new product development. See copy of Hauptbüro file notice concerning capital procurement and "cell construction," June 15, 1932, DMM JA Flugzeugbau 0301/28/65.

169. See the more detailed discussion in Blunck, *Hugo Junkers*, 260–63.

170. On November 29, 1930, a high-level meeting between representatives of the Defense, Foreign, and Transport Ministries agreed to ignore the Treaty of Versailles provision banning stockpiling of aircraft. Attendees included Ernst Brandenburg and Defense Minister Wilhelm Groener. See Homze, *Arming the Luftwaffe*, 33.

171. Budrass, *Flugzeugindustrie*, 268–69.

172. Ibid., 270–72.

173. Transcription of notes of Junkers, September 25 and 26, 1932, DMM JA Flugzeugbau 0301/29/24. Public opinion had turned against Junkers after attacks on the professor's leadership of the firm appeared in National Socialist newspapers in July 1932. These attacks relied on information provided by Sachsenberg and other former Junkers employees in two "brochures." The first,

known as the "yellow brochure" and entitled "Korruption um Junkers," appeared on July 25, and the second, or "white brochure," entitled "Answer to Professor Junkers," appeared one month later on August 25. These revelations damaged Junkers's public reputation and encouraged calls for his removal and replacement. At all levels, from local to national press outlets, National Socialist propaganda repeatedly attacked Junkers and his firm, abruptly ceasing their attacks once the nationalization concluded.

174. See settlement proposal in insolvency proceedings of Junkers, October 6, 1932, DMM JA Flugzeugbau 0301/19/27.

175. Blunck, *Hugo Junkers*, 263.

176. Memoranda from Junkers to Junkers Works, November 14 and 28, 1932, DMM JA Flugzeugbau 0301/29/39.

177. See letter from Junkers & Co. to Robert Bosch AG, November 19, 1932, DMM JA Flugzeugbau 0301/29/35.

Chapter 5

1. The following discussion draws on the pioneering work of Lutz Budrass, whose description of the events between the National Socialist "takeover" in 1933 and Junkers's death in February 1935 represents a major revision of traditional interpretations, such as those of East German scholars Olaf Groehler and Günter Schmitt, who see the events leading to Junkers's death as centrally coordinated actions of the new Fascist state (*Flugzeugindustrie*, 320–32).

2. This letter was signed only with a swastika. See copy of excerpt in Schmitt, *Hugo Junkers*, 313.

3. Letter from Hauptbüro to Staatsminister Müller, December 8, 1932, DMM JA Flugzeugbau 0301/29/32; and copy of letter from von Sydow to IFA Director Mühlen, January 26, 1933, DMM JA Flugzeugbau 0301/31/3.

4. Homze, *Arming the Luftwaffe*, 49–50. Homze perceptively comments: "It is ironic that the centralization of aviation agencies, initiated and given impetus by the desperate shortage of funds, should occur at precisely the time a deluge of money became available. It is doubly ironic that the military, which so long and jealously fought for independent army and navy units, finally could agree to a united control of aviation, only to see it slip from their hands. The Nazis had stepped into a ripe situation and turned it to their advantage."

5. Budrass, *Flugzeugindustrie*, 322–23. Budrass also observes that Klaus Junkers joined the SS in 1933.

6. See Junkers/Reich, list of important dates, March 9, 1934, DMM JA propaganda box C1, 1234; and letter from Junkers to Göring, February 21, 1933, DMM JA propaganda box C1, 1175.

7. JUMO file notice, March 8, 1933, DMM JA propaganda box C1, 1175.

8. See Hauptbüro file notice concerning Junkers's opinions regarding the re-

lationship between Junkers and the Reich, March 16, 1933, DMM JA propaganda box C1, 1175; and notice for Junkers, March 30, 1933, DMM JA propaganda box C1, 1176. On March 27, Junkers remarked that the "the aim of the Reich, to force Junkers into fulfilment of the settlement terms through withholding of orders and payments is in reality an expensive and inflammatory fight against windmills that endangers the entire concern." See Hauptbüro shorthand transcript entitled "Declaration of Hugo Junkers's Position Regarding Actions Taken by the Reich against Him," March 27, 1933, DMM JA propaganda box C1, 1176. The RVM demonstrated its displeasure of Junkers's recalcitrance by excluding him from the unveiling of Deutsche Lufthansa's second G-38, named "Field Marshal von Hindenburg," at Berlin's Templehof Airport on April 29.

9. These figures derived from a series of eighteen confidential reports on the activities of the Junkers Works produced in May 1932. These reports were designed to give potential buyers of the concern an overview of IFA's current activities and, therefore, contained information concerning military orders. Five of these reports had been given to Junkers trustee Privy Councilor von Buttlar, who according to Junkers company records only returned three copies. Buttlar apparently gave one of these reports to Oskar Henschel, and the whereabouts of the other report remained a mystery. When Dethmann attempted to determine the location of the two missing reports, Buttlar did not reply, and the publication of material within the report in November led to Dethmann filing suit against Buttlar. See Junkers/Reich, list of important dates, March 9, 1934, DMM JA propaganda box C1, 1234.

10. The decree curtailed fundamental rights granted under the Weimar Constitution, including freedom of movement and of the press, freedom of association and combination, and the individual right to privacy. The decree greatly increased police powers; legalized telephone, mail, and telegraph surveillance; and granted far-reaching powers of search and seizure. See Schmitt, *Hugo Junkers and His Aircraft*, 214. Historical interpretations of the causes of the Reichstag fire tend to infer some element of National Socialist involvement, although no conclusive evidence survives to prove this connection.

11. Lämmler had been present at the meeting between Milch and Interior Ministry representatives on March 10 and was therefore aware of Milch's agenda. See Schmitt, *Hugo Junkers*, 318.

12. Fiala was deported on March 26. Dethmann and Drömmer remained in custody until May 26 and were then released but remained barred from returning to Dessau and faced concentration camp incarceration for contravention of this obligation. See copy of declaration of Oberstaatsanwalt Lämmler, May 26, 1933, within DMM JA propaganda box C1, 1176.

13. Junkers/Reich, list of important dates, March 9, 1934, DMM JA propaganda box C1, 1234. Two days earlier, Junkers appeared at the offices of the Anhalt State Ministry and declared his readiness to "accept the wishes of the

Reich regarding personnel changes." See copy of declaration of Junkers, April 5, 1933, DMM JA propaganda box C1, 1176. See also Budrass, *Flugzeugindustrie,* 323–24.

14. Protocol of meeting and agreement between Junkers and the Reich Commission for Aviation, April 7, 1933, DMM JA propaganda box C1, 1176.

15. A meeting held by the Reich Commission for Aviation later amended the deadline for a formal proposal to one week after Easter 1933. See file notice on the meeting with Reich Commission for Aviation, April 12, 1933, DMM JA propaganda box C1, 1176.

16. Letter from Sander (Dessau police) to Junkers, April 28, 1933, DMM JA propaganda box C1, 1176. The next day Junkers Press Chief Fischer von Poturzyn drew up a series of points that refuted Lämmler's accusations and argued that Junkers's actions since the end of the war had "always conformed to the interests of national defense." This list noted the work of Junkers to hide military material from the Allies after the war and attributed the leaking of material related to the Fili Affair to the press in 1925 as a "consequence of the current parliamentary system." See remarks of Junkers on April 29, 1933, DMM JA propaganda box C1, 1176.

17. Transcript of telephone conversation between Klaus Junkers and RLM Assistant Secretary Panzeram, May 6, 1933, DMM JA propaganda box C1, 1176.

18. Budrass, *Flugzeugindustrie,* 324. Copies of these transfer agreements signed by Junkers on June 2, 1933, can be found within DMM JA propaganda box C1, 1176.

19. Letter from Milch to Junkers, June 12, 1933, DMM JA Flugzeugbau 0301/31/14.

20. See chapter 4, notes 132 and 133. For the specifics of this information, see Budrass, *Flugzeugindustrie,* 324, note 122.

21. The ABC (Albatros, Bayerische Flugzeugwerke [BFW], and AEG) program, developed by Erhard Milch and the Air Ministry, involved significant changes in the German aircraft industry, including the use of licensees and "shadow plants" to increase production, the introduction of standardized production techniques across the industry, and workforce de-skilling to allow simplified mass production. See Homze, *Arming the Luftwaffe,* 77–78 and 104–5.

22. Budrass cites an excerpt of an August 1934 report given to Göring by Victor Lutze, then chief of staff of the Sturmabteilung (SA), that illuminates the thinking of the RLM during 1933: "During the long years of collaboration between the Junkers concern and the Reich, the behavior of Professor Junkers and his employees always led to friction. In earlier years however, the parliamentary state of Weimar made a move against Junkers impossible due to Junkers's good and varied connections with all leading parties. These connections on the one hand allowed to him to always receive new support, and on the other hand allowed him to knowingly escape scrutiny through exertions of influence. This

situation fundamentally changed on January 30, 1933. . . . The Reich has the right, obligation and ability to examine the national and economic reliability of leading private executives. . . . Such an examination of Junkers leads to unacceptable conclusions." Report from Lutze to Göring, August 8, 1934, cited by Budrass, *Flugzeugindustrie*, 324–25 and note 124.

23. Budrass, *Flugzeugindustrie*, 325.

24. Schmitt, *Hugo Junkers*, 323.

25. Appointed by the Anhalt National Socialists, Müller's responsibilities included supervision of the Junkers Works throughout 1932 and 1933.

26. Transcript of meeting at Chamber of Commerce, October 17 and 18, 1933, DMM JA Flugzeugbau 0301/31/19.

27. See copy of the receipt of this "Judas payment" within Schmitt, *Hugo Junkers*, 327.

28. Budrass, *Flugzeugindustrie*, 329.

29. Both Schmitt and Budrass cite this perception as the ultimate reason behind Junkers's removal from Dessau and the insertion of outside management. This view reflected a consensus within the RLM, as other officials such as Albert Kesselring, chief of the RLM's Administration Office and later general of the Luftwaffe, shared Milch's view. See Homze, *Arming the Luftwaffe*, 63–68; and Budrass, *Flugzeugindustrie*, 326.

30. Budrass, *Flugzeugindustrie*, 327.

31. Ibid.

32. This meeting took place in the wake of Germany's withdrawal from the League of Nations on October 12, 1933, during which time many officials feared foreign military intervention. Heinrich Koppenberg attended the meeting and later recollected the scene: "In addition to the Ministry's top officials I saw not only aircraft and engine factory chiefs but also senior directors of the industry producing light-weight and heavy raw materials. State Secretary Milch presided over the assembly. He appealed to the dependability, loyalty, ardor, and patriotism of those present, and indicated that for Germany the hour had struck for the creation of a new air force." See Irving, *Rise and Fall*, 36.

33. Junkers/Reich, list of important dates, March 9, 1934, DMM JA propaganda box C1, 1234.

34. For details see Blunck, *Hugo Junkers*, chapter 13, passim; and Hauptbüro file notice, August 23, 1933, DMM JA Flugzeugbau 0301/31/6.

35. Besides Leutgebreune, Junkers contracted the services of Georg Eschtruth, a district leader of the Berlin branch of the National Socialist Legal Association, and Attorney Betz, legal adviser to the SA leadership in Munich. Both Betz and Eschtruth were old associates of Deputy Führer Rudolf Hess. Junkers also wrote directly to Ernst Röhm in November 1933 and January 1934 asking for assistance; these pleas went unanswered. See letters from Junkers to Röhm, November 23, 1933, and January 4, 1934, DMM JA NL 21, folder 22, cited also by Budrass,

Flugzeugindustrie, 329. Junkers also attempted to cultivate relations with prominent "new men" of the National Socialist regime, particularly from other districts and states as a counterweight to the local authorities. See Hauptbüro file notice, August 23, 1933, DMM JA propaganda 703; and memorandum of Fischer von Poturzyn entitled "Instructional Work in the New State," September 13, 1933, DMM JA propaganda 703.

36. See document entitled "Report of the Junkers Affair," April 26, 1934, DMM JA propaganda box C1, 1306.

37. Ibid. See a transcript of the discussion between Junkers and Munich police officials in Schmitt, *Hugo Junkers*, 326–29.

38. See the discussion and convincing dismissal of Lämmler's claims within Schmitt, *Hugo Junkers and His Aircraft*, 216–17.

39. Report of the Junkers Affair, April 26, 1934, DMM JA propaganda box C1, 1306.

40. Letter from Eschtruth to Keppler, August 24, 1934, cited within Budrass, *Flugzeugindustrie*, 331.

41. On April 23, Milch declared "any mercy shown to the Professor is misplaced." Göring stated his intention to "completely destroy any individual who sought to hinder state or political interests." See Groehler and Erfurth, *Hugo Junkers*, 57.

42. Budrass, *Flugzeugindustrie*, 331.

43. See copies of these obituaries in Schmitt, *Hugo Junkers and His Aircraft*, 218. International obituaries are located within the Junkers Archive at the Deutsches Museum, Munich.

44. Irving, *Rise and Fall*, 37.

45. Reiss, "Die Junkers-Tragödie," 38.

46. Budrass, *Flugzeugindustrie*, 332.

47. Homze, *Arming the Luftwaffe*, 193–94. By 1944, Junkers's workforce increased to 135,000, including tens of thousands of forced laborers from all over Europe.

48. Fritzsche, *Nation of Flyers*, 3.

49. Ibid.

BIBLIOGRAPHY

Archives

Archiv der Deutsches Museum, Munich, Federal Republic of Germany (DMM)

Junkers-Archiv (JA)
NL 21 - Tagebücher, Private Papers and Correspondence of Hugo Junkers (TB)
NL 123 - Conzelmann Archiv (CA)
Teilbestand Propaganda (Propaganda)
Flugzeugbau and Verwertung (Flugzeugbau)
Hauptbüro (HB)

Landeshauptarchiv Sachsen-Anhalt, Abteilung Dessau, Dessau, Federal Republic of Germany (LSA)

Secondary Sources

Beilke, Anja. *Der Mythos "Hugo Junkers" in der deutschen Literatur: Exemplifiziert am Roman "Die Besessenen" von Wulf Bley*. Norderstadt: Grin Verlag, 2011.

Blunck, Richard. *Hugo Junkers: Der Mensch und das Werk*. Berlin: Wilhelm Limpert Verlag, 1943.

Bohme, Klaus-Richard, and Ulf Olsson. "The Swedish Aircraft Industry." In *War, Business and World Military-Industrial Complexes*, edited by Benjamin Cooling, 146–70. Port Washington, WI: Kennikat Press, 1981.

Bongers, Hans. *Es lag in der Luft: Erinnerungen als fünf jahrzehnten Luftverkehr*. Düsseldorf: Econ, 1971.

Boog, Horst (ed.). *The Conduct of the Air War in the Second World War*. New York: Berg Publishers, 1993.

Budrass, Lutz. *Flugzeugindustrie und Luftrüstung in Deutschland 1918–1945*. Düsseldorf: DrosteVerlag, 1998.

Byers, Richard, "An Unhappy Marriage: The Junkers-Fokker Merger," *Journal of Historical Biography* 3 (Spring 2008): 1–30.

Carsten, Francis. *The Reichswehr and Politics, 1918 to 1933*. New York: Clarendon Press, 1966.

Cooling, Benjamin (ed.). *War, Businesses and Military-Industrial Complexes.* Port Washington: Kennikat Press, 1981.

Corum, James. *The Luftwaffe: Creating the Operational Air War, 1918–1940.* Lawrence: University Press of Kansas, 1997.

Crouch, Tom. *Wings: A History of Aviation from Kites to the Space Age.* New York: W. W. Norton, 2003.

Davies, R. E. G. *Lufthansa: An Airline and Its Aircraft.* New York: Orion Books, 1991.

de Syon, Guillaume. *Zeppelin!: Germany and the Airship, 1900–1939.* Baltimore: Johns Hopkins University Press, 2007.

Dierickx, M. L. J. *Fokker: A Transatlantic Biography.* Washington, DC: Smithsonian Institution Press, 1997.

Feldman, Gerald. *The Great Disorder: Politics, Economics and Society in the German Inflation, 1914–1924.* New York: Oxford University Press, 1993.

Fritzsche, Peter. *A Nation of Fliers: German Aviation and the Popular Imagination.* Cambridge, MA: Harvard University Press, 1992.

Groehler, Olaf. *Hugo Junkers.* Berlin: Militärverlag der DDR, 1989.

Groehler, Olaf, and Helmut Erfurth. *Hugo Junkers: Ein politisches Essay.* Berlin: Militärverlag der DDR, 1989.

Hayward, Keith. *The British Aircraft Industry.* New York: Manchester University Press, 1989.

Higham, Robin. *100 Years of Airpower and Aviation.* College Station: Texas A&M University Press, 2003.

_____. *Armed Forces in Peacetime: Britain, 1914–1940, a Case Study.* London: Foulis, 1962.

Homze, Edward. *Arming the Luftwaffe: The Reich Air Ministry and the German Aircraft Industry 1919–1939.* Lincoln: University of Nebraska Press, 1976.

Hotson, Fred. *The Bremen.* Toronto: Canav Books, 1988.

Irving, David. *The Rise and Fall of the Luftwaffe: The Life of Field Marshal Erhard Milch.* Boston: Little, Brown and Company, 1973.

Ittner, Stefan. *Dieselmotoren für die Luftfahrt: Innovation und Tradition im Junkers-Flugmotorenbau bis 1933.* Oberhaching: Aviatik Verlag, 1996.

Junkers, Hugo. "Grundsätze technisch-wirtschaftlicher Forschung, entwickelt aus ihren Zielen und nach eigenen Erfahrungen." Unpublished manuscript of speech given by Junkers at the Haus der Technik in Essen, October 11, 1932.

———. "Eigene Arbeiten auf dem Gebiete des Metall-Flugzeuges," In *Berichte und Abhandlungen der Wissenschaftlichen Gesellschaft für Luftfahrt*, Book 11. Munich, 1924.

———. *Eine Chronik des Flug-Gedankens bis zum Luftverkehr im Dienste der Völkerverbindung*. Berlin: Licht und Schatten, 1930.

Kinney, Jeremy, *Airplanes: The Life Story of a Technology*. Baltimore: Johns Hopkins University Press, 2008.

Kleffel, Walther. "Zum Jahreswechsel." *Luftfahrt* 32 (January 7, 1928): 2–3.

Kolb, Eberhard. *The Weimar Republic*. Translated by P. S. Falla. Boston: Unwin Hyman, 1988.

Leary, William. *Aerial Pioneers: The US Air Mail Service, 1918–1927*. Washington, DC: Smithsonian Institution Press, 1985.

Mason, Herbert. *The Rise of the Luftwaffe: Forging the Secret German Air Weapon, 1918–1940*. New York: Dial Press, 1973.

Mommsen, Hans. *The Rise and Fall of Weimar Democracy*. Translated by E. Foster and L. Jones. Chapel Hill: University of North Carolina Press, 1996.

Morrow, John. *Building German Airpower, 1909–1914*. Knoxville: University of Tennessee Press, 1976.

———. "Connections between Military and Commercial Aviation in Germany: Junkers, Heinkel and Dornier through the 1930s." In *From Airships to Airbus: The History of Civil and Commercial Aviation, Volume 2: Pioneers and Operations*, edited by William Trimble, 153–67. Washington, DC: Smithsonian Institution Press, 1995.

———. *German Air Power in World War I*. Lincoln: University of Nebraska Press, 1982.

Peukert, Detlev. *The Weimar Republic: The Crisis of Classical Modernity*. Translated by Richard Deveson. New York: Hill and Wang, 1993.

Radandt, Hans. "Hugo Junkers - Ein Monopolkapitalist und Korrespondierendes Mitglied derpreussischen Akademie der Wissenschaften." *Jahrbuch für Wirtschaftsgeschichte* 1 (1960): 53–133.

Rae, John. *Climb to Greatness: The American Aircraft Industry, 1920–1960*. Cambridge, MA: MIT Press, 1968.

Reiss, Curt. "Die Junkers-Tragödie: Ein Dokumentarbericht über den Pionier der deutschen Luftfahrt," *Münchner Illustrierte* 33, August 13, 1955: 38.

Schmitt, Günter. *Hugo Junkers: Ein Leben für die Technik*. Planegg: Aviatik Verlag, 1986.

———. *Hugo Junkers and His Aircraft*. Translated by C. Scurrell. Berlin: VEB Verlag, 1988.

Siefert, Karl-Dieter. *Der deutsche Luftverkehr 1926–1945: Auf dem Weg zum Weltverkehr*. Bonn: Bernard und Graefe Verlag, 1999.

Wagner, Wolfgang. *Der Deutsche Luftverkehr: Die Pionierjahre 1919–1925*. Coblence: Bernardund Graefe Verlag, 1987.

————. *Hugo Junkers: Pionier der Luftfahrt: Seine Flugzeuge.* Bonn: Bernard und Graefe Verlag, 1996.

Widerhold, Konrad. "Die Wahrheit über Junkers" (The Truth about Junkers). In *Die Weltbühne* 22, no. 21. Potsdam: Verlag der Weltbühne, 1926: 806–10.

Winter, Frank, and Van der Linden, Robert. *100 Years of Flight: A Chronology of Aerospace History, 1903–2003.* Reston, VA: American Institute of Aeronautics and Astronautics, 2003.

Wissmann, Gerhardt. "Zur Geschichte des Junkers-Flugzeugwerkes in Fili bei Moskau (Konzessionsbetrieb) in den Jahren 1922 bis 1925. Grundlagen, Triebkräfte und Entwicklungder Zusammenarbeit zwischen Hugo Junkers, der Heeresleitung der Reichswehr und der Roten Armee 1921 bis 1925 auf dem Gebiet des militärischen Flugwesens: Die Auseinandersetzungen zwischen dem Junkers-Konzern und der Heeresleitung um das Junkers Flugzeugwerk Fili und deren Auswirkungen bis zum Jahre 1935 als typische Erscheinungs formen des staatsmonopolistischen Kapitalismus," PhD diss., University of Dresden, 1964.

Wohl, Robert. *A Passion for Wings: Aviation and the Western Imagination, 1908–1918.* New Haven, CT: Yale University Press, 1994.

Zeidler, Manfred. *Reichswehr und Rote Armee 1920–1933. Wege und Stationen einer ungewöhnlichen Zusammenarbeit.* Munich: Beiträge zur Militärgeschichte, 1993.

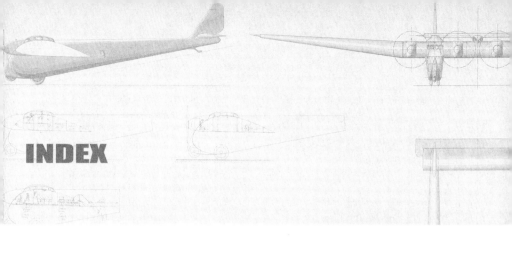

Notes: Aircraft not otherwise labeled are Junkers aircraft. Central photo gallery begins following page 102.